Medieval Culture and Society

General Editor: Miri Rubin
Advisors: Jean Dunbabin and Robert Stacey

Medieval Culture and Society provides a frame-work for the study of an array of themes in the history of medieval Europe, including some which are looked at comparatively, and approaches them in the light of the new theoretical reflections.

The books in the series will be useful to students, to a wide range of scholars, and to the general reader. Written in clear and elegant prose, they concisely present new sources and their interpretation and also highlight underlying method and theory.

Published titles

Jean Dunbabin CAPTIVITY AND IMPRISONMENT IN MEDIEVAL EUROPE, 1000–1300

Elisabeth van Houts MEMORY AND GENDER IN MEDIEVAL EUROPE, 900–1200

Phillipp R. Schofield PEASANT AND COMMUNITY IN MEDIEVAL ENGLAND, 1200–1500

Medieval Culture and Society Series

Series Standing Order

ISBN 0–333–75058–6
(outside North America only)

You can receive future titles in this series as they are published by placing a standing order. Please contact your bookseller or, in case of difficulty, write to us at the address below with your name and address, the title of the series and the ISBN quoted above.

Customer Services Department, Macmillan Distribution Ltd
Houndmills, Basingstoke, Hampshire RG21 6XS, England

PEASANT AND COMMUNITY IN MEDIEVAL ENGLAND, 1200–1500

Phillipp R. Schofield

palgrave
macmillan

To Mum

First published 2003 by
PALGRAVE MACMILLAN
Houndmills, Basingstoke, Hampshire RG21 6XS and
175 Fifth Avenue, New York, N.Y. 10010
Companies and representatives throughout the world

PALGRAVE MACMILLAN is the global academic imprint of the Palgrave Macmillan division of St. Martin's Press, LLC and of Palgrave Macmillan Ltd. Macmillan® is a registered trademark in the United States, United Kingdom and other countries. Palgrave is a registered trademark in the European Union and other countries.

ISBN 0–333–64710–6 hardcover
ISBN 0–333–64711–4 paperback

This book is printed on paper suitable for recycling and made from fully managed and sustained forest sources.

A catalogue record for this book is available from the British Library.

Library of Congress Cataloging-in-Publication Data

Schofield, Phillipp R., 1964–
    Peasant and community in Medieval England, 1200–1500 / Phillipp R. Schofield.
        p. cm. – (Medieval culture and society)
    Includes bibliographical references and index.
    ISBN 0-333-64710-6 – ISBN 0-333-64711-4 (pbk.)
    1. England–Rural conditions.   2. England–Social conditions –
1066–1485.   3. Peasantry–England–History–To 1500.   I. Title.
II. Series.

HN398.E5 S43 2002
307.72'0942–dc21   2002025830

10   9   8   7   6   5   4   3   2   1
12   11   10   09   08   07   06   05   04   03

Printed in China

CONTENTS

ACKNOWLEDGEMENTS

In writing this book, over too long a time, I have accumulated many debts from family, friends, colleagues and students, and it is a pleasure to acknowledge them here. During its writing, I have moved from Oxford to Cambridge and, then, to Aberystwyth, and have benefited from the insight and encouragement of a good number of people along the way. At Oxford and Cambridge, Michael Bevan, Chris Briggs, Cliff Davies, Ralph Evans, Ros Faith, Simon Loseby, Yoko Miyoshi, Zvi Razi, Leigh Shaw-Taylor, Jane Whittle and Margaret Yates, and at Aberystwyth, where most of this book was written, Lesley Abrams, Aled Jones, Maureen Jones, Peter Lambert, Sîan Nicholas, Martyn Powell, Llinos and Beverley Smith, as well as other members of staff and students in the Department of History and Welsh History, have all supported, in one form or another, this endeavour. I have also gained greatly from discussions with Christopher Dyer. I owe particular thanks to Richard Smith and to Barbara Harvey who have both offered foundation to my work and presented me with the opportunity to write this book.

Miri Rubin, as series editor, has been both patient and encouraging; she has offered invaluable comment on earlier versions of the book, as have the series advisers, Jean Dunbabin and Robert Stacey. Terka Acton, Felicity Noble and Sonya Barker at Palgrave have cajoled me along with a kind constancy. Anstice Hughes has been the most careful and considerate of copy-editors. I must also express my thanks to Amil Rigdus.

Sections of this book have been given at meetings and conferences at the University of Leicester, summer 1996; Economic History Society conference, Leeds, spring 1998; University of Wales, Aberystwyth, autumn 1999; Economic History Society conference, Glasgow, spring 2001; Kalamazoo, summer 2001; University of Leeds, summer 2001. I am grateful to those who were present for their comments. I am also very grateful to the Dean and Chapter of Westminster Abbey for permission to cite the Abbey muniments.

This book could not have been written without the support of my family. My parents always encouraged my efforts and my Mum continues to do so. It is with love, and in the memory of my Dad, that I dedicate this book to her. Jane and Bethany were with me throughout and Thomas arrived to see it completed; I could not begin to hope for more or for better than that.

Llansantffraed
August 2002

1

INTRODUCTION: PEASANT AND COMMUNITY

This book is an attempt to explore the limits of peasant society in medieval England. In the last thirty or more years, the study of the medieval English peasantry has moved in new and significant directions. The inter-disciplinarity of the post-war period, the growth of new social history, the encouragement to engage with history from below, and the development of women's studies and gender studies, have all informed research into the medieval peasantry. Two strands in recent decades are particularly prominent and both have, to an extent, borrowed their approaches from other disciplines, namely the social sciences and demography. The social science approach has been most obviously employed by those who have studied with and under J. A. Raftis at the Pontifical Institute, Toronto. Close investigation of the medieval village has been attempted by Raftis and his pupils who have employed manorial court rolls to examine such issues as the peasant family, landholding and inter-peasant dealing.[1] In undertaking this work, these historians have tried both to distinguish between social and economic groups within the village, stratifying that community according to certain criteria (office-holding, for example), and have also attempted to chart changing social relations within the community over time. The other strand, that of demography, has set out to explore both the role of population movement as a causative factor for change (in this respect, the influence of M. M. Postan is more than considerable).[2] Borrowings from demography have prompted investigations not just into long-term population movement but also into the dynamics of the peasant family and household, age at marriage, the onset of fertility, life expectancy, incidence of migration, and so on.

1

These reflections, whilst they have generated their own debates amongst demographic historians, have also permeated other investigations of the medieval peasantry.[3] Questions of capital formation, labour opportunities, the viability of the family farm, diet, standards of living, and morality in the village, have all grown out of or found common ground with this broadly demographic agenda.[4]

Alongside and allied to examination of village society and the medieval peasant family/household formation, there have been associated studies of other features of peasant life. Prominent amongst these has been the study of the peasant land market. The transfer of land was already on the agenda, as an adjunct to studies of, for instance, lordship or villeinage. In the late 1940s R. H. Hilton described the boost in the peasant land market in the late Middle Ages and the social consequences of such a departure. Generally, and this was as true of Hilton as of other historians, the medieval peasant land market was defined as limited and late. Preconceived notions of a peasant economy, borrowed to a degree from studies of more recent peasantries (especially that supplied by A. V. Chayanov), underpinned views of the medieval peasantry and its motive force. As will be discussed more fully in a later chapter, the view of an essentially acommercial peasantry is also evident in the writings of Postan, whose introduction to the *Carte Nativorum* (The Charters of the Villeins) provided a 'key-note' address on peasant economy and land market in the early 1960s. His argument, which essentially concerned the nature of exchange in village society and its dependence on changing family size, remained a canon of the literature for at least two decades and still retains no little currency. Hyams's salvo against this view, delivered in the early 1970s, whilst it proved damaging, did not wholly derail a Chayanovian conceptualisation of the medieval peasantry, as later studies of the land market clearly evince.[5]

But the study of the peasant land market was, by then, a seedbed for alternative views of the peasant economy. Studies by King (Peterborough) and Smith (Bury St Edmund's manors) had begun to show that the market was 'real'. In other words, not just a redistributive mechanism dependent on family-cycle, it responded to economic forces.[6] The work of Smith, in particular, encouraged others who recognised, as Postan had done fifty years earlier (but not for the peasantry), that high and late medieval England was, at least partially, 'commercial'.[7] Studies of commercialisation and the role which the peasantry played in the development of the market have done much to alter the view of the medieval peasantry. In so doing, they have also encouraged a reinvestigation of issues that belonged to a historiography that predates the one so far considered here. In the most recent work on the medieval English peasantry, historians have turned their attention to institutions and forms that might support commercial endeavour and, most importantly, may have been misunderstood or misapplied by a previous generation of historians. This, in particular, has prompted a new interest in aspects of law: the nature of leases, the instruments of credit and the mechanisms which support it, peasant comprehension of courts other than the manor court, the restrictions of villeinage. Additionally, historians of the peasantry, in conceiving of a peasantry engaged beyond the boundaries of manor and vill, have looked to other sources than manorial records to support their investigations: records of county courts, borough court rolls, taxation assessments, nominative listings, have been re-employed, this time as sources for the study of the peasantry. Historians now look for and find peasants in contexts beyond the manor and villages, in markets, in county courts, in military levies, or on pilgrimage.

This reacquaintance with non-manorial institutions is, in small part, a return to an older and established historiography. The main elements of a pre-*c*.1960 historiography – serfdom, villeinage, the manor, the village community and its antecedents – can be characterised as the investigation of institutions. The agenda of the early investigators into English peasantry was established, unsurprisingly, by a discipline which, at the close of the nineteenth century, was preoccupied with the great institutions of the state, not least of which was the law. Maitland's famous but brief examination of the manorial records of a Cambridgeshire vill (Wilburton) was not an early investigation into peasantry but into landholding and estate policy.[8] The same can be said of a number of studies which soon followed, including Davenport's study of a Norfolk manor and A. Clark's research into Essex villeinage.[9] At the same time, these, and others, were important works which provided a foundation for subsequent studies. Vinogradoff on the manor and villeinage; Maitland on the manor court, on Bracton and serfdom, on tenure: these are the staples of a 'peasant' historiography. They persist until the present in legal works and in the close regard for institutions which informs so much of the study of the medieval peasantry.[10] Thus, throughout the last century, starting with the work of Levett on Winchester, estate studies have thrown much light on the condition of tenants, that is, members of the peasantry.[11] Other work on institutions also informs our understanding of the medieval peasantry: Kosminsky's work on the Hundred Rolls, for instance, has provided the basis for a general conception of diversity amongst the peasantry, whilst work by 'political' historians on taxation and the records of the Exchequer has thrown up further avenues of investigation. Discussion of serfdom as an institution also persists.[12] Another hugely important development of this early historiography, and again one linked to an abiding interest in institutions as well as one that continues to have a significant impact, was the 'programme' of publication, typically the work of local record societies, which produced series of edited court rolls and associated manorial documents. Local record societies also published editions of national or non-local records relating to their locale and furnished historians with immensely useful series of taxation assessments, church court material, wills and probates, feets of fine (records of dealings in free land), and so on.[13]

Between this legalistic/institutional/constitutional historiography and the social science historiography of recent decades, there have been a few evident links. There were early indications of a movement into new territory, notably the formidable advance made by R. H. Tawney, whose *Agrarian Problems in the Sixteenth Century* (1912) offered some extraordinarily apposite insights into the late medieval peasantry. Tawney recognised the potential for an aggressively acquisitive peasantry to take full advantage of conditions in the medieval village. Tawney's work found some sympathetic resonances in the early study of the fourteenth-century land market by Hudson.[14] But, interestingly, the views of Tawney and, less surprisingly, Hudson remained largely overlooked, incompatible with the perspective that took hold from the post-war period. In terms of a general view of peasantry, overall passivity, at least in economic terms, was the order of the day. Homans's study of English villagers in the thirteenth century places the peasant family at the centre of the rural economy, in much the same way as did later studies by Raftis and Postan.[15] One approach that also emerged during this period was the Marxist study of the medieval English peasantry, which, with some irony, can also be accommodated, in its shared general sense of a coherent village community, with the work of Raftis and of Postan and their respective followers. For historians such as Hilton, working from the 1940s on English peasantry, the recognition of the peasantry as a 'class', and its consciousness as such, not least in its opposition to lordship, is of fundamental importance. All other forces, social or economic, lose out to this bond. What all of these works achieved, despite their very different agendas, was a paradigm shift which helped move the focus of historians' attentions away from institutions, such as lordship and the manor, and onto the peasantry.

The renewed emphasis on the peasants themselves, as outlined at the beginning of this chapter, challenges certain notions traditionally associated with the peasantry. Narrow definitions of 'peasantry' or 'village community' cannot easily be accommodated within a thesis that sees peasants engaging in a variety of contexts beyond the family farm and the local community. The concept of 'community' has powerful resonances in the historiography of the English peasantry and has been employed as a by-word for solidity, an antidote to the friendless anonymity of urban life.[16] 'Community', in the context of the medieval village, means self-regulation, mutual support, resistance, ceremony, collective piety, but it also implies remoteness, insularity and shared assumptions. Rubin has recently expressed some concern that the concept of community 'obscures rather than reveals' since it hides the nuances of internal conflict and difference.[17] It is certainly an accusation not infrequently levelled at historians of the medieval village that they have been insufficiently aware of tensions and differences within the village, either because they have preferred to see any such tension as secondary to external conflict with lordship (and have accordingly identified the peasantry as essentially a 'class') or because they have defined difference according to rigid and fairly arbitrary criteria.[18] The development of a more nuanced conception of community requires, therefore, an explicit acknowledgement of that difference and an exploration of the factors that created differences within the village community and its smaller units, including the peasant family. Rigby, in his attempt to employ closure theory as a device to help explicate the function of late medieval English society, has perhaps done most to challenge any remaining complacencies over the concept of 'community'. For Rigby, community in the Middle Ages is as likely to be constructed around issues of exclusion as it is around issues of inclusion. Further, and most importantly for what follows in this book, membership of communities is fluid and insecure, determined by a variety of motives, agendas and exogenous forces. Finally, and also of vital importance, individuals are capable of multiple memberships, able to belong to numbers of communities. None of this is, of course, especially surprising, but in its application to the high and late Middle Ages and to the medieval English peasantry, various levels of analysis are admitted, levels which have not been at the centre of earlier investigations of the medieval peasantry. Thus, we are encouraged to think of peasants as members of family, household, neighbourhood, village, county, nation-state; of parish, guild, sect; as co-parceners, as parties and partners; as suitors, litigants, jurors; as administrators and petitioners; as employers and as labourers; as villeins, neifs, freemen; as 'kulaks', the poor, even the landless.

With this diversity comes the challenge to community which Rubin has described: these multi-identities wreak havoc with any more simplistic notions of community ethos or collective endeavour. However, it is also the case that acknowledgement of a multiplicity of memberships extends the concept of community. In recognising that peasant membership was not confined to the close(d) communities of family and village, examination of the nature of family and village community gains significant new dimensions. This diversity of experience and membership also calls into question monolithic concepts of 'peasantry'. Any rigid, economic definition of the peasantry has been roundly dismissed by historians of the medieval peasantry, and, in its place, implicit in the work of some, explicit in others, is the recognition that 'peasant' is a label which can be applied generously. Medievalists have been, generally speaking, most comfortable with the flexible definition most evident in the work of anthropologists such as Thorner. Thorner's criteria of the peasant economy – that it should be primarily agricultural, that it should exist within a 'territorial state', that there should be towns which can be sustained by that agriculture, that the principal unit of production should be the peasant family – also acknowledge other likely variables, including a shifting degree of serfdom or 'semi-freedom' and, to a limited extent, market integration.[19] As more than one commentator has noted, it is in the degree of involvement with the 'non-peasant' sector that the definition of peasantry is determined. Most especially, in economic terms, it is the degree of market involvement and the extent to which individuals produce for consumption or for the market that needs to be carefully scrutinised. Undoubtedly, there were individuals in the high and late Middle Ages, especially the kulaks of the medieval village, who tested these boundaries, but in their proximity to their landholding, their membership of local communities, and, frequently, in their legal status as serfs, the term 'peasant' still seems entirely appropriate.

If definitions of peasant and community have proved fluid and open to debate for this period, an explanation lies in the period itself. The three centuries between 1200 and 1500 were a time of enormous change which saw the first stirrings of capitalism and the decline of 'feudalism'. The process by which a society based upon systems of mutual dependency, in which labour and rent obligations were exacted by lords from their dependent tenantry in return for promises of protection, evolved into one in which, increasingly, relations were dictated by the market and settled for money or money's worth, is explicable in a number of ways. The extraordinary demographic shifts of the period, with population rising to a high point of c.5–6 million around 1300, possibly declining before the plagues of the mid-century, which cut numbers by half, and then stagnating until the late fifteenth century when began a slow recovery, have been acknowledged as a significant cause of social and economic change.[20] Against population movement, others have set endemic social and economic discord, or class struggle, which precipitated the end of feudal society.[21] The search for the cause of these momentous changes remains a potent force in medieval historiography but all parties are generally agreed that the medieval England of c.1500 was a different place to the medieval England of three hundred years earlier.

As well as population change and a limited redistribution of political, legal and economic powers, the historical landscape had altered in other ways. Physically, a greater proportion of the population lived in towns by the end of the fifteenth century than had done so c.1200; less land was cultivated by 1500 and more of that land was given over to pasture. The economy by the end of the fifteenth century was far more dependent on the export of finished goods than it had been in the thirteenth and fourteenth centuries. Changes in standards of living and diet are also evident with a general indication of improved conditions by the fifteenth century. Individuals re-employed their surplus in consumption but also in expressions of piety. They also invested, especially in land. The broad distinctions persisted, however. Southern and eastern England enjoyed a measure of prosperity and a degree of market intensity that was not to be found in the highland zones to the west (north and south). Whilst some areas developed as centres of rural industry, others, such as parts of Cornwall, Derbyshire and Cumbria, had always been home to industries, such as mining, and, as such, dual economies.

These differences, whether temporal or spatial, affected social structure, local and regional economies and the basic tenor of peasant societies. We will need to return to this diversity of experience, across time

and between regions, in the following chapters. It is in that diversity
that the multiplicity of the experiences of peasants and their communities is located and it is from that diversity that multiple explanations
and historical anomalies begin to look like different but still reasonable
explanations. It is as an exploration of that difference and the various
consequences of that broad membership that this book is written.

Part I

Land

In the opening part of this book, an attempt will be made to describe some of the more fundamental aspects of peasant life. Reserving discussion of family for Part II, the principal aim here is to offer a sense of landholding amongst the peasantry of high and late medieval England. In the first chapter of Part I, discussion of differences in tenure, rents owed and the size of landholding will establish the considerable disequilibrium of the medieval countryside, a disequilibrium which was revealed not just across time and between regions but within villages and hamlets. The following two chapters will explore such disparities. In Chapter 3, the causes of differences in rent, tenure and holding size will be scrutinised. Here the aim is to show the range of influences capable of effecting changes in landholding. In the final chapter of Part I, Chapter 4, the transfer of land will be considered in similar terms.

Land was, of course, of vital importance for peasants in this, as in any, period. It helped define their nature, their economy, their legal status and their family form. In some cases, as we shall discuss in later chapters, landholding was of paramount importance in constructing the range of opportunity and the expectations of the individual landholder and his family. In the simplest terms, availability of land and the limits of its uses affected, in the most immediate terms, the living standards of the peasantry. Decisions about landholding and the use of land also influenced the nature and organisation of local communities and the expectations which lords made of their tenants.

Not all peasants were or could be as closely tied to the land. A proximity to the soil, epitomised in images of the patient, plodding ploughman, does not have a general application. The diversity of land-holding amongst the medieval peasantry is testimony both to the range of factors which played upon rural dwellers and also to the possibilities and the forces that encouraged and compelled peasants to engage with individuals, families and institutions beyond the family farm. That the landholding patterns of the tenantry, their tenures and their obligations, also changed over the period of this study is testimony to that engagement. The simple but important point in what follows is that land did not mean the same thing to all peasants at all times in this period and, in fact, for some it mattered far more than it did for others. However, it was through an enduring association with land, whether that association was substantial or relatively minor, that villagers were identified by contemporaries, and it was in that proximity to the soil that they may, perhaps, have continued to identify themselves.

2

LAND: TENURE, LANDHOLDING AND RENT

This chapter will be concerned with the land of the peasantry: the size of holdings, the different ways in which land could be held, and the rents and other obligations which individuals owed their lords for holding land. Discussion of the range of influences which played upon peasant landholding and the transfer of that land within the peasant community will be reserved for the following chapters. For the moment, discussion of landholding and its obligations offers us a point of access into the expectations which society made of peasants in the high and late Middle Ages and an insight into the disparities which existed in the medieval countryside. It will also permit us to establish some of the more significant developments in the economic and societal life of the peasantry during the three centuries between 1200 and 1500. It is an obvious but important point that even something as immobile as land was not immune from historical developments; nor were those who lived upon the land isolated from wider economic and social trends.

Land held by the peasantry in this period fell into three broad categories: *unfree land*, that is land held typically, but not exclusively, by villein or servile tenants of a manorial lord according to the custom of the manor (hence also *customary* land) and over which the lord held sway;[1] *free land*, land which was held directly or indirectly of the king and, as a consequence, disputes concerning which could be referred to the king's courts and the common law; and *leasehold*, or contractual tenancies, which provided the tenant, or more accurately the lessee, with an interest in the land, whether free or unfree, for a period of time, be that for a term of years, the life of the lessee or some other person, or for some indeterminate period (at the will of the lord, say). Leasehold could be actionable at common law or it could be granted by the lord to his unfree tenantry and governed by the custom of the manor. As shall be more fully discussed in the next chapter, a combination of different landscapes and institutions helped determine the quality and relative distribution of peasant tenures in the late Middle Ages; before we consider the influences that played upon peasant land-holding we need to describe its variety. We shall begin with an overview of tenurial differences and follow this with short discussions of size of landholding and rent.

Landholding: Tenure

Serfdom and tenure in villeinage

In Anglo-Saxon and early Norman England, the peasant tenantry is broadly to be distinguished from slaves. To employ the terminology of Domesday Book, in the late eleventh century the peasantry was divided between *villani, cotarii, bordarii, servi, bovarii, coliberti*. The *villani*, but also the *cotarii*, and *bordarii*, could stand on a par with the sections of the freer elements in the eleventh-century countryside, notably the *sochmanni* or sokemen. Although all owed obligations to their lord, relativities of freedom were indistinct and *villani* and their like were, as we shall see, not 'serfs' in a thirteenth-century sense of the word. Instead, they were husbandmen or farmers who held land and were restrained only by the particular expectations of lordship but not formally distinguished as unfree. Essentially, they enjoyed rights at law.[2] By contrast the *servi, bovarii* and *coliberti* were servile or of servile origin and, as such, were obliged to labour upon their lord's demesnes in roles that would, in later centuries, be filled by paid estate workers or *famuli*. Their rights were extremely limited and, at least in the eyes of Anglo-Saxon laws, they existed more as chattels than as individuals. In particular, they did not enjoy a right to leave their lord's demesne at will.

Between the eleventh century and the thirteenth century, and more particularly between the late twelfth and the early thirteenth centuries, the concept of unfreedom was extended and offered definition – or redefinition – by common law. As landlords sought to restrain their labour force and maximise the advantages from their tenantry, they sought mechanisms which enabled such restraint and control.

Although it has recently been suggested that significant changes in legal status and conditions of tenure were under way from the eleventh century, it is most often argued that the creation of a common law villeinage was no more than an appendage to a developing law of real property under the Angevins.[3] In the late twelfth century, during the reign of Henry II, possessory actions at common law distinguished between freeland, which could be recovered through the king's courts, and land which was held unfreely, which could not. In defining freedom, it has been suggested, common lawyers inadvertently set the seal on unfreedom as well.[4] Thus, those who may once have held by a degree of freedom relatively weak in comparison with their immediate superiors were now firmly distinguished as unfree, their access to the king's courts barred in actions against their lord.[5] The dividing line was drawn between the *villani* and the *sochmanni*, the former unfree as regards their access to the common law, the latter free.

By the thirteenth century, the distinctions between neifs or serfs (*nativi* or *servi*), those unfree by birth, and villeins (*villani*), those who may have become unfree, possibly by acquisition of unfree land, had blurred (at least in the record). Historians tend to adopt a shorthand of 'unfree' in referring to that group of tenants who held from and were the *de iure* property of their manorial lord but, as we have seen, the likelihood is that, of the two constituent elements, the servile tenants were the descendants of Anglo-Saxon slaves whilst villeins were descendants of freemen who had fallen into a state of serfdom, probably as a result of the extension and clarification of a common law of villeinage in the twelfth and early thirteenth centuries.[6]

However, such distinctions continued to resurface and to be tested at law throughout the remainder of our period. By the thirteenth century, the important distinction between villeinage and serfdom was, essentially, that those who held in villeinage were associated with serfdom by tenure, but those who were serfs (*servi*) or neifs (*nativi*) were born into a condition of serfdom; they were neifs by blood (*nativi de sanguine*) and their condition was inescapable. Effectively the chattels of their lord, they could be bought and sold along with his other property; consequently, their offspring were often referred to as brood or litter (*sequelae*). The concept of neifty in blood constituted an element of serfdom which survived, in legal theory, even into the sixteenth century; in reality, however, servile tenures based upon birth had all but been extinguished by the early fifteenth century. The Fellows of Merton College, Oxford, lords of the manor of Kibworth Harcourt,

Leicester, agreed, for example, to stop using the term 'nativus' of their tenants there in 1439, whilst 75 years earlier the same term had been outlawed on certain manors of the estates of the prior and convent of Durham. In 1364 an injunction issued at West-Raynton to 'all tenants of this vill and of the vill of East-Raynton' ordered that 'none of them should call anyone of the same vills "neif of the lord"'.[7] That said, the association of servility with birth meant that, even as, during the fourteenth and fifteenth centuries, unfree tenures developed and loosened their association with servility and, as a consequence, those who were serfs through tenure experienced an amelioration of their position, there remained some families whose members were born into serfdom and who could not shake off the stigma of serfdom, just as there were some lords who resolutely refused to abandon the concept. In the late 1530s William, earl of Arundel, could write of one Thomas Goodfreye that 'he is in truth my bondman, as all his progenitors have been, and if I made him free it would be to the prejudice of my inheritance for ever'.[8] However, even if, in principle, lords such as Arundel could still think of serfdom in terms familiar to their high and late medieval counterparts,[9] by the early sixteenth century the nature of unfree tenure had altered almost beyond recognition.

It was the development of villeinage, serfdom by tenure rather than serfdom by blood, that paved the way for the eventual disappearance of all aspects of servility, including serfdom by blood – a process that, if we followed it to its conclusion, would carry us far beyond the early sixteenth century. Instead, we should content ourselves here with the development of villein tenure in the high Middle Ages, its variety of forms, and its adaption in the late Middle Ages. The legal reforms of the twelfth century, by extending the common law of real property and the protection which it offered those who held land freely, effectively denied access to those who did not hold land by free tenure. Essentially, to hold land unfreely or by lease was defined by the failure to hold it freely, as the thirteenth-century jurist Bracton explained,

> a free tenement is a tenement which a person holds to himself and his heirs. . . . But a tenement cannot be called free which he possesses for a certain number of years. . . . Likewise a tenement cannot be called free which he holds at the will of lords, precariously. . . . Likewise a tenement is called free to distinguish it from villeinage. . . .[10]

Those who held their land from their manorial lords 'in villeinage' or 'in bondage' had no recourse against their lords in the king's courts, that is, at common law.[11] For a defendant to defeat a plea in land at common law, it was only necessary to prove that the plaintiff was his serf or held from him in villeinage. Proof came, in the case of neifty or serfdom by blood, from the servile lineage of the plaintiff or, as regards those who held in villeinage, in the obligations which a lord had managed to extract from his tenantry. When, in 1233, Emma, the widow of Reginald of Bradebroc, pursued the abbot of Abingdon at common law for her rights as a widow to one-third of her late husband's lands, the abbot refused to respond on the grounds that Reginald had held his land as a villein. A jury supported the abbot, reporting to the court that Reginald

> had held in villeinage because he could not arrange the marriage of his daughter without payment of a fine to the lord (*merchet*), and that, in marrying off his daughter, Dionisia, he had paid the same abbot half a mark (80d.); and also that the same abbot could raise tallage from him; and also that he had four sons, of whom the youngest remained as tenant in villeinage, whilst the three others took land wherever they could.

These three damning pieces of evidence, the payment of two arbitrary fines (*merchet* and *tallage*)[12] as well as the practice of inheritance by the youngest son (ultimogeniture or Borough English), proved the unfree status of Reginald and his widow and assured victory for the abbot, irrespective of the reasonableness of Emma's claim.[13]

Doubtless, to be a serf or to hold land in villeinage was to be insecure and to hold your property and live your life at the whim of your lord. Aside from the demands of lordship which, by the beginning of our period, were exacted in a variety of forms, as the Bradebroc case illustrates, the lord enjoyed the potential for arbitrary action. In addition to the more usual penalties associated with unfree tenure – heavy labour services, occasional pecuniary levies (*tallage*), fines to be paid for the right to leave the manor (*chevage*), to marry (*merchet*), to succeed to property (*heriot*), to compensate for illicit sexual unions or their product (*leyrwite* and *childwite*), to sell livestock (*tolnetum*) – it was, for instance, theoretically possible for the lord to evict his tenant or to impose upon him or her in a number of other ways. As Hyams has attempted to show, a defining criterion of villeinage by the thirteenth century was the lord's ability to change what was deemed customary, in other words to bring uncertainty to obligations which his tenants might have imagined as sure and fixed.[14] Furthermore, there is some indication, especially in the thirteenth century, that lords increased the burdens of customary service, especially labour service, whilst, where circumstances permitted, some also attempted to adjust the burden of unassessed *ad hoc* payments, such as entry fines.[15]

That said, it is important not to overstate the impediments which villeinage or serfdom brought. Although, in theory, the unfree tenant went to bed not knowing what his next day would bring, in reality much of the requirements of unfree tenure were enshrined in custom which, although far from immutable, offered considerable protection. By the thirteenth century the labour services and other elements of rent which a lord could demand from his or her tenant were already largely well established; unfree tenants were unlikely to be ejected from their holdings unless they failed repeatedly to maintain them in good order; contrary to legal theory, which held that a serf or villein had no rights in property since they themselves were the property of their lords, their heirs could expect to inherit land whilst, increasingly, it was common for unfree tenants to have the right to sell or otherwise alienate their holdings; the fines and penalties which an unfree tenant was likely to pay were, if not necessarily protected by custom, ameliorated by the vigilance of the village community which, through the manorial court, *inter alia*, restrained the excesses of the lord.[16]

Furthermore, nor were all villeins equally disadvantaged. As we shall see, the expectations which landlords brought to their unfree tenantry varied significantly and, importantly, were constrained by a variety of impediments, conditions and past histories. A special case, in particular, can be made for the so-called 'villein sokemen' of ancient demesne, that is, manors held directly by the crown, such as Havering-atte-Bower in Essex. The king's villeins, effectively protected by the interests of the crown which, in the twelfth century, had sought to preserve the wealth of its own tenantry for its own economic advantage, enjoyed certain advantages over the villeins of other lords. In particular, unlike other villeins, they were accorded rights of access to common law. Interestingly, their advantage increased in the thirteenth century as they managed to exploit their peculiar circumstance, a circumstance initiated by their lord, the crown, to eke further benefits from that same lordship. Most recently, McIntosh, in discussing the development of the ancient demesne at Havering, has suggested that the particular advantages of the king's tenantry there were, at least in part, a product of ill-considered seigneurial policies in the mid-thirteenth century. The fixing of low rents, possibly intended to attract new tenants to the manor, further improved the advantage of these unfree tenants and helped, as we shall see, encourage a rash of litigation as tenants on other manors attempted to claim similar status.[17]

The unfree tenure of land and the condition of serfdom or villeinage, concepts which the early law courts had helped develop and which were not dependent upon the definition of statute, were never abolished but simply dwindled into abeyance. Although serfdom (bondage) and tenure in villeinage persisted throughout the Middle Ages, the taint of serfdom undoubtedly remaining – for those who suffered it – as demeaning and unwelcome as ever, for the majority of those who held by unfree tenures the institutional reality of serfdom was markedly different by the close of the fifteenth century than it had been two hundred years previously. In the first decades of the fifteenth century, at Kibworth Harcourt in Leicestershire, tenure 'in bondage' gave way to tenure 'at the will of the lord'; here it seems that the tenantry insisted that their lords, the Fellows of Merton College, Oxford, replace the older tenurial formula, so strongly redolent of servitude, with the rather more neutral wording. Elsewhere, the disappearance of tenure 'in bondage' or 'in villeinage' was not always so abrupt but, generally, tenures strongly suggestive of bond servitude gave way to unfree tenures whereby the tenant held 'at the will of the lord according to the custom of the manor'. In fact, there was enormous variety in the development of tenurial forms in the late fourteenth and fifteenth centuries;[18] if there was a defining principle behind this mutiplicity of forms, it was still to be found in the assumption that the tenant held from his lord according to manorial custom and not, therefore, from the king according to common law.[19] It was only in the sixteenth century, with the development of a common law of copyhold, that tenants of land descended from unfree tenures fell under the protection of the common law.[20] If, then, in the minds of lawyers at the close of the Middle Ages, the fundamental distinction between unfree tenures and free tenures remained, *de facto* the tenure of unfree land was no longer so onerous as once it had been, a reality that owed more to economic change than to legal wrangling. This is a point to which we shall return later in this chapter; before we do, however, we should briefly consider the development of leasehold and, even more briefly, free tenure, in this period.

Leasehold

Although most of the unfree peasants held land as tenants from their lord, that is they held according to some form of unfree tenure for an interest which was very likely to be hereditary, there were some villagers who held, in the strict sense, not as tenants but as lessees. In such cases they normally held for a set period, often a term of years. There were, in some parts of the country, forms of leasehold which were already well established by the thirteenth and early fourteenth centuries. On the estates of the Duchy of Cornwall, established in 1337, the predominant peasant tenure was a seven-year lease at a market rent and with right of renewal.[21] Elsewhere, at this time, leasehold was much less common. In the late thirteenth and early fourteenth centuries, leases between lord and peasant, when they occurred on manors in southern, central and eastern England, tended to be for fairly short terms and were less likely to involve the leasing of a servile holding than they were the lease of a portion of the lord's demesne. That said, on occasion tenants might group together and lease substantial parcels of demesne for lengthy terms.[22]

Leases of servile holdings, if they occurred at this time, were often temporary measures employed by the lord to ensure a holding remained tenanted during some hiatus. For instance, in 1316/17, during the worst year of the Great Famine, on the Westminster Abbey manor of Birdbrook, the deaths of five of the lord's 29 unfree tenants, possibly as a result of food shortage or associated disease, caused the lord temporarily to lease parts of the holdings to local freemen. On the Suffolk manor of Mildenhall, a Bury St Edmunds manor, many holdings were held at farm by the early fourteenth century.[23] On the estates of the bishop of Ely, something closer to a policy of leasing complete holdings was already making its appearance by the close of the thirteenth century; at Littlebury (Essex), for example, three tenements were leased to the peasantry by 1299. That these Littlebury tenants now held by lease for a fixed annual money rent (or, more correctly, 'farm') rather than by villein tenure for rent predominantly in the form of labour service, represented a growing tendency reflected elsewhere on the estate and one which responded to a retreat from direct management of the demesne by the lord.[24] It also hinted at a trend that would gain its full momentum in the second half of the fourteenth century.

It seems to have been the demographic collapse of the mid-fourteenth century that had the greatest effect on tenures and, in

particular, precipitated the widespread adoption of leasehold. Returning, for the moment, to the Westminster Abbey estates, it is clear that
there the monks, as landlords, attempted to ensure holdings remained
occupied after the first and subsequent outbreaks of plague; with survivors of the plague apparently increasingly reluctant to hold land by
the traditional customary tenures, the monks were obliged to grant
leases of those same holdings which came into their hands as the previous tenants died.[25] The situation on the Westminster Abbey estates
also applied elsewhere, as investigation of the late medieval estates of,
for instance, the bishop of Worcester and the prior of Durham have also
revealed.[26]

Leasehold, therefore, was frequently an alternative offered by landlords to tenants who were not, in the late fourteenth century, prepared
to hold large holdings by unfree tenure in return for labour services.
Since, then, lords often saw leasehold, in the late fourteenth and early
fifteenth centuries, as a temporary measure, much perhaps as they had
in the first half of the fourteenth century, the anticipation remained
that tenure in villeinage and all that was associated with it, most importantly labour services, would one day be restored. Most measures taken
in the second half of the fourteenth century seem to reflect this uncertainty. There was, during this period, considerable variety in the form
that leases of customary holdings took from one estate to the next; furthermore, the length and degree of security of the lease on any particular estate also underwent considerable changes during our period.
Thus, on some of the manors in the West Midlands, leases granted
after the first outbreak of plague were often for a term of years or for
a life but many granted towards the end of the fourteenth century were
far shorter than this, reflecting the uncertainty of both lord and
tenant.[27] Similar developments can be found on the manors of the
prior of Durham; after the Black Death leases for life were most
common but by the early fifteenth century leases of nine years or less
accounted for about half of all leases taken up. By mid-century, three-
and six-year leases had become the rule.[28] On the Westminster Abbey
manor of Birdbrook, in north Essex, 12-year leases gave way to shorter
terms so that, by the close of the fourteenth century, lessees were
typically admitted for a single year.[29]

Inevitably, not all manors saw the same developments. On some
manors, leasehold was not adopted; instead customary tenure was
simply modified and, presumably, ameliorated. At Kibworth Harcourt
in Leicestershire, as we have already seen, land which had been held

'in bondage' in the fourteenth century came to be held 'at the will of the lord';[30] on certain estates in the West Midlands tenants continued to hold in customary tenure, but the labour service component was everywhere replaced by an assized rent from the beginning of the fifteenth century.[31] Outside of central England, particularly where fragmentation of the large labour service holdings had occurred early, the introduction of leasehold, which elsewhere was essentially an innovation of landlords keen to retain their tenantry and some level of income from rents, would not have been so important. In eastern England, where the larger traditional units of landholding had all but vanished on many manors by the thirteenth century, where land was dealt with in very small parcels, where labour services were relatively light or non-existent, and where unfree tenants enjoyed extensive rights of alienation over their property, lords did not need to resort to leasing to ensure their holdings remained populated. Instead, as at Hakeford Hall in Coltishall (Norfolk), land remained a saleable commodity; unlike certain other parts of the country, tenants here, possibly with less to fear from the burdens of serfdom, were prepared to continue holding their land in servitude whilst lords, whose ultimate strategy was not to enforce labour services on the demesne but to oversee and, thereby, to reap the benefits of a peasant market in land, did not see the *status quo ante* disrupted in ways which more 'traditional' landlords had witnessed.[32]

Discussion of leasehold cannot be complete without some acknowledgement that peasants could also be lessees not from their lords but from their fellow villagers. Sub-letting of holdings to under-tenants was a common, if not especially well documented, feature of medieval peasant landholding. Short-term leases of unfree land, of a year or two, were not always registered in the manor court and nor was there an expectation that they should be. On the estates of St Albans Abbey, for instance, inter-tenant leases of short duration did not require the lord's consent.[33] Longer terms between tenants were subject to registration and the payment of an appropriate conveyancing fee, an entry fine. If lords on some manors were slow to develop leasehold for larger holdings, it seems very likely that their tenants were employing leasehold at a much earlier date.

Freehold

Although discussion of the peasantry in high and late medieval England has tended to focus upon the unfree tenantry, principally because they feature more prominently in surviving records, the free peasantry was a very important contingent within the countryside, especially in those parts of the country where population continued, even into the high Middle Ages, to be able to expand into new land. Free tenants, often holding very small plots of land, provided a significant element of the rural workforce whilst the presence of substantial areas of freeland affected considerably the timbre of rural life.[34]

In the centuries before the Conquest a situation loosely analogous to that which followed it can be described but, instead of forcing a distinction between freemen and serfs, a distinction can be drawn between freemen and slaves. The process whereby in the centuries after the Conquest a part of the once free tenantry, the villeins or *villani*, was, to all intents and purposes, absorbed into the unfree population also left in its train a substantial body of freeholders. The number of free tenures and free tenants had also increased in the century and more after the Conquest; this growth can be explained in terms of population growth and the consequent colonisation of new land, which ate into woodland, moorland and poorer grade land, the 'waste'. Hilton distinguishes between regions where free tenure abounded and those where it was sparsely represented, suggesting that free tenure was more evident in those parts of the country where new land had been cleared from the waste or assarted; precocious commercialisation in some parts of the country may have also encouraged a spread of free tenancies. He notes however that even in areas where colonisation of this kind was possible in the twelfth and thirteenth centuries, during a time of wholesale expansion and population growth, powerful lords, such as large monastic houses, managed, during the same period and in the same regions, to impose villeinage and weighty obligations upon their own tenants. The Hundred Rolls of the late thirteenth century, which provide our best view of the distribution of tenures in the Middle Ages after Domesday Book, show that over one-third of tenants were free in those parts of England covered by the rolls; in certain areas of central and eastern England perhaps 70 per cent of tenants were free whilst in others no more than 20 per cent held land freely.[35]

To hold land freely was certainly to enjoy advantages over your unfree neighbours. Principally, free tenants enjoyed the protection of common law against their own lords, especially in the particular form of the possessory assize of novel disseisin which originated in the late twelfth century and offered remedy for a free tenant ejected from his holding. They could also freely alienate and inherit land, although the extent of these rights was contested. Issues of alienation and of inheritance had social significance, not least in the challenges that they posed heirs and lords. By the end of the thirteenth century, however, the rights of free tenants to perform both were evident and confirmed by statutes, particularly *Quia Emptores* (1290).[36] That peasant tenants were alert to legal developments in free tenure and recognised the benefits is also clear. On the Westminster Abbey manor of Birdbrook in July 1294, a free tenant, John Parkgate, present in court, said that he held his land 'according to the statute [of *Quia Emptores*], directly from the lord and without anyone between them so that the service owed the lord, as rent, should be for his portion of the tenement only.'[37]

These developments in tenure were, as we have already seen, the consequence of changes in law and administration; they also, especially in the emergence of leasehold in the place of customary tenures, reflected seigneurial policy. Importantly, therefore, the way in which the peasantry held land was not static and it was certainly not uniform, issues which will be considered in more detail in the next chapter. As we shall now see, differences in land tenure were also mirrored in the size of tenant landholdings and the obligations which they owed.

Landholding: Size and Rent

The familiar view of the peasant holding in the Middle Ages is of a fairly substantial holding, perhaps of 30 or 40 acres, divided into strips, scattered throughout the common fields. Tenants of these holdings, which were referred to variously as yardlands, bondlands, virgates, bovates, oxgangs, were serfs or villeins and, again, according to the traditional picture, owed their lord rent principally in the form of labour on the lord's portion of a manor. Such holdings undoubtedly did dominate landholding on many manors in late medieval England. Even on those manors where these standard holdings occupied the core of the tenant land, there also existed other units of landholding, including smaller plots of unfree land, freeland held both as smallholdings but also as extensive blocks (effectively manors in their own right), and, in addition, acres of demesne arable and pasture held by lease from the lord. On the bishop of Winchester's Somerset manor of Orchard, in the mid-fourteenth century, there were, as well as five free tenancies, ranging between 1 and 15 acres in extent, 30 tenants 'in bondage', in other words holding for some form of customary rent; of these last 30 tenants, 13 seem to have held virgates, or more precisely fractions of virgates, in return for weekly labour services or their money equivalents. A virgate at Orchard was 40 acres but no tenant held as much as this, most (eight) holding a quarter-virgate, whilst one tenant held half a virgate and two held eighth-virgates.[38] The remaining unfree tenants held small plots, often little more than a cottage and garden. The greater proportion of the tenant land, which was estimated at approximately 200 acres in total, was therefore held as fractions of virgates (110 acres), with most other holdings comprising no more than a couple of acres.[39]

Even on manors where these large standard holdings existed and where they accounted for most of the tenanted land, they were likely to be held by a minority of the tenant population. In fact, as Kosminsky's famous analysis of the Hundred Rolls of 1279 indicates, the majority of tenants in parts of eastern and central England, the area covered by the surviving rolls, held substantially less than even a quarter-virgate, 10 acres or less. On some manors in the same areas of open-field country, the virgate and its larger fractions was no more than a documentary fiction, and, even by the late thirteenth century, almost all tenants held very small plots indeed.[40] On other manors, where the virgate and its fractions persisted as more than simply a unit of account, there were also tenants holding much smaller plots of land. Beneath the ranks of the middling tenantry, those who held a half or quarter virgate, in those areas of open-field or champion agriculture, essentially a broad central band of the country, there were small landholders who held no more than their residence, a garden and, perhaps, a small plot of land. At Orchard, in addition to the virgates, there were, as already noted, also five freeholdings, the largest of which was 15 acres. All of the others were under 10 acres, all but one of these under 5 acres. Of the remaining unfree tenements, 26 in all, none was larger than 5 acres and the majority (21) were in extent no more than a cottage with garden or a single acre.[41] Beyond the boundaries of the open-field region, smallholdings were even more in evidence.

Hardly surprisingly, perhaps, there was, in the late Middle Ages, some correlation between regional types and landholding size. If we begin with a broad distinction between the lowland and highland zones of England, we find that the far west of England, both north and south, situated outside of champion or open-field country, displayed quite different patterns of landholding from that found within the broad band of open-field husbandry stretching from the south coast to the north-east. Beyond the boundaries of open-field agriculture were areas where a system of standard holdings and heavy labour services had never existed and where much land was already enclosed, in some cases for centuries; there, units of landholding seem generally to have been quite small. In Cornwall, for example, the large standard holdings, or virgates, were less in evidence, nor was there much recourse to labour services; the landholding of the tenants of the duke of Cornwall in the first half of the fourteenth century fail to evidence the relative uniformity of the manors of central and southern England and, instead, a very few tenants held enormous tracts of land (in one case as much as 400 acres) whilst the majority seem to have held much smaller plots of 10 or so acres; in parts of the north-west, landholding patterns were also quite distinct from that to be found in the regions of open-field agriculture.[42] There is a similarly disparate quality to landholding in the east of the country and in Kent. Throughout considerable stretches of Norfolk, Suffolk and Essex, tenants in the generations before the arrival of plague held often very small plots of land, frequently much less than five acres; although at Redgrave, a Suffolk manor of the Abbey of Bury St Edmunds, the largest holding was 40 acres, the mean holding size seems to have been less than five acres and it is estimated that almost 30 per cent of holdings comprised less than a single acre.[43] The common rents paid to the abbot of the Cistercian Abbey of Sibton in 1328 include the rents of tenants for the manor of Sibton, a few miles inland from the coast at Dunwich (Suffolk), six of the tenants are described as neifs (*nativi*) and they held some of the largest plots, typically three or six acres, which were fractions of large standard holdings. Most tenants at Sibton held less, either cottages or messuages, sometimes with odd acres attached.[44] In Kent, similarly, land appears to have been often held in small parcels; at Gillingham, in 1285, half or more of the holdings were of two acres or less.[45]

If size of landholding could vary so markedly, it is also likely that disparities increased over the period. By the late thirteenth century, a smallholding class had existed for centuries but the origins of all smallholdings were not the same and, most importantly, the number of smallholdings was, by the thirteenth century, proliferating. In certain cases some or all of the smallholdings of a manor were the tenurial descendants of similar pre-Conquest holdings, a feature reasonably evident in the case of some freeholdings on the estates of the Abbey of

Bury St Edmunds, for instance. On the Bury manor of Hinderclay seven *sochmanni* held, between them, 40 acres at the time of Domesday; this looks to have been divided amongst even more tenants by the end of the eleventh century and more still at the close of the twelfth. By the end of the thirteenth century, the same holding was in the hands of one freeholder 'and his tenants', but the number of these is undisclosed.[46] The tenure of very small parcels of land could be the product of recent processes, typically those spurred by population growth in the two centuries immediately prior to 1300; we have already considered the possibility that, on some manors, ancient large holdings, such as virgates, had sub-divided so that, by the early fourteenth century, few tenants held anything approaching a full virgate or even one of its larger fractions. This fragmentation was especially evident in areas where inheritance was partible and where lordship condescended to allow a market in land, points that will be returned to in later chapters.[47]

Even more closely related to population growth in the high Middle Ages was a process of colonisation, as a land-hungry populace carved additional holdings from the 'waste'. The greatest colonising activity in this period was reserved for the lands beyond the central band of open-field agriculture where new land, such as moorland in the north and west and fen and marsh in the east were exploited, sometimes perhaps for the first time; by contrast, in the champion regions of central and southern England there were limited opportunities for expansion. In rather more piecemeal fashion, in both champion England and beyond, tenants might seek to add to their own holdings by enclosing small plots of land (purprestures) next to their own properties, such as, for instance, the stretch of road outside their houses; they might also seek to transform local woodland or marsh into arable. Essentially, however, the vast majority of land in lowland central England that could be tenanted was already under the plough even before population began to rise in the eleventh and twelfth centuries. As a consequence, the opportunities for colonisation of large tracts of land were limited; instead a movement into 'new land' in the high Middle Ages served mostly to create fairly minor holdings, reflecting as much the efforts of the poorer villagers to eke out a living as the aggrandisement of the lord or the wealthier tenantry. Both processes are revealed at the Forest of Bernwood, on the Oxfordshire–Buckinghamshire border, where, in the fourteenth century, licensed enclosers carved out substantial plots but others managed to create illicit assarts of no more than an acre, or sometimes less.[48] Beyond lowland England, in the highland zones to the north and far west, opportunities for the poorer peasant to nibble at the 'waste' were greater; in the thirteenth century, small-scale colonisation of moorland, for example, created large numbers of smallholdings on land that was often of poor quality.[49]

If the broader story of the thirteenth and early fourteenth centuries is the morcellisation of landholding and the expansion of a class of smallholders, a different process was under way in the second half of our period. The demographic collapse of the mid-fourteenth century gave a, perhaps vital, encouragement to a growing entrepreneurialism amongst the tenantry which, in the last decades of the fourteenth century and throughout the fifteenth century, was revealed in the eager accumulation of substantial plots of land, including numbers of large standard holdings or their fractions. This process was under way, on a relatively modest scale, in certain parts of the country, such as East Anglia and Cornwall, before the plague, but it became more general in the post-plague period. The effect of this accumulation of holdings was an inevitable polarisation of landholding and the emergence of a proto-yeomanry.[50]

These distinctions of landholding size were also reflected in the type and size of the obligations which tenants owed their lords. As with size of holdings, discussion of rent has tended to centre on the labour services owed by standard holdings of the manors of central and southern England; historians have also long recognised that to restrict the view of rent in this way is to limit that view both spatially and temporally. It has been estimated that, by the early fourteenth century, regular labour services were performed by no more than one in six of all households.[51] This proportion was set to decrease still further as the fourteenth century progressed so that, by the fifteenth century, very few unfree tenants indeed held their land in return for regular labour services.

That said, in the thirteenth century and in the first half of the fourteenth, labour services owed by tenants of standard unfree holdings continued to provide a substantial proportion of rent on numerous demesnes throughout large parts of England, whilst the additional burdens and obligations of these holdings were an important element of manorial income. To return to the example from the Winchester estates referred to earlier, at Orchard the tenant of a quarter-virgate, a holding of 10 acres plus a messuage (a dwelling with a surrounding yard, outbuildings and the like) typically owed the lord a rent of 3s. 10d. or 2s. 10d. a year as well as one labour service per week during the winter (or a $\frac{1}{2}$d. money equivalent), mowing service in late June and July (or 10d. in its stead), reaping in August and September (or a payment of 3s. 4d.), a day's ploughing in winter and sowing at Lent. The tenant was also to help in the construction of haystacks; he also owed suit of court and of mill, which meant that he was obliged to attend the lord's manor court to aid in its administration, and to grind his grain at the lord's mill. In addition to these regular dues, there were also irregular payments (*consuetudines non taxatas*) which unfree tenants, including the holders of these standard tenements, made to their lords. Tenants at Orchard, as elsewhere, would have paid fines to leave the manor, to marry, and to educate their offspring; the heir of an unfree tenant also paid a duty, normally the best beast of the tenant's livestock, on that tenant's death, a convention known as 'heriot'. The lord could also demand occasional and arbitrary sums, known as tallages, from his tenants and, in addition, on the accession of a new lord, the tenants would be expected to pay a fine of 'recognition'. As well as ensuring that the lord's tenants helped furnish the lord with a ready source of revenue, the payment by an individual of such fines to the lord could also serve, as we have seen, as evidence confirmatory of the unfree status of that individual and thereby help secure him or her within his or her lord's domain.[52] In other words, land held in this way, merely by the fact of its existence, helped confirm lord–tenant relations and, as such, standard holdings of this quality provided the foundation of the 'typical' manorial economy. At Orchard, the unfree tenants of such holdings owed almost 45 per cent (44.3 per cent) of all money rents on the manor and 95 per cent of all labour rent. Their combined contribution accounted for just over 25 per cent of the manor's value to the lord. Tenants of cottages and of free land at Orchard mostly paid smaller rents. Their relative worth to the manorial economy, compared with the standard holdings owing substantial labour services, was light. At Orchard, as the rental income shows, free tenants and unfree cottagers paid the bulk of money rent (55.7 per cent) but very little in the way of labour services (5 per cent); together free tenants and cottagers contributed 15 per cent of the value of the manorial economy.[53] Similarly, in the late thirteenth century, on the Merton College manor of Cuxham (Oxfordshire), the unfree tenantry was composed of two distinct groups, eight villeins holding half-virgates, each of about 12 acres, and 13 cottagers, who held no

more than a cottage and small plot of land. In addition to the normal
occasional burdens of villeinage, the villein tenants of the half-virgate
holdings owed quite substantial labour services, roughly two days'
work per week throughout the year as well as additional services at
harvest; villein tenants also owed various customary rents in kind,
including fixed amounts of grain and seed, and poultry; by contrast,
the cottagers paid money rents of between 1s. 2d. and 4s. per annum.[54]

Although standard holdings owing labour services were familiar in
villages throughout considerable areas of England, and could count
for the greater proportion of tenant land on certain manors as well as
the bulk of the lord's rental income, throughout the country they were,
as we have seen, of less significance, proportionately, than were smaller
plots of land, both free and unfree, which were held predominantly
for money rents. Unlike their contemporaries in the open-field areas
of England where arable husbandry predominated, tenants in areas of
ancient enclosure or in regions where pastoral husbandry, by-
employments or proto-industries predominated were much less
likely, throughout the period, to pay a large proportion of their rent
as labour. Outside of a block of counties running from central to
eastern England, labour services, where they existed, were relatively
light. Instead, money rents tended to dominate. Labour services on
the Cornish manors of the earldom of Cornwall had always been light
and, by the early fourteenth century, were almost completely obso-
lete.[55] Furthermore, fixed customary and free rents also appear to have
loomed less large beyond champion England in comparison to other
non-customary levies. In eastern England, as Smith has shown, the
relative proportion of rent to income from the manor court indicates
that rent, as a proportion of manorial revenue, was less important
than it was on manors where a more 'traditional' manorial economy
operated. Whilst the ratio of manor court income to money rent at
Redgrave (Suffolk) was in the region of 0.4, at Orchard, the ratio was
closer to 0.04, the high ratio at Redgrave explicable in terms of an
active land market which, administered through the manor court,
generated 'conveyancing' revenue for the lord.[56]

Some manors and regions were dominated not by tenant land held
unfreely but by free tenancies. The long-established freeholds owed
rents which had been established generations previously; not only were
they immutable, they were, in comparison with the rents of the customary standard holdings, also very low. On some estates, free tenants
holding as much as 60 acres owed annual rents of no more than 2s.

or 3s.[57] These ancient freeholds might also owe additional 'customary elements', the relics of obligations once owed not to lords but to the 'state'. Free holdings might owe suit of court, small parcels of labour rent and other vestiges of ancient services; the tenure of freeholdings also attracted fines for marriage (*maritagium*) and for inheritance (*relevium*). Given the obvious similarities between the obligations of these freeholdings and those of unfree land, considered earlier in this chapter, if we are to detect a real difference it lies both in the designation of status accorded by lordship and sanctioned by common law and, in economic terms, in the relativities of scale of the exactions.[58] A mid-twelfth century inquiry into tenure at Cirencester noted that 'no man is so free that he must not plough and carry', whilst the similarity of obligations in the twelfth and early thirteenth centuries and the lack of distinct measures of unfreedom caused real uncertainties.[59]

Elsewhere, the number of freeholdings increased in the twelfth and thirteenth centuries. In areas of post-Conquest colonisation, as in areas of the Fens surrounding the Isle of Ely, where much land had only been reclaimed for cultivation in the twelfth and thirteenth centuries, manors were composed almost entirely of newly colonised land, assarts, whose tenants were free or semi-free and paid almost all of their rent in money, as was the case in hamlets of the manor of Wisbech in Cambridgeshire. Rents for assarts grew as the thirteenth century progressed; assarts held as free land, as many assarts were, generated higher rents as population increased in the twelfth and thirteenth centuries. On the Westminster Abbey estates it has been observed that manors which, at the time of Domesday Book (1086), included large areas of woodland, evidenced, by the close of the thirteenth century, a large proportion of free tenants. Lords, keen to encourage colonisation in the twelfth and thirteenth centuries, were less needful of large virgated holdings owing labour services than they were holdings which could generate money rents and entry fines.[60] There was, therefore, little effort on the part of even the most conservative lords to force all such newly created holdings into villeinage. A good deal of the new land colonised in the high Middle Ages generated large numbers of small free tenancies paying rents that did, at their inception, follow inflationary trends. On the manor of High Ercall (Shropshire), customary tenants holding additional land colonised from the waste paid as much as four times the rent per acre they paid on their customary holdings.[61]

In addition to the advantages which assarting brought to the seigneurial sector, lords' rental income also increased as their unfree tenantry bought up available free land. Lords were chary of permitting their villein tenantry to hold free land and, as we have seen, they frequently insisted that free land, when it came into the hands of their villeins, should be held for a 'new rent' according to the will of the lord. This 'soiled land' (*terra soliata*) was held by the tenant for a nominal rent, often a penny, in addition to the free rent.[62] Where villein tenants were permitted to hold free land, the lord benefited financially both from the increased rent and also from the boost which such seigneurial latitude may have given the local land market, where sales of land also brought in income to the lord through the process of conveying the land. As we shall see, not all lords were prepared, even by the close of our period, to risk trading the integrity of their claims over their villein tenantry for the potential benefits which might accrue from a villein land market in small plots of free land; typically, these lords persisted with customary rents and cherished dreams of a return to a period of demesne farming.

Finally, as well as freehold and land held unfreely, there was also, as we have already seen, land held by what are termed contractual tenures, leasehold. Although some leasehold was really quite ancient by the mid-thirteenth century, leaseholds tend to be categorised alongside rents from newly colonised land, as true 'economic' rents, unfixed and unprotected by custom. Early introduction of leasehold rents on the estates of the bishop of Ely has been characterised as an 'attempt to develop new types of rent which were more flexible, more precarious, more easily changed as economic circumstances changed'.[63] Contractual rents or 'farms' could be set at levels that more truly reflected the value of the land. In the mid- to late-thirteenth century, when population was near or at its medieval peak, land's worth increased exponentially but fixed customary rents remained at the levels set in earlier centuries. Customary money rents for unfree land were typically in the region of 4d.–6d. per acre.[64] Conversion of heavy labour services into their financial equivalent could increase the rental value considerably, however. To return to the Orchard example quoted above, if all of the annual rent owed by a tenant of a 10-acre quarter-virgate was converted into its money equivalent, he or she would owe approximately 1s. per acre. This comes close to the size of money 'farms' which landlords hoped to extract from lessees who held by contractual terms. In the thirteenth century, when high population also meant low wages, some lords recognised that their real economic advantage lay not in the exploitation of their land by their own tenants as labour rent but the extraction of money rent from their tenantry and the purchase of labour for their demesnes. By the late thirteenth century, leases of tenements in the Cotswolds to Gloucester Abbey tenants were desired by both lord and tenant, judging by the size of the premiums paid by lessees.[65] In early fourteenth-century Cornwall, lords turned unfree tenures into conventionary tenures with adjustable rents.[66]

The early moves towards contractual money rents gathered pace in the fourteenth century and were given a significant boost by the Black Death which, as was discussed earlier, encouraged landlords to employ leasehold as an interim measure. During the late fourteenth and early fifteenth centuries, the extent of leasehold increased considerably, and appears most marked on manors which had, until then, solely attempted to extract customary rents. As in the previous period, the size of contractual rents in the late fourteenth and fifteenth centuries tended to reflect the true worth of the holding; contractual rents were unprotected by custom and look to have responded to supply and demand. In the pre-plague period, this generally seems to have worked to the advantage of the landlord and, if contractual rent moved in any direction before 1350, it was upwards. At Ely, for instance, contractual rents doubled and quadrupled between the mid-thirteenth and early fourteenth centuries. Thereafter, the general direction of contractual rents was downwards. On the Westminster Abbey estates, leasehold farms, which often originated, in the third quarter of the fourteenth century, at 1s. 8d. per acre, declined to closer to 1s. per acre by the early fifteenth century.[67]

What is more, in real terms, by the mid- to late-fourteenth century, contractual rents, unlike a century earlier, were principally beneficial to the tenant, and not the landlord. At Birdbrook, the monetary value of customary rent owed by tenants of quarter-virgates, including labour services, was, according to the manorial accounts, less than 8s.; in the second half of the fourteenth century, annual farms of the same holdings were between 12s. and 13s. 4d. Despite this disparity, in 1386/7, Andrew Paternoster, tenant of a quarter-virgate at Birdbrook, was permitted to hold for the higher money rent of 13s. 4d. rather than for 'services and customs . . . for so long as the lord wills on account of his poverty (*causa paupertatis*)'. By the 1380s, as a result of the ravages of plague, the value of labour had increased considerably; the manorial accounts continued to offer a monetary value of labour services based on early fourteenth-century wage levels but, almost a century later, the wages of a day labourer had increased threefold and so, consequently, had the *de facto* costs of customary tenants such as Andrew Paternoster who were still expected to perform roughly two-thirds of regular labour services on the lord's demesne. In such circumstances, contractual rents were inevitably viewed as preferable by customary tenants who, as well as the economic costs, may have seen less stigma in leasehold than in servile tenure.

In this review of rent, we also need to recognise that the general movement was towards money rent in some form. In the first place, it is important to recognise that even those rents – labour services, rents in kind, fixed money rents – which appear to have been relatively isolated from market movements and secured by custom were hardly untouched by movements of prices and wages. The cost of labour or the price of livestock was not constant in our period; consequently, rents, even customary rents, which were composed of such elements, effectively rose and fell accordingly. The hidden costs of unfree tenure, not least the possible need of a tenant to hire wage labour to perform his or her labour services as a surrogate meant, for instance, that, if wages rose, tenants who were obliged to pay others to perform services in their stead faced higher costs whilst tenants performing their own labour services lost potentially lucrative employment opportunities elsewhere. Generally, then, no rent was entirely divorced from the market and the trend appears to have been to intensify the degree of market integration.

The rise of contractual rent, leasehold 'farms', was accompanied by the long-term conversion of labour rent and rent in kind into their money equivalents. A process of commutation, the transformation of labour services into money rent, had been under way in England since at least the eleventh century. The vestigial service component in ancient freeholds was evidence of a process which, over centuries, would see the replacement of all services by fiscal equivalents. By the thirteenth century, many landlords had largely abandoned reliance on labour services from their unfree tenantry and had chosen to convert the majority of their labour rents into money rents or rents of assize (*redditus assise*). As we have seen, other landlords, for a variety of reasons (which we will be discussed in detail in the next chapter), chose to continue to exact substantial proportions of their rent in the form of labour services. However, even where labour retained an importance in the manorial economy, lords did not claim their full allocation of labour in each year; instead, they 'sold' labour rent to their tenantry in a piecemeal and irregular commutation. In this sense, the monetary component of a tenant's rent could alter from year to year. By the early fifteenth century, very few lords expected to receive labour rent and had either contented themselves with 'farms' from contractual leaseholds or had already long been in receipt of customary or freehold money rents.

3

DETERMINANTS OF PEASANT LANDHOLDING

Having set out the ways in which land was held, its extent, its obligations and its legal tenures, it is evident that no simple uniformity of peasant landholding existed in medieval England. In order to comprehend this diversity, it will be useful to consider the combination of factors that might have contributed to it. The range of these is, of course, very considerable: they include the landscape, patterns of settlement, regional customs and inheritance practices, and the initiatives of the peasantry themselves. Developments in these, increases or diminutions in the importance of each, were of signal importance in the lives of the peasantry and, above all here, the ways in which they held and worked their land.

Certain of these influences had a degree of universality – legal developments and the impositions of common law and government, although not necessarily carrying the same weight throughout England and certainly not in the Marches, did have a general force. The same could be said of the larger economic and demographic developments of the period, although even here we need to be aware of regional aberrations. Closer to home, the peculiarities of a more regional and local character had obvious influences on land tenure and the extent of its obligations. Landscape, soil quality and local markets were important determinants of the local economy and the role which the peasantry could play in it. Additionally, earlier patterns of settlement and the shared cultural heritage of a region (including deep-rooted assumptions about family and forms of inheritance) also mattered, as did, perhaps most immediately, the expectations of landlords and the tenants themselves.

Importantly, these influences cannot obviously be separated one from the other. Thus, developments in forms of tenure, such as the growth of leasehold, were both dependent upon and created by long-established legal and administrative machinery, the expectations of landlords and their tenants, demographic upheaval, and so on. To treat each in isolation, as will be attempted on more than one occasion in this book, is to disguise their interconnectedness. In the last chapter of this part, we will attempt to use discussion of the peasant transfer of land in this period as a 'test-case' for the effect of these and other influences on one vital aspect of land use and tenure in the Middle Ages, whilst in the following part, the range of influences which affected the form and function of the peasant family will be considered. In this chapter, the intention is to consider the extent to which peasant landholding was determined by this variety of influences. Since the tenantry inevitably held its land from lords (landlords), the focus of this chapter will be the lords themselves and the ways in which lords served as 'filters' for the range of exogenous influences also to be considered here.

As we have already had cause to discuss, the development of land tenure was a product of law and government. The early organisation of the emergent nation-state employed tenure as a basis of obligation to the state. Free tenants, as we have seen, owed duties of defence and of taxation for the land that they held. From long before the Norman Conquest, distinctions of status had also been attached to tenurial differences, with varieties of landholders designated according to their function. Thus, to follow the gradations of the early- to mid-eleventh century *Rectitudines Singularum Personarum* (an estate management treatise on 'the rights and ranks of people'), the tenantry can be divided between *thegns* who owe, amongst other things, armed service, *geneats*, who hunt and guard their lord, cottars, whose obligations are 'according to the custom of their estate' but also involve elements of guard, and *geburs*, whose services include significant elements of labour.[1]

After the Conquest, as has also been described, the extent of service in the form of labour looks to have increased. This appears to have been at the initiative of new Norman landlords who, as can be clearly seen in certain parts of the country, eradicated some free tenures in the first decades after 1066.[2] The growth of a common law of real property, itself the product of an extension of rule of law in the twelfth century, forced, as we have also seen, more concrete distinctions between the free and the unfree. In this sense, it has been argued, expansion of law and government under the Angevins had, as a consequence, redefined tenure and, importantly, had assured unfreedom by providing it with a common law identity. The emergence of a common law of real property provided, then, a framework for lord–tenant relations in the thirteenth and fourteenth centuries, a framework in which rent assumed a significant role as legal proof. As has already been discussed, to be a villein and to be subject to one's lord was to hold land for certain obligations, such as merchet, tallage, heavy labour services, and so on. This legal framework helped confirm landlords in their intransigence since it placed such a significant degree of emphasis on forms of rent; tenants, in the meantime, also saw rent as a mode of proof and attempted to claim immunities from their present predicaments by presenting claims to ancient and more liberal obligations.[3] It was, therefore, developments in law and government in the twelfth and thirteenth centuries that had extraordinary and far-reaching effects on land tenure in the ways already described. Later developments, most especially the protection of unfree tenure by Chancery in the fifteenth century and common law in the sixteenth, although of undoubted importance, seem rather more to have been responses to ongoing social and economic developments, especially the special pleading of new non-peasant copyholders who sought additional security for their servile holdings. As well, therefore, as law and government, we need to look to economic change as a further influence on landholding in this period.

Social relations and the economy underwent dramatic change between 1200 and 1500: markets proliferated in the thirteenth century but the number of market centres had contracted by 1500; wool, the mainstay of the export economy before the plague, was replaced by cloth in the 150 years after c.1350; grain remained the staple element of the diet throughout the period but its importance was reduced somewhat by the late fifteenth century as meat consumption increased, reflecting a general rise in the standard of living. The principal indicators of these movements were prices and wages. From the late twelfth century, inflation meant that prices, although fluctuating dramatically, tended to rise. This rise continued until c.1380 when the trend was reversed. By contrast, wages behaved oppositely, remaining low in the thirteenth and early fourteenth centuries but beginning to rise by the late fourteenth century. By the end of the fourteenth century, if we were to graph those movements, we would see wages and prices parting company, with the price of foodstuffs falling as wages continued to rise. Such movements, themselves the effect of a variety of influences, including shortage of coin and bullion, climate changes and crop yields, population movement, and levels of taxation, had clear implications for rent. In the first and most obvious case, money rents altered in their real value according to the behaviour of wages and prices. When, for instance, prices were high, fixed money rents were of less immediate benefit to the landlord; as we have seen and shall discuss in a little more detail later, landlords attempted to remedy this by creating more unfixed rents, such as new free rents arising from assarts or leaseholds, which were unprotected by custom.[4] These new rents could be altered according to market conditions, something that made the renewable terms of short leaseholds especially attractive to landlords. However, this is not to say that customary or fixed rents were immune to the vagaries of prices and wages. Although the bulk of unfree rents and the older free rents were fixed and, thereby, afforded a degree of protection, this did not mean they were isolated from these wider economic shifts. Just as a fixed money rent of 4d. per acre altered in its *real* value according to the purchasing power of that 4d., so rents in kind and labour services also changed their value according to price and wage fluctuations. To take labour services as an example, in the thirteenth century, wage levels were low; by contrast, in the late fourteenth century, wage levels had increased considerably. In the later period, all other things being equal, labour services effectively cost the tenant more than they did in the earlier period, a fact which appears to be supported by the desire in the late fourteenth century for landlords to hold on to or even revert to labour services, while tenants increasingly opted to take contractual tenancies.[5] How we explain these changes remains a matter of some debate amongst historians, with, most obviously, some historians taking a monetarist line and preferring to see fluctuation in wages and prices in terms of the money supply (itself a product of bullion availability) whilst others have argued a thesis in which price and wage movement behaviour is explained as a product of population change.[6]

Although it is, to say the least, neither a simple task to separate the range of historical causes which explain fluctuations in these indicators nor to ascribe a rank ordering to their importance, historians have tended to grace population with a primary role. Most obviously, the demographic crises of the thirteenth and fourteenth centuries have attracted the attention of historians as potential determinants of change in the medieval economy. Mortality arising from the dearths of the thirteenth century, the Great Famine of the early fourteenth century, the initial outbreak of plague in the mid-fourteenth century and its recurrence throughout the fifteenth century, affected tenure and land use variously. Neither was it just demographic crises that challenged existing economic institutions. Population movement occasioned by changing fertility levels or regional population change which was the product of migration could, for instance, create conditions of high or low population which had important consequences for levels of rent.[7]

Demographic shifts offered opportunities for both landlord and tenant to negotiate levels of rent and forms of tenure. At no point during this period were the parties to these 'negotiations' equal: in the thirteenth and early fourteenth centuries, a very high level of population worked to the advantage of landlords who were able to increase their rental income accordingly; by contrast, the decline in population from at least the mid-fourteenth century had the effect of bringing down rents. Importantly, as has already been considered, customary rent, although malleable to a degree, was largely static; rents established in the twelfth and early thirteenth centuries or earlier were, from the view of the landlord, increasingly uneconomic as prices rose in the late thirteenth and fourteenth centuries. Instead, landlords attempted, with some success, to increase the returns from the non-customary, non-rent element of tenants' obligations. Most obviously, entry fines, irregular dues paid by tenants upon entering purchased land, increased considerably in the thirteenth century, an apparent consequence of population pressure and a means for landlords to capitalise on such shifts.[8] This was especially the case where lords, presumably uninhibited by local concerns, were able to charge exorbitant fines of outsiders entering customary land. On many estates in the late thirteenth and early fourteenth centuries, outsiders paid double the going rate to enter land.[9] Landlords also sought to exploit those rents which could be adjusted to respond to changing economic conditions; thus, in the decades around 1300, new rents arising from assarts increased as a proportion of the rental income from land. By contrast, in the late fourteenth and fifteenth centuries, as the levels of rent fell, the relative size of customary rents increased and, in these decades, the tenantry may have viewed such fixed rents as increasingly unattractive. Interesingly, then, in the decades after 1350, when population had halved and landlords fought hard to keep tenants on their lands, it was the tenants themselves who now preferred the insecurity of elastic rents unprotected by custom. Most importantly, in terms of the decline of customary rents in the manorial economy, many landlords found themselves increasingly obliged to abandon customary labour rents in favour of contractual rents, a process that, as we have seen, accelerated quite dramatically in the late fourteenth and fifteenth centuries. These contractual rents could also fall, as demand for land waned in the years around 1400, a feature clearly evident on estates and manors throughout England.[10]

Aside from the more general political, economic and demographic developments during the period, there were also regional and local features that helped dictate forms of landholding and their obligations. In the most obvious sense, landscape, soil quality, geology, all had enormous influence on how land was held and the expectations which tenants and their lords could place upon it. In areas of pastoral or wood husbandry, the demands which landlords made of their tenantry were, inevitably, different from those made in the cereal-growing areas of open-field husbandry. Thus, for instance, charcoal-burners and other forest workers were typically smallholders. John the charcoal-burner (*carbonarius*) in Feckenham Forest (Worcestershire) held a small plot of land and a cottage for which he owed 2s. rent, a 'cauk' of charcoal, and three days a year haymaking, harvesting and weeding.[11] Where the natural landscape provided alternative outlets for the economy, the relationship between lord and tenant was modified to reflect that influence. In some cases, this was simply revealed in forms of rent that were appropriate to the local economy. In Hilgay (Norfolk), in the Fens, in the early thirteenth century, the tenants of the Abbey of Bury St Edmunds 'had always paid, as rent, eels which are known as Foreles, that is Wedingeles and Skeringeles'.[12] Elsewhere, the particular nature of that economy affected landholding and the tenurial structure in ways that were wholly distinctive; areas still capable of extensive colonisation in the period, as for instance the poorer soils of the north-east, encouraged large numbers of small freeholdings, held for relatively large rents. Similarly, where industry was located in the countryside, especially the extractive industries such as lead-mining in Derbyshire or tin-mining in Cornwall, the capital and employment generated thereby fostered a rather different regional economy than elsewhere. The most distinctive features of that economy, all of which had important effects upon lord–tenant relations, landholding and forms of rent, were a proliferation of smallholdings and a degree of landlessness, a concomitant polarisation of landholding, a substantial proportion of freeholdings, and a preponderance of money rents.

It was not simply topography that produced difference. Early patterns of settlement were potentially as important. Pre-Conquest processes of colonisation, for instance the Danish invasions and settlements of the eighth to eleventh centuries, created cultural differences and regional inconsistencies as regards the conceptions of landholding and forms of tenure. The settlement of the Danes in eastern and northern counties established a regional distinctiveness, identified as the Danelaw, which was characterised by, amongst other things, scattered settlements and a large proportion of free tenants.[13] By contrast, in the eleventh century, the southern and western counties, the focus of the pre-Conquest kingdom of Wessex, displayed rather different features, especially more intensely manorialised settlements, and a higher proportion of slaves and servile tenants. Such differences were not entirely swept aside by post-Conquest developments but were maintained in modified form. Although the number of free tenancies suffered a general decline in the late eleventh century, as we have already seen, the relative numbers of free tenants remained high in northern and eastern counties. There, free rents and obligations attached to pre-Conquest freeland also persisted into the late Middle Ages and restricted the potential of lords to foist new labour rents on a well-established and durable tenurial structure.

Such distinctions were also maintained through custom and long usage. In particular, customary practices of inheritance affected landholding, the organisation of land use, and the demands which landlords could place upon the tenantry. In historical discussion of variants in inheritance practice, the root of that variance has been identified, though not with general acceptance, as ethnic. Pre-Conquest colonisation movements, it has been suggested, imported a variety of modes of tenure and transfer, notably a tradition of partible inheritance in eastern England, including Kent, East Anglia, and sweeps of northern England. Whilst, as we shall see, subsequent forces for change, notably lords and their tenants, could effect important alterations in these customary practices, and may indeed distort our sense of the pre-Conquest regionalism in forms of inheritance, the possibility remains that a broad distinction of inheritance practices (monogeniture in champion England, partibility elsewhere) was the product of differences between ethnic groups.[14] Inheritance practices which were inimical to fragmentation of holdings but encouraged the persistence of large standard holdings also helped provide the foundation for a manorial economy based upon labour rents and family farms. Where partible inheritance was practised instead, holdings were much smaller, and the rationale of the single family holding was less easy to sustain. In such circumstances, landlords were more likely to commute labour rent than they were to attempt to employ it directly.[15]

In order for customary practices to have had an impact on, *inter alia*, landholding and rent, they had not only to be established but maintained. The role of local communities in storing and modifying custom was an important element in many aspects of land tenure. In the first instance, the body of tenant landholders served as a collective source, a memory of obligations owed by the tenantry as well as the ways in which land was held and transferred. Whilst lords increasingly relied upon written documents, such as manorial accounts, custumals and rentals, to record the dues of their tenantry, they also had to turn time and again to their tenants or the leading representatives of the tenantry for confirmation. Tenants advised on the customs of inheritance and the typicality of obligations attached to holdings of a particular type. At Crowland (Cambridgeshire) in 1323, an inquest jury pronounced on inheritance custom within the manor, stating that the heir should apportion part of the holding amongst his surviving brothers. At Methley (Yorkshire), in 1340, the jurors declared that an oxgang (i.e. a virgate or standard holding) of land should not be divided amongst surviving sisters and that no tenant could disinherit his heirs by alienation of parcels of land. Here, in two different scenarios, pronouncements upon inheritance served both to encourage and to discourage fragmentation.[16] In the Methley case, in particular, we sense that the priority was to maintain the integrity of the oxgang, or standard holding. The pronouncements of local juries could be more specifically directed at the issue of rent and tenure. These could include general statements on obligations or more specific testimonies. At Rastrick (Yorkshire) in the early fourteenth century, a villager, Henry Steven, denied that he owed ploughing services for 12 acres which he held. An inquest of 12 jurors was called and determined that Henry 'ought to render the Earl [Warenne – the lord of the manor] a custom of ploughing, viz. 4d. for a whole ploughing, and 2d. for half a plough, yearly'.[17] An inquiry in the manor court at Walsham le Willows (Suffolk) in 1332 was made of the lord's tenants in order to discover 'who holds [the tenement Skut, the tenement of Robert of Fornham and the tenement formerly called Margery's tenement] and

how much each one holds separately, and to apportion the said tenement . . . under penalty of 20s'. At the same court, the villagers were
to divide an additional and ancient pecuniary levy (sheriff's aid)
amongst those tenants 'who should be apportioned'.[18] Those obliged
to render unassessed obligations, the *consuetudines non taxatas* such as
heriot and merchet, were also identified by inquest juries. Jurors also
pronounced on custom with regard to such exactions. At Birdbrook
(Essex) in 1338, an inquest jury, having inspected the manorial court
rolls for earlier examples, declared that widows holding their land as
dower were liable to heriot.[19]

The same individuals who pronounced on landholding were also
instrumental in affecting the tenor of tenure. As jurors and manorial
officers, these representatives of the village community could reduce
or increase an individual's obligations in a number of ways. Their role
in the manor court, for instance, as assessors of fines and dues
(affeerors), afforded them the opportunity to limit the weight of certain
customary and non-customary dues. Although, for instance, lords must
have had a significant say in the level of entry fines paid by incoming
tenants, it is also clear that local knowledge and the designs of the community were important in establishing levels of payment. This is especially apparent in the distinctions made between local entrants to land
and strangers.[20]

Equally importantly, being the eyes and ears of the lord in the local
community, village officers could fall conveniently blind and deaf when
circumstance required. Although, as we saw a little earlier, the inquest
at Rastrick revealed that Henry Steven did owe ploughing services,
the community was fined 6s. 8d. because they had concealed Henry's
obligation for ten years, during which time he had failed to perform
his service. Manorial officers, in their capacity as assessors of property
and overseers of labour could deliberately overlook chattels and
moveables owed to the lord and ignore services badly performed or
not performed at all. Attempts to conceal livestock liable as death-duty
payments (heriot), for instance, were, on occasion, made with the
connivance of village officers. Manorial court records also abound with
references to non-performance of labour services and orders to fine
manorial officers, such as the reeve, bailiff or the hayward (*messor*), for
inadequate supervision. The same also applies to sales of land and,
most obviously, short-term transfers of land by lease where the strong
suspicion is that leading members of the community were aware of
and sanctioned illicit transfers extra-curially, the effect of which was

to ease the financial burden of the parties to the transaction and to deprive the lord of any profits arising from the conveyance, notably the entry fine.

Finally, if village administrators and manorial officers behaved in a manner inconsistent with the expectations of their lord, this undoubtedly reflected their adherence to a different agenda, that of the community in which they lived. The extent to which the community could and did attempt to reduce the burden of rent imposed upon it by landlords has been a central issue in histories of the English peasantry, especially of Marxist discussions of lord–tenant relations. It is a topic to which we shall return in a later chapter.[21] Here we need to establish the role of the village community in determining levels of rent. In establishing any resistance to the excessive demands of lords or others who claimed rents, the tenants' simplest approach was to refuse or to limit payment. Rent-strikes by the tenantry, both in terms of money rent and labour services, are well attested in this period. They are, for instance, a feature of the crisis years of the late thirteenth and early fourteenth centuries. Refusal to pay could result in its own severe penalties, including seizure of land and expulsion from holdings, but it is also evident that villagers were able to build up arrears of rent over many years. Poor- and non-performance of rent and services were possible because of a collective policy of concealment, a feature already discussed in the context of the village officials.

It may prove impossible to establish whether the more substantial villagers, as has been suggested for early modern England, imposed their own moral agenda on the village or whether the leading villagers took their lead from a grass-roots morality.[22] It does seem plausible, however, that the behaviour of manorial officers was conditioned in part by their sense of local audience. Litigation, especially trespass and defamation cases, may indicate that manorial officers who were overzealous in their duties to their lord became objects of common censure. Certainly, if exercises in concealment of poor- or non-performance of rents and services were to be successful, manorial officers and the wider community had to collude. A moral agenda could also be extended beyond lords and their officers to peasant rentiers and sublessors who, if they sought to take excessive advantage of their peers, could suffer the outrage of fellow villagers, a point that will be explored in fuller detail in later chapters.[23] By the same token, villagers could increase the effective rent burden of their peers, or individuals amongst them, by false, malicious or simply zealous presentations,

choosing to inform lords of abuses of rent or evasions of fines rather
than look the other way. At Osset (Yorkshire), in 1316, the suitors in
the manor court 'concealed the heriot due on the land of Hugh Pees'
and were, 'with the exception of William de Heton', fined 6s. 8d. Elsewhere, jurors and suitors may have been more forthcoming.[24] In such
cases, individual life histories, enmities and alliances played no small
part in determining the extent to which tenants were fully obligated
to their lord.

The potential for a collectivity of communal enterprise and its
impact on rent and landholding is perhaps best revealed in concerted
efforts to contest seigneurial dues. We will reserve detailed discussion
in this respect for a later chapter. We should, however, note at this
point that tenants were not beyond resisting the expectations of their
lords in ways other than rent-strikes and refusals to co-operate. Active
resistance came in a number of forms. The tenantry might make direct
appeal to their lord for amelioration of conditions; they might also
appeal to other or higher authority, taking claims regarding status and
obligation into the king's court. Finally, and most obviously, they could
resist through violence and quasi-political acts. Minor, that is to say
geographically or numerically limited, attacks on lords and their officials could well develop into full-blown revolt, as the Peasants' Revolt
or English Rising of 1381 most clearly illustrates. Such uprisings were
not just about rent and tenure, although the famous petition of the
rebels in 1381 includes the demand 'that there should be no more
villeins in England, and no serfdom nor villeinage but that all men
should be free and of one condition'.[25] In so far as they were successful, there is some reason for suggesting that sporadic outbreaks of such
extreme discontent reminded landlords of the need to tread carefully.
In the case of the Peasants' Revolt, although it is unlikely that the revolt
effected a *volte face* on the part of lords, it may have helped confirm
a growing sense that, in the changed social and economic climate of
the later fourteenth century, labour services and non-customary dues
attached to villeinage were no longer easily realisable.[26]

Given the influence of such long-established and immense elements in
the determination of the rights and obligations of the tenantry, the role
of lordship in this determinative process might appear relatively
limited; that said, by the late Middle Ages in certain regions, the impact
of lordship was certainly considerable in helping to ensure that long-
established patterns of land use and inheritance were maintained or

modified. It is frequently stated that certain parts of England were subjected to 'weak lordship', others to 'strong lordship', suggesting that landlords were able to impose obligations in some parts of the country, typically the midlands and southern England where a regime of relatively uniform holding size and labour services persisted into the fourteenth century, whilst they were unable to do the same elsewhere, a failure reflected in fragmented and unequal holdings, commutation of labour services and money rents. In fact, it seems as useful to think in terms of lordly strategies, lords tending to work not always to a standard estate policy but rather to simple expectations of necessity and income from manor and estate, in which case lords, possibly with the exception of some of the more conservative landlords such as the great Benedictine houses, may have tended to work with rather than against local conditions and conventions.

This should not, however, be seen as an attempt to minimise the role of lords in the lives of their peasant tenantry. If certain fundamentals of peasant life, such as the nature of the soil and the practice of inheritance, were largely (but not entirely[27]) beyond the control of lordship, the strategy which a lord might adopt in order to realise (if not necessarily maximise) income from his landed resources impacted greatly upon the peasantry. In some parts of the country and under certain lords this impact was greater and was endured for longer than elsewhere.

There were a number of 'concerns' which might have affected lordly attitudes towards rent. Important amongst these were the requirements of the lord's economy, his or her engagement with the market, and his or her anticipated means of constraining and exploiting the tenantry. In dealing, briefly, with each here, the intention is to illustrate the extent to which the peasant tenantry of landlords was subject to a variety of seigneurial decisions, a theme that will resurface more than once in what follows. We can begin with the seigneurial economy.

At the close of the twelfth century, during a period of intense inflation which saw grain prices rise to unprecedented levels, landlords, who had been content to lease their demesnes to farmers in return for an annual money farm, recovered their lands and chose to work them directly.[28] A return to demesne farming also reflected a concern that farmers might be about to gain an effective freehold interest in the demesnes they leased.[29] The thirteenth century has been characterised as a period of 'high farming' during which, as population continued to rise, all available land was exploited as arable. In order to further this exploitation, some landlords used, in so far as they were able, their tenants as a labour force, insisting that their servile and villein tenants performed, as part of their rent, a range of labour services on their demesnes.[30] Given our earlier discussion of the variety of tenures and forms of husbandry as well as the differences in the rank and scale of lordship in the later Middle Ages – a point to which we shall make some brief return below – we should, of course, not be surprised to find that not all landlords were in a position to use their servile tenants in this way. Some landlords must have been largely reliant on hired labour; we should also note that not all demesnes were taken in hand by landlords, some remaining leased throughout the period.[31]

A retreat from this general position of high farming was already under way by the early fourteenth century. In the Welsh Marches, demesnes of some manors were leased in the early fourteenth century. On the estates of the earldom of Cornwall a number of manors were leased in the early 1320s.[32] However, for the greater part, until towards the close of the fourteenth century, landlords preferred to keep their holdings under direct management. The most likely reason for the long duration of a policy of direct farming was a period of high prices, with grain prices in particular reaching spectacular levels during the famine years of the early fourteenth century but also remaining high for three decades after plague had cut the population by half in the mid-fourteenth century. Interestingly, most landlords seem to have ridden out the first, and heaviest, outbreak of plague without having to alter drastically the tenurial regime; new tenants were found on manors throughout England and Wales to replace those who had succumbed and these, often relatives and, if not, neighbours, continued to hold by customary tenure. There were exceptions, of course, especially where mortality was particularly extreme: at Wood Eaton, in Oxfordshire, the two surviving tenants would have fled the manor unless the lord had renegotiated their tenures[33] but, mostly, lords, at least the larger lords, managed to maintain the manorial economy in much the same form as that familiar from the thirteenth and early fourteenth centuries. Thus, during these decades, tenants on some estates – typically the larger ones – continued to perform labour services; Postan, in a famous essay, noted that 'the fluctuation of labour services requires no other explanation than that which is provided by the ordinary interplay of supply and demand'.[34] Whilst the demesnes remained under the direct management of the lord, services were regularly exacted on a number of estates. For example, on the Battle

Abbey estates labour services continued to be used into the late fif-teenth century;[35] estates where labour services were maintained also needed to maintain their villein tenantry. Before the close of the four-teenth century, therefore, there was little retreat from the direct farming of the previous 150 years. In these years, some lords fought hard to retain their tenantry and many entries in the manor court rolls list the names of villeins who have fled and describe efforts made for their forced return to the manor. This period, an Indian Summer of demesne farming and, hence, a time of seigneurial reaction, did not last.

As well as a fall in the supply of customary labour as a result of recur-rent high mortality and increased mobility – as disaffected neifs fled their manors and sought opportunities further afield – there was a decline in demand as prices fell.[36] Consequently, by the last years of the fourteenth century and the first decades of the fifteenth century, as prices fell and wages continued to rise, the lords began to lease their demesnes in ever increasing numbers. Again, the chronology varied and some landlords, particularly the smaller gentry, continued to manage their demesnes directly, but the general trend was to lease. Towards the end of the fourteenth century, demesnes on some of the estates of the nobility, such as those of the Clares, were leased; of West-minster Abbey's demesnes only one was still in hand by 1420, the majority leased in the late fourteenth and early fifteenth centuries. Similar stories could be told for most monastic estates in England. Some demesnes were leased *en bloc*; others piecemeal. The retreat of landlords from direct farming opened the door to lessees once again and now, as in the period of demesne leasing 200 years earlier, the lessees included villagers, neighbouring townsmen and merchants, as well as the minor gentry and other local lords.[37] In some parts of the country this retreat also signalled an end to arable husbandry; in its stead, land was given over to grass and to livestock, including the sheep flocks which furnished the native cloth industry. By the early sixteenth century, the English countryside, shorn of half its population and with a greater proportion of its land given over to pastoral husbandry, must have looked a rather different place than it had three centuries earlier.

This general pattern, as already intimated, does not hold good for all landlords, nor is it wholly representative of developments through-out all parts of England; if it is representative of a type, it represents the experience of the great lords of the larger ecclesiastical and lay estates, whose records have survived in relative abundance. Of great importance in forcing a distinction between the likely impact of different types of lord on his or her tenantry is the fact that the size and structure of the manor mattered: smaller landlords who possessed large demesnes but few villeins would have been obliged to hire most of their labour and were, perhaps, less likely to have insisted that their villein tenants perform heavy labour services. Minor landlords would, therefore, not necessarily have been in a position to take the same policy decisions as their more substantial neighbours; in particular, demesne leasing in the later Middle Ages may have been less of an option for minor landlords.[38]

The general pattern of a period of direct management and subsequent retreat by landlords had important repercussions for the tenantry. As we have seen, during the period of direct management at least some landlords insisted upon rents in the form of labour service from their unfree tenants. Again, the levels of these exactions varied but they could be onerous. Importantly, for landlords, these labour rents constituted a vital and relatively inexpensive element in the extraction of demesne produce and, as a consequence, they were jealously guarded. Further, since this was labour *rent*, the obligation was attached to tenure and, thus, the lord's decision to demand rent in this form often had an important influence on the pattern of landholding on the manor, notably through the lord's insistence that units of landholding, typically yardlands, virgates, bondlands, or fractions of the same, remained intact. The lord achieved this, through the agency of the manor court and his manorial officers, by actively restricting the twin evils of fragmentation – the trade in parcels of these holdings – and accumulation – the acquisition by an individual of more than a single holding.[39] With the decline of direct farming, the leasing of the demesnes and the shrinkage of arable, such restrictions were relaxed and, as a consequence, a market in these large holdings which owed labour services came into existence. In the fifteenth century, therefore, we find peasant entrepreneurs who had managed to accumulate small empires composed of yardlands and portions of yardlands, totalling tens and hundreds of acres. Inevitably, of course, this general picture, the broadly 'traditional' explanatory model of change in peasant landholding, although clearly holding true for certain lordships in certain parts of the country, cannot be applied universally. As we shall see in the next chapter, the ease with which land could be transferred varied enormously from one manor to the next, and an explanation for that variety is not solely, or even largely, dependent on lordship; instead, a number of influences, including long-established inheritance customs and the local geography, may have also been very significant factors.

In addition to the long-term shifts, which affected tenants and their lords in ways that were certainly not uniform, the day-to-day conditions of the peasantry were also, in part, dependent upon the particular expectations and 'character' of their lord. Some lords may, for instance, have been more assiduous in their efforts to exact all they could from their tenants. It is clear that the wealthier and more powerful lay, ecclesiastic and monastic lords could command the range of resources, in terms of officers and administration, that would permit a close management of their estates, even if that management, unlike the lordship of minor knights and gentry, resident on their manors, was at a physical remove.

Although neither major nor minor landlords were entirely insulated from the market, we might wish to draw a distinction between the expectations which different landlords made of their manors, or at least some of their manors. Whilst major landlords, abbots, bishops, earls and barons, may have seen some, but certainly not all, of the manors on their estates as predominantly sources of supply for their households, it has been suggested that minor landlords, such as minor gentry holding perhaps a single manor, were more concerned to maximise production of their demesnes, their gaze fixed squarely on the marketable potential of their produce. Britnell, however, testing some of Kosminsky's conclusions, has noted that both major and minor landlords sought to optimise market opportunities in so far as they were able, and that, in fact, minor landlords with fewer resources may have been less able to take full advantage of the market.[40]

Despite this general willingness of landlords to engage with the market, it is evident that not all unfree tenants of the same lord fared equally, an inconsistency explicable, at least partially, in terms of the perceived role of different manors in meeting the lord's needs. We might, for instance, wish to draw a distinction between the experience of the tenantry on those manors on the large estate of a single lord, the demesnes of which were considered to be suppliers of the lord's household, and those manors of the same estate which were perceived as producing for the market. The domanial manors administered by the prior and convent of Westminster Abbey in the early fourteenth century provided approaching 40 per cent of the grain needs of the prior and convent; by the 1350s and 1360s this had risen to 80 per cent. Importantly, not all manors on the estate provided grain but rather an identifiable, administratively distinct, group of manors were answerable in this way to the convent whilst other manors rendered cash rather than kind.[41] Those manors which provided for the household and not for the market permitted major landlords a degree of self-sufficiency in the running of their estates, and insulated them, to some extent, from the vagaries of the market and the movement of prices; by contrast, on the manors where production was aimed more at the market, there will have existed both a greater vulnerability to fluctuations in external supply and demand and a heightened need to adjust the management of their estate or manor accordingly. Costs of production, in particular, mattered more on manors where produce was destined for the market, and may have meant, for example, that in years when grain prices were low or falling, it may have made greater economic sense to use labour rent on the demesne rather than to commute those services in return for cash and to purchase waged labour from beyond the villein tenantry; by the close of the fourteenth century, when grain prices were in decline but wages continued to rise, this would certainly have been the case, but by that time a landlord's ability to insist on the performance of labour services would have been much reduced.[42] Most importantly, by engaging more directly with the cash economy, market-orientated manors evidenced a greater degree of flexibility and 'modernity' in the relationships between lord and tenant. By contrast, on manors feeding the domestic economy of an estate, landlords encouraged a form of practice that responded as little as possible to external stimuli, and appear to have insisted, in so far and for so long as they were able, on the obligations of serfdom irrespective of wider developments in society and the economy.

Finally, in this review of seigneurial determinants of rent and tenure, we need also to consider the additional concerns that landlords brought to such issues. Rent and tenure, as earlier discussion (Chapter 2) has been intended to show, mattered not just in purely economic terms but as evidence of status and general obligation. In managing their estates and adapting tenure and rent to changed circumstance, lords had to be mindful of the legal consequences of their actions. Most especially, as a common law of villeinage developed in the twelfth and thirteenth centuries, the obligations of tenure, rent, became, as we have seen, vital indices of tenurial status. If a tenant paid merchet, performed labour services, sought licence of the lord to alienate his land, then the lord's case that his tenant was also his villein was strengthened.[43] Relaxation of these obligations constituted or might be deemed to constitute an implied manumission, transforming the villein into a freeman. Whilst some lords chose to take this step in this period, partly as a gesture but also for economic reasons, others refused to contemplate this turn of events; hence their persistence with customary rents and obligations throughout the late Middle Ages.[44]

For the greater part, however, lords, throughout the country, adapted to changing political, economic and environmental conditions and their tenantry was obliged, often to their advantage, to adapt with them. The period between 1200 and 1500 witnessed, then, enormous developments in the relationship between lord and tenant, a relationship which can, not unreasonably, be defined in terms of economic rent. Essentially, the demands that landlords were able to make of their tenantry shifted over these three centuries whilst their general expectations of what their estates should deliver also altered. These decisions and responses by landlords had major implications for tenure, for landholding and for rent. Harvey notes that there was a general retreat of lordship from the community of the vill between the eleventh and the fifteenth centuries, one closely associated with a narrowing of the range of the lords' interests to those that were largely economic; interests that did not threaten the lords' purse were left to his tenants and the wider community of the vill.[45]

However, the determinants of rent outlined here illustrate the extent to which the condition of the peasantry was influenced by factors other than lordship and its own expectations. Even lordship, the most immediate influence on rent and tenure, was conditioned by external influences. If the obligations of the peasantry and their landholding were conditioned by so many factors, the same was also true for land transfer.

4

THE TRANSFER OF PEASANT LAND

The diversity of forms of landholding had implications for and was, in part, a condition of the transfer of the land itself. Where, for instance, land was held in substantial parcels and was perceived, by tenant and/or by lord, as the unit of support for a peasant family and the provider of particular services for the lord, then the conditions which affected ease of transfer were likely to be rather different from those pertaining where landholding was more fragmented and the hopes and expectations of tenant and lord were directed elsewhere. The influences upon landholding, discussed in the previous chapter, apply, therefore, in certain measure to the transfer of land, and we will need to revisit some of these here. We will also reserve some consideration of the motive force of land transfer for later sections, notably discussion of the market and commercialisation, where the role of land as a capital investment will be given some treatment.[1] We will also postpone consideration of the transfer of land between family members, both in terms of *post-mortem* transfer or inheritance and *inter-vivos* transfer, that is, transfer conducted between living parties. For the present, the aim is to consider, within the society and economy of the medieval peasantry, the role of the *inter-vivos* transfer of land and to describe that transfer of peasant land within the context of the wider political, social and economic community.

The tenure and transfer of land are of singular importance in the peasant economy but also in peasant society. It is obvious that a transfer of landed resources is fundamental to the needs of a family of peasant producers dependent upon land for their sustenance. Furthermore, it is an observation often made by those studying peasant communities that, given that the peasant family defines itself and is defined by its landholding, the degree to which land is transferred freely and beyond the family has been taken by historians not only as an index of the mores determining peasant behaviour but also as a measure of the extent to which the society under observation can be categorised as 'peasant' at all.[2]

It has been suggested that a standard of 'true' peasantries is that peasant families retain holdings for generations, parting with them only at moments of dire necessity or when extinction of a line places a new name upon the land. This 'family–land bond' has been observed by commentators on peasant landholding in later medieval England and has served historians as a staple in their description of the transfer of peasant land in the centuries either side of the Black Death in the mid-fourteenth century. Although, as we shall see, it has been generally acknowledged that close familial association with particular peasant holdings tended to disappear in the decades after the arrival of plague, it has also been generally accepted that, before the mid- to late-fourteenth century, peasant families tended to remain on the same plots of land for generations and that, as a consequence, transfers of land tended to be *post-mortem*, through inheritance by kin, rather than *inter-vivos*, by sale or gift to non-kin.

In such conditions of relative stability of landholding and consequent inelasticity of supply in terms of landed resources, some relief, it has been argued, came through the *inter-vivos* transfer of small plots and odd acres of land, traffic in which operated outside of the normal constraint of familial attachment. According to the majority of historians writing on this subject in the middle decades of last century, and indeed through at least into the early 1980s, the prime mover for these occasional transfers of small parcels of land was biology; as individual peasant families increased in size they looked to take on more land, and, conversely, as they declined, so they released part of their landholding to those peasants with newly burgeoning families. As a consequence of this process of redistribution between 'natural sellers' and 'natural buyers', small plots of land were bought and sold in order to readjust the sizes of the main peasant holding which, as we have seen, was itself typically transferred within the family by inheritance. This demographic model of peasant land transfer is usually accredited to A. V. Chayanov and was widely adhered to by M. M. Postan and his 'school' in describing the transfer of land amongst the English peasantry during the later Middle Ages. Postan's extremely influential introduction to an edition of peasant charters, published in 1960, employed the Chayanovian model to make sense of the transfer of land in English peasant communities in the thirteenth century, concluding that 'the balance of evidence suggests that the main stimulus for traffic in land was generated within the peasant community', and reflected the impetus of 'certain abiding features of peasant life'.[3]

The impression of land transfer in peasant communities is then essentially one of relative timelessness,[4] an impression that has been modified by more recent research on the peasant land market which has endeavoured to show that the transfer of land was strongly influenced not only by the life-cycle of the peasantry but also by a range of short- and long-term factors, including the quality of the harvest, local commercial expectations, the dictates of landlords, and the demands of the state. In other words, what has sometimes been characterised, at least before the mid-fourteenth century, as essentially a wholly natural and inevitable consequence of peasant life has come increasingly to be described in terms of responses to external stimuli; inevitably this also means and helps explain why the frequency of transfer of land, as with so many other aspects of peasant landholding in the later Middle Ages, varied considerably across regions and over time.

The English peasantry in the late Middle Ages did, broadly speaking, possess an alienable interest in land but that interest was, as we shall see, constrained to varying degrees and by a range of factors, notable amongst which was lordship. That said, the period between, say, the early thirteenth century and the late fifteenth century experienced a shift from a time when the preponderance of peasant land was distributed between kin at moments coinciding with vital events, notably marriage and death, to a time when the majority of land transactions, as well as the greater part of land transferred, took place between non-kin in commercial transactions which were less likely to be occasioned by the life-cycle of the individual or his or her family. At Halesowen, where, it has been suggested, land transfers between family members persisted long into the fifteenth century and *post-mortem* transfers far outweighed *inter-vivos* transfers in the first decades of that century, the overall tendency was both for non-kin transfers to supplant transfers between family members and also for inheritance to give way to *inter-vivos* exchange, notably sales and purchases of land.[5] On many manors throughout England and Wales, the last decades of the fourteenth century and the first of the fifteenth saw a considerable

upsurge in land market activity and of entry into holdings quickly
vacated by others. In the Welsh Marches, for example, the land market
in the decade 1390–9 was far more extensive than that of 1340–8.[6]
Elsewhere, in midland and southern England, although the chronology might vary by decades, similar patterns emerge. In Berkshire,
more land changed hands in the 1390s and 1400s than at any time
since immediately after the Black Death; similarly, in Bedfordshire, the
turnover of customary holdings increased in the early fifteenth century
and, on the manor of Willington, a number of tenements passed into
the lord's hands for want of an heir.[7] On the estates of Westminster
Abbey, the larger family holdings of peasant land tended to be transferred through inheritance until the fifteenth century when a combination of factors saw *inter-vivos* transfers replace inheritance, even for
the large units of landholding, such as virgates. By the last two decades
of the fifteenth century at Birdbrook, Essex, the *inter-vivos* transfer of
customary standard holdings had, for the first time since relevant
material appears for this manor in the late thirteenth century, replaced
post-mortem transfers and grants from the lord of the manor as the
dominant form of transfer.[8] On the estates of the bishopric of
Worcester, there is a marked increase in transfers between non-kin
during the fifteenth century which reflects 'an intensification of the
land market'. By the early sixteenth century, as population began to
recover, land became relatively scarce and, as those who had acquired
land in the late fifteenth century endeavoured to keep the family name
upon it, there was a partial return to an earlier scenario, with a greater
frequency of transfer between kin.[9]

Historians noting these developments have tended to describe this
period in terms of the disruption or extinction of the family–land
bond. In the late Middle Ages, it has been suggested, a system of
peasant landholding, in which each peasant family held roughly
similar extents of land and where distribution of holdings was greatly
dependent upon inheritance, collapsed.[10] In its place there arose a
system increasingly dependent upon a land market for distribution
and where it was possible for holdings to accumulate in the hands of
fewer and fewer individuals. Hilton, in an important early study,
described how, on manors such as Stoughton (Leicestershire), substantial holdings were gathered together in the hands of single tenants,
so that, by the third quarter of the fifteenth century, some tenants
held two or three virgates, in other words, holdings in excess of 70
acres.[11] In addition to accumulation, or engrossment, some customary

tenements distintegrated in the second half of the fourteenth century
and the early fifteenth century. To quote one example amongst many,
at Rothwell (Yorkshire), a customary tenement called Walkeroxgang
had fragmented into several small plots by 1425.[12] A fall in demand
for land in the late fourteenth and early fifteenth century meant that
the forces, such as lordship and familial commitment to a holding,
that held tenements together could dissipate, offering opportunity for
cheap land acquisition.

This model does not follow the same chronology in all instances and,
again, East Anglia stands out as quite distinctive in its precocity. But
even there we are forced to acknowledge that, although *inter-vivos*
transfers of small plots were an important element of the history of
land transfer in that region, the *post-mortem* transfer of the main family
holding retained, as elsewhere, its significance well into the post-
plague period. That said, it is in eastern England, as historians have
long acknowledged, that a market in peasant land is likely to have
made its earliest appearance.[13] Certainly by the early thirteenth
century there are suggestions that the members of peasantry in East
Anglia were buying and selling land from each other. On the estates
of the bishop of Ely, for instance, there is some strong indication that
a significant redistribution of holdings was under way even in the
twelfth century. Similar observations could be made of the estates of
the Abbey of Bury St Edmunds, where, from the earliest court rolls,
that is, by the mid-thirteenth century, there is clear indication of the
energetic buying and selling of small plots.[14]

As already discussed, changes in the size of the peasant family
holding are, according to some historians, explicable simply in terms
of changes in the size of the peasant family: in such conditions, the
peasant land market serves only as a redistributive mechanism
responding to the local needs of a largely self-contained community.
The land market, in such circumstances, is not driven by commerce or
desire for profit or aggrandisement but principally by the need to
maintain a family of a particular size. The constraints which play upon
it are essentially those of simple supply and demand. There were,
however, in the late Middle Ages, factors other than peasant family
life-cycles which could have prompted a land market amongst the
peasantry. As the discussion of regional and temporal distinctions has
already implied, not all of these factors were necessarily present at the
same time nor were they evident in all parts of the country. Further,
in certain regions or at certain periods, the same general factors may

have helped generate an active market in land while in other regions or at other moments in time they served only to depress it. Thus, topography and historical patterns of landholding, lordship and seigneurial policy, local and regional economies, manorial custom, and patterns of inheritance, could all promote the frequent and unfettered transfer of land, but they could also restrict it. To attempt to isolate the determinants of the land market is, however, to investigate the factors which explain broader developments within the peasant family and community. Hardly surprisingly, it is in the combination of short- and longer-term factors that we can comprehend the motive forces of land transfer in the later Middle Ages and, in the particular prevalence of certain of these factors, that we can explain significant regional and temporal variations. Most especially, it seems reasonable to draw a distinction, in the most general terms, between, on the one hand, such longer-term or relatively autonomous determinants of landholding and land transfer as landscape and topography, patterns of settlement and the proximity of urban or market centres, economic and political developments, demographic shifts, population movement and the role of inheritance and, in the shorter term, lords and peasant, those who held the land and made choices regarding its management. We shall begin, therefore, with a brief review of factors that will have helped determine patterns of landholding in medieval England before considering how lords and peasants responded to such patterns.

Pre-determinants

Landscape and topography had, inevitably, a vital role to play in the initial distribution and organisation of landholding, as we have seen.[15] Landscape and soil type, in one sense, helped define the arrangement of land long before the twelfth century and, in so defining it, may have set early limits upon the land market. In the simplest terms, some parts of the country were less able to support large bodies of population than were others: population density varied to a considerable degree, with the highest populations tending to centre upon and around areas of better soil and relatively high yields. In north-east Norfolk, for instance, in the eleventh century, population density was almost four times the calculated national average, a pattern generally repeated when the surviving sources of the fourteenth century next permit such an analysis. By contrast, the northern marches of Northumbria,

Westmorland and Cumbria, suffering from the predations of frequent
outbreaks of warfare, relatively isolated from major markets and urban
centres and lacking good quality arable, were sparsely populated.
Whereas, by the late fourteenth century, most of East Anglia was settled
with more than 16 persons per square kilometre (km), the Scottish
borders had densities of less than 3.5 per square km.[16]

Areas of early colonisation and of relatively intensive arable husbandry, such as parts of southern and central England, tended,
inevitably, to be managed differently from areas where pastoral husbandry predominated. It was, in part, in the presence or absence of
colonisable waste that the nature of the peasant community and the
consequent attitudes, on the part of both lords and the tenant peasantry was partially founded. Beyond 'champion' England, opportunities for late colonisation of woodland and moorland had, as we
have seen, created communities of smallholders, often holding their
land by free tenure.[17] In this preponderance of free tenures and in
the ubiquity of smallholdings, but also in the high frequency with
which individuals held both free and unfree land simultaneously and
in the precocity of an active peasant land market, such communities
contrasted markedly with those of central, open-field, England. In
'champion' England, a process of colonisation had, for the most part,
been completed centuries earlier and the patterns of landholding
which existed in the late Middle Ages had, perhaps, been established
before the eleventh century. There was, therefore, a rigidity of landholding in parts of central England which augured against a fluid and
vibrant market in land.

Further variable features of topography and landscape which could
impact upon the rural land market and the transfer of land were the
degree of market integration and the proximity of urban centres. Discussion of the relationship between towns and their rural hinterlands
can be reserved for a later section of this book but, for the moment, it
will not be possible to discuss the changing attitudes to land and its use
in this period without acknowledging the potential impact of towns
and their trade upon peasant landholding. The growth of towns and
local markets in the thirteenth century, their relative decline in the
fourteenth century and the emergence of new centres of industry in
the fifteenth century all impacted in significant ways upon the local
land markets, particularly land markets within the hinterland of urban
and mercantile centres. London merchants, throughout the period,
invested their profits in land, a feature that becomes increasingly

evident in the fifteenth century. On the manor of Tottenham (Middlesex), for instance, craftsmen and artificers from London made frequent incursions into the land market there.[18] Trade between towns and their hinterlands also promoted inequalities in rural land markets; the greater success of certain villagers in their trading ventures allowed them to re-employ their capital in the purchase of land, a feature especially evident in the land markets of the East Anglian countryside by the late thirteenth century.[19] Finally, towns acted as lures to local rural populations, exerting a centripetal force: migration into towns freed up landed resources which could then be redistributed. The reverse was, of course, true of rural industry. During the period, there were, for instance, significant incursions of the cloth industry into the countryside. The transformation of villages in rural Berkshire, Somerset and the Essex–Suffolk border into centres of cloth production meant that their populations were swollen by in-migrants who looked to purchase plots of land. At Castle Combe (Wiltshire), the growth in local cloth production from the mid-fourteenth century encouraged an influx of clothiers, labourers and apprentices. It was clothiers, in particular, who invested in land.[20] We might also add here that certain areas encouraged not only investment in industry but also the influx of capital in other ways. The wool-producing areas of central England, such as the Cotswolds, were regularly visited by Italian wool merchants who bought not just from lords but also from peasant producers; elsewhere, wealthy peasant cornmongers were also dominant in local land markets.[21]

Perhaps less obvious than trade and the economic pull of towns, church and state and their various organs also affected land transfer amongst the peasantry. In the first place, simple demands made by the church and by the state, the former in the form of tithe, the latter as direct taxation, entered into the budgetary calculations of peasant families and may have encouraged certain 'policy changes' with regard to land and perceptions of its worth.[22] In late thirteenth-century Hinderclay (Suffolk), it is possible that wealthier villagers, anticipating direct taxation of their moveable goods, reinvested their moveable wealth in land to hide it from the assessors.[23] In such cases, taxation spurred the land market and, by encouraging buyers into the market, enhanced the real value of land. Of course, taxation could have the opposite effect – by draining the resources of poorer villagers, high levels of taxation could oblige villagers to sell plots in order to meet the demands of the state.[24] We shall revisit these questions in Part II

when we consider the influences which played upon the peasant family
and its economy.

The impact of the state on peasant land transfer extended beyond
the immediacy of taxation and economic pressures. Most importantly,
developments in law had significant implications for the tenure of land
and its ease of transfer. In terms of free land, the thirteenth century
witnessed a struggle to facilitate a market in freeholdings, a market for
long hampered by lords' concerns over the fragmentation of their tenanted lands and their concomitant dues. The replacement of a legal
principle of subinfeudation, whereby if tenant A, who holds from lord
X, sells free land to B, then B simply becomes tenant of A who still
continues to hold from X, with substitution, in which A sells to B and
B replaces A as X's tenant, worked to the advantage of both lords and
their free tenants. Statute, notably *Quia Emptores* (1290), which effected
the introduction of substitution in place of subinfeudation, confirmed
the free tenant's right of unimpeded alienation. Earlier, in the late
twelfth century, Angevin government had provided free tenants with
a growing range of legal remedies which may have served to embolden
tenants and helped foster an incipient market. As we have already seen,
the emergence of a secure freehold, protected by possessory assizes,
also, as a by-product, brought into existence a common law of
villeinage. While security of tenure may have encouraged a market in
free tenements by the mid-thirteenth century, the reverse was the case
for unfree land which, unprotected at common law, undoubtedly lost
some of its lustre in the eyes of freemen buyers.[25] On manors and
estates where lords persisted in their expectations of a manorial
economy dominated by serfdom, it was generally not until the last
decades of the Middle Ages, when tenure in villeinage had thrown off
most of its more blatant associations with servility, that free men felt
once again sufficiently encouraged to invest in unfree land. Elsewhere,
where lords were less exercised about their rights over their villein tenantry, the free had made earlier inroads into lands held in villeinage,
a point to which some brief return will be made later in this chapter.

This distinction between free and unfree tenures should not,
however, imply that an active market in free land was the counterpoint
to a sluggish market in customary or unfree land; while it is true that,
on certain manors, lords resisted any attempts at piecemeal sale of
villein holdings on other manors and estates there was an energetic
market in unfree land by, at the latest, the mid-thirteenth century.[26]
The important difference was that, while free land was transferred

through the mechanisms of common law, unfree land changed hands through the private jurisdiction of the lord and his manor court. We shall return to seigneurial attitudes to the transfer of unfree land later in this chapter but, for the moment, we need simply acknowledge that developments in common law from the twelfth century had, as we have just observed, real implications for the transfer of free land and 'cultural' and, *de facto*, 'real' implications for the transfer of unfree land. In the case of unfree land, this 'cultural' effect was manifested in the transmission of legal concepts and devices from common law into the local courts of lords.[27] Common law developments in forms of proceedings, of protection and of recovery, were quickly aped in manor courts, the lords of which, it has been suggested, hoped to divert business into their own jurisdictions.[28] Importantly for our present discussion, common law forms of conveyancing were, at least in part, mirrored in customary law manor courts by the late thirteenth century. The emergence, during the thirteenth century, of transfers in unfree land which accorded rights of admittance, inheritance and alienation to the transferee and his heirs has been perceived as an important stimulus to a less-encumbered market in unfree land. Would-be villein vendors and emptors, increasingly protected at customary law through the adopted devices of common law conveyancing, entered with growing confidence into markets in land. Lords, as we shall see, perceived economic advantage in such markets while the land market itself promoted further elaboration and sophistication of conveyancing practice. By the close of our period, the transformation of tenure in villeinage into copyhold, a tenure which in the sixteenth century would increasingly enjoy the protection of both equity and the common law, was both partial cause and effect of a revived market in 'unfree land' by the end of the Middle Ages.[29]

Inheritance practices also had an important influence upon land-holding and land transfer in medieval England. Customs of inheritance, broadly divisible into monogeniture or impartibility (inheritance by a single, male heir) and partibility (joint inheritance by, in the first instance, male siblings), were long established by the thirteenth century in England. As Faith and others have shown, despite at times an effective homogeneity of practice, there were in the medieval countryside significant regional differences to practices of inheritance, notably a concentration of the practice of partible inheritance in eastern England and Kent. It has been suggested that, whereas partibility (and ultimogeniture) may have been the typical form of inheritance practice amongst the peasantry of Anglo-Saxon England, monogeniture, or more precisely primogeniture, came to replace it in the decades and centuries after the Conquest.[30] The presence of one or other particular form of inheritance practice had potential implications for the land market in that, whereas primogeniture tended to ensure the integrity of holdings, both partibility and ultimogeniture encouraged their fragmentation or parcellisation. Whilst, therefore, impartibility, by maintaining holdings intact, acted against a peasant land market, partibility, by reducing holdings to small, saleable holdings, encouraged such a market. Although the potential of inheritance practices to determine local landholding and, thereby, the nature of the local peasant land market, has elicited certain expressions of reservation by historians, the frequent correspondence of, in particular, partibility, small plots of land, and an early and active market in that land is compelling. We will, however, reserve a fuller discussion of the forms of inheritance and their implications for, *inter alia*, land transfer until the next part of this book.

Finally, and obviously of no small importance, the short- and long-term demographic developments of the period were not without consequence for the peasant land market. The growing population of the high Middle Ages, the dearths and famines of the late thirteenth and early fourteenth centuries, the dramatic losses of the mid-century and the concomitant stagnation of population in the late fourteenth and fifteenth centuries, all had effects upon the market in land. The land hunger of the thirteenth century gave way, by the late fourteenth century to a relative land abundance and, increasingly, an active market in relatively cheap holdings. In the shorter term, moments of demographic crisis, such as the famine years of the second decade of the fourteenth century, encouraged, where such markets already were active, a volatile response amongst buyers and sellers.[31]

The nature of the environment, patterns of settlement, the development of commercial enterprise, the financing of national and international politics, incidence of disease and famine, were likely then to determine, in significant ways, the choices in the management and distribution of land and, thereby, the presence or absence of an active land market. As we shall now see, those who occupied the land could react either fairly passively to these determinants, allowing their use of the land to be formed and directed by a combination of these exogenous factors, or they could act rather more energetically, making clear choices either to react against such factors or to attempt to exploit them fully.

Lord and Tenant

Obviously, not all of these factors were necessarily immune from the influence of those who held the land, the landlords and their tenants. Although, therefore, lords and peasants may have been constrained by a range of factors wholly or largely beyond their control, the choices they could make and the initiatives they could promote were capable, perhaps singularly capable, of easing or restricting the potential for the *inter-vivos* transfer of land. It is, in particular, in the persistence of long-established patterns of land use and in the appearance of novel approaches to the land, that we can chart the variety of attitudes both to the tenure and to the transfer of land in this period.

Fundamentally, many of the elements from which the landscape of medieval England was composed – the patterns of landholding, the organisation of field systems, the management of woodland, the extraction of resources – were, of course, the products of long-standing choices made by those who worked the land during earlier centuries. From before as well as during our period, lords and peasants effected considerable changes in the landscape of rural England. The efforts of both lords and peasants to mould their landscape had important implications for land transfer in the late Middle Ages since choices made regarding land use were posited upon distribution of land amongst the tenantry and, to a greater or lesser extent, were dependent upon that distribution. Where such dependency was considerable, as, for instance, in the case of the open-field system, both lords and their peasant tenantry were careful to control the extent of land transfer.

In various parts of England, and, again, we can draw a crude and sweeping distinction between 'champion' England and the zones to the east and to the west, attitudes to land use and the development of the landscape tended, in the earlier part of our period, to follow the patterns determined much earlier.

Thus, in central England, an adherence to open-field agriculture survived, at least on some manors and estates, into the fifteenth century. The open-field system, with the two or three great fields divided into furlongs, with each furlong composed of strips, and with a tenant's holding distributed in strips throughout the open fields, was a response to the particular quality of land and its workability. The organisation of the open fields, characterised by economists as a policy of risk aversion,[32] became, for the lords of southern, midland and north-eastern England, a foundation of their manorial economies, while village communities organised their agricultural routine in accordance with the limits and potential of the open-field system. The particular features of the open field, a form of agricultural organisation dependent upon collectivity and a rough equality of holding size, may have discouraged a free market in strips of land since neither lords nor tenants saw their advantage in permitting individuals to accumulate large holdings or to concentrate those holdings in the more advantaged areas of the open fields. The response of both lords and villagers to the transfer of customary land – composed as it was of strips spread within the open fields – may, therefore, have been conditioned by their expectations of and concerns over the limits of open-field agriculture. Consequently, preoccupations on the part of the lord over the retention of labour services and, amongst the peasantry, concerns to maintain a loosely egalitarian structure based upon mutual co-operation, may both have militated against an unrestricted market in customary land. In the late fourteenth and fifteenth centuries, there were, however, significant changes in land use. Most marked of these was the decline in arable husbandry in parts of central England and the rise of pastoral husbandry in its stead. Allied to this development was the accumulation of holdings by individuals who, increasingly, ran their land as commercial enterprises and were able to contemplate specialisation for the market.

Elsewhere, beyond the fringes of 'champion' England, colonisation and the creation of small freeholdings maintained their progress into the early fourteenth century, slackening only with demographic decline and subsequent collapse in the mid-fourteenth century.[33] Here, concerns over land use were not necessarily of paramount importance for lord or tenant. Lords, principally concerned with the income that their lands could generate, were, depending upon their other policies of estate management, as likely to see economic advantage in the transfer of land as they were disadvantage. For the tenantry, also, apprehensions over the impact of unconstrained land transfer on the exploitation of land were more likely, in such circumstances, to be mediated by perceptions of economic advancement or security which investment in land could help generate.

It is with these broad contrasts in mind that we can now turn to consider the particular attitudes of lord and tenant to land and its transfer. As we shall see, for lords, the tenantry and the wider community of the village, land transfer had legal and social implications which went far beyond immediate concerns over the exploitation of land as a resource. Certain of these aspects will be investigated here whilst others, land as inheritance and as a family 'possession', will be treated more fully in the next two chapters.

Lords

It is evident that lords on many estates attempted to ensure that customary holdings, typically those that owed labour services, remained intact, at least into the early fifteenth century, and that careful regard was given to each holding. The reasons for this seem clear and relate to the expectation of the lord in terms of the functioning of the manorial economy and administration. In particular, as we have seen, a proportion of landlords in late medieval England continued to extract labour services from their tenants as a form of rent even into the fifteenth century. The continued preoccupation with labour rent on the part of some landlords throughout much of this period was reflected in a concern that the viability of the customary standard holding as a unit of labour rent should be preserved at almost all costs. Even by the close of the fourteenth century, when it was increasingly evident that tenants prepared to perform labour services were in short and diminishing supply, landlords on certain estates continued to hold on to the increasingly vain hope that their manors would once again be populated by a servile tenantry fulfilling a proportion of its rent requirements in the form of labour. Faith, in her study of Berkshire manors, describes tenancies which were, according to the qualifying clause, held 'until a tenant shall be found who will perform the due and accustomed services'.[34] Similarly, tenants entering leases of holdings in the Welsh Marches in the last decades of the fourteenth century were admitted until (*quousque*) a tenant willing to hold by customary services could be found.[35] With such expectations it was important for lords to ensure that the services of individual holdings were not forgotten and could one day be reimposed. As a consequence, during the period of high farming in the thirteenth and early fourteenth centuries, landlords who utilised labour services in the running of their demesnes institutionalised restraints upon a potential peasant land market; the persistence into the late fourteenth and fifteenth centuries of a strong desire to maintain labour services meant that landlords and their policies remained a frictional drag on the peasant land market on manors in certain parts of the country throughout most of the period.

Strong resistance to a market in customary standard holdings from the thirteenth century through to the fifteenth is especially evident on some of the larger ecclesiastical estates. Fears that the buying or selling of customary holdings owing labour rents or fractions of those holdings would threaten their ability to exact services are evident in a strong resistance to accumulation and/or fragmentation of customary holdings.[36] This control of the market by landlords is particularly evident on the estates of Westminster Abbey where, on the majority of manors, the monks, as landlords, were keen to preserve standard holdings intact. Their concerns over fragmentation were reflected in seemingly punitive additional rents attached to the fragments of holdings sold by tenants while the rent of the remaining portion of the holding was not allowed to decline; similarly, efforts on the part of the tenantry to accumulate holdings were constrained by high rents and entry fines.[37] It was only when landlords lost sight of this hope, or were presented with an alternative which shook them from their reverie, that customary standard holdings in areas of heavy manorialisation could be truly said to have entered a real land market.

Not all landlords were as chary of permitting a market in peasant holdings. Where landlords had jettisoned any great dependence on labour services or where they had adjusted their strategies to accommodate the prevailing physical, economic and social conditions, the market in land was vibrant long before the end of the thirteenth century.[38] In regions beyond the champion belt of central England, there is evidence to suggest, as we have seen, that lords opted much earlier than did their counterparts on 'champion' manors for a more monetised form of estate management. On manors and estates in eastern England, for instance, lords were less dependent on labour services and more inclined to pay for the labour of their demesnes. Instead of the hidden profit of labour services, lords sought to generate income through money rent but also through entry fines generated by an active, and actively encouraged, land market. Income from *inter-vivos* transfers on the manor of Redgrave, a manor of the Abbey of Bury St Edmunds in Suffolk, although considerably less than annual rent from land, was equivalent to approximately 40 per cent of rental

income by the early fourteenth century and, in extreme years, such as
the famine year of 1317, land transfers, the majority prompted by des-
peration, yielded as much income for the lord as did rent. Further, a
comparison of revenue generated by *inter-vivos* and *post-mortem* transfers indicates that, at Redgrave, by the end of the thirteenth century,
the buying and selling of tenant land by the peasantry produced three
times as much income for the lord as did revenue arising from
inheritance.[39]

Where lords perceived their financial advantage to reside in an
active land market, the practical needs which affected the decisions of
landlords on 'champion' manors were less in evidence and, most
importantly for us here, careful regard for the integrity of the customary standard holdings could be abandoned. On these manors and
estates, there were moves towards the accumulation of holdings and
the reconstruction of holdings from odd acres much earlier than is
found in other parts of England. There was also, at least from the thirteenth century, a considerable disparity in size of landholding which
was promoted by a largely unconstrained land market. In the late thirteenth century, at Redgrave, just under half of all holdings comprised
less than 2 acres, whilst just over 10 per cent of holdings were larger
than 10 acres, with less than 4 per cent holding in excess of 18 acres.
This disparity was both reflected in and a consequence of the con-
tinual buying and selling of land. At Redgrave, between 1260 and
1319, there were 2756 *inter-vivos* transfers of land, an average of 7.3
transfers per court. A comparison of *inter-vivos* transfers and transfers
post-mortem, effectively inheritances, for the years between 1305 and
1319, reveals that, while there were only 108 *post-mortem* transfers in
this period, there were 1039 *inter-vivos* transfers. Although the total
amount of land transferred *inter-vivos* was not significantly greater than
that transferred *post-mortem*, the larger family holdings tending to pass
at death to heirs while the smaller plots of land were traded piecemeal,
as we have seen, the revenue that the *inter-vivos* transfers generated for
the lord was a highly significant element of annual income. Further, it
afforded opportunities for the acquisitive and advantaged members of
the community to buy up land and create relatively substantial landholdings, a point that we shall return to below.[40]

As we saw in the previous chapter, landlords in late medieval
England tended to respond to the conditions that already prevailed
within their lordships and adapted their policy to accommodate the
variety of conditions. The factors discussed earlier in this section –

landscape, established agrarian practices and inheritance customs – provided the template with which lords had to work. It is for this reason that a single landlord might manage different manors on his estate differently, as can be seen on the Westminster Abbey estates, where the lords, although generally antipathetic to an unrestricted market in customary land, were prepared to countenance such a market on 'manors of a certain type'.[41] On manors such as Aldenham in Hertfordshire or Pyrford in Surrey, early assarting from the waste had created a structure of landholding which, in its preponderance of smallholders and freeholders, was unlike the pattern of landholding centred upon the standard holdings in evidence on most of Westminster's manors. On these manors there is considerable evidence for both accumulation and fragmentation of customary standard holdings in the thirteenth and early fourteenth centuries, practices that would not have been permitted on other Abbey manors.[42]

Neither were landlords beyond forcing their circumstances to conform to their own expectations. Lords were heavily involved in schemes to colonise the 'waste', to drain marshland, to erect sea-defences in order to protect farmland, to maintain woodland.[43] There were evident ramifications for land transfer if landlords sought to effect changes in agrarian conditions – for instance, by promoting colonisation of new land or by restricting access to the waste[44] – or to encourage local commerce, notably through the creation and subsequent encouragement of local markets.[45] The ready availability of colonisable land, for instance, had implications for a peasant land market by offering relatively easy access to small plots and generating an atmosphere in which frequent dealing in land was the established norm; similarly, proximity of commercial centres, such as local markets or small towns, encouraged the creation of surplus capital which may, as we have already discussed, have found its way back into a peasant land market as investment.

There is, similarly, a strong sense that landlords could dictate inheritance practices and encourage changes as fundamental as a shift from primogeniture to partible inheritance or vice versa. At Gressenhall in Norfolk in the late thirteenth century, it has been suggested, the lord of the manor initiated the introduction of partible inheritance 'because he wants more tenants' while on the estates of Westminster Abbey and the bishopric of Worcester, at an earlier date, the lords engineered the opposite, replacing partibility with primogeniture in order to reduce the risk of splitting holdings and the consequent threat to labour services.[46] Such developments would, as has been briefly discussed and as we shall see more fully in a later chapter, have important implications for the facility of the peasantry to buy and sell or simply to exchange land.[47]

Tenants

Lords were, however, not the only parties who may have, at different times and for a variety of reasons, attempted to restrict or to encourage a market in customary land. In addition to lords, the peasant tenantry could be strongly resistant to alienation but, just as their lords, tenants also displayed contrary tendencies and, at different moments and in different places, they promoted the *inter-vivos* exchange of land. Undoubtedly, as in the above discussion of the role of lordship in encouraging or confining a market in peasant land, the particular attitudes of the peasantry were forged, at least in part, by the landscape in which they lived and worked and the customs which they held as their own. That is not to say that the peasantry, as their lords, did not regard custom or landscape as immutable. They were prepared to contemplate change if it appeared to accord with their own advantage. The physical organisation of the rural landscape was as dependent upon the choices of the peasantry as it was of lords; it was frequently the members of the village communities of medieval England who were responsible for the setting out and organisation of open-field systems; it was also villagers who, with an eye to their customary rights, protected commons and waste from encroachment just as it was the peasantry who spear-headed campaigns, especially, in the thirteenth century, to transform 'marginal' land into arable. Finally, it was also the wealthier peasants who were in the vanguard of the move from arable into pasture in the fifteenth century. However, like their lords, the attitudes of the peasantry to the exchange of land and their control of the degree of that exchange were inextricably linked to custom and forms of landholding; as such they were conditioned responses and not altogether their own.

To begin with restrictions, there are a number of features of peasant behaviour in the later Middle Ages that suggest resistance to an unrestricted market in peasant land: these include evident concerns over the integrity of the family holding and a presumed preoccupation with the preservation of links with the 'family land', the efforts of individuals to prevent alienation of land they considered rightfully their own, collective censure of land market activity that could lead to the impoverishment of members of the village community or the withdrawal of cherished communal rights. Each of these will be considered in turn before we explore ways in which the peasantry actively encouraged a market in their land.

The 'family–land bond' has featured prominently in much that has been written on the peasant land market in late medieval England. Studies, particularly of the manors of central England, have encouraged historians to the view that the peasantry had a close emotional attachment to their land, or at least to the core of their holdings, and that alienation of such land was contrary to the ethos of the late medieval peasant family.[48] Discussion of the 'family–land bond' has, in turn, prompted much debate regarding the nature of rural society in late medieval England, a debate which can be omitted here.[49] The important point for us is that, although historians tend now to argue against the existence of a 'family–land bond' but, instead, tend to grace one or other factor as determining the nature of land exchange in late medieval England, there is, at least, some indication that the peasantry could, through, *inter alia*, emotional attachment to holdings, restrain the local land market.[50]

As we shall see in the next chapter, individuals attempted to contest inheritances, claiming prior and better rights of inheritance. There were also, clearly, individual concerns over alienation of family land and the *inter-vivos* sale of land which should, by right, have passed to surviving relatives. Rivalry between siblings may have stood in the way of *pre-mortem* alienations by parents keen to provide in some measure for all of their offspring. Similar restraints on the free transfer of land came from widows; the recovery of land by widows of men who had alienated it during their lifetimes without their spouses' permissions may have served as a restraint of the land market both in the actuality of the recovery of transferred land and the sense of insecurity that it bred in the minds of buyers.[51] Not all such restraints necessarily emerged from tension and rivalry, however: in areas of partible inheritance where, as might be reasonably imagined, inheritance practice effected division of holdings and helped promote a land market in very small plots of land, a single heir can often be observed buying out his siblings' shares in order to consolidate the holding. In such cases, family ties presented individual family members with effective pre-emption rights.[52]

It was not only family that acted as a drag upon land transfer in medieval England. The wider village community also had a part to play in containing the force of the land market. We have already discussed the likelihood that, in areas of champion England, community could have looked unfavourably upon an active land market that challenged the integrity and function of open-field agriculture. In addition we have to consider the real possibility that other 'concerns' of community, the appropriate rule of customary law and the maintenance of established practice, the preservation of village harmony and the protection of the interests of individual villagers, will all have had an impact upon land transfer in this period. Once again, these are themes to which we shall necessarily return in the next chapter but, for the moment, we need briefly to consider aspects of law and socially accepted norms of behaviour in the village. In the first place, the village community was, as we shall see in more detail in a later chapter, a store of collective memory. In particular, the more substantial male tenants fulfilled functions within the village and within local lordships which necessitated their familiarity with legal mechanisms and their willingness to inform on past practice. As an effective source of customary law, the wealthier sections of the community enjoyed some influence over the transfer of land and could either encourage or restrict such practice. In Winslow (Buckinghamshire) in 1341 an inquest jury in the manor court rejected a widow's claim to land previously granted as a lease by her late husband. The jurors insisted that her claim should lose because no dower rights existed for widows in land held for a lease and where that lease had yet to expire. The potential force of custom and the role of the jury in interpreting it are neatly revealed here, not least because, as Beckerman has shown, the jurors had actually ruled incorrectly in this case.[53] The role of the community and its representatives in determining the form and velocity of land transfer occurred in many other ways: officials in the manor court, affeerors, established the size of entry fines and revealed their local knowledge in reducing fines for relatives or those who were not strangers and whose credit-worthiness was already established.[54]

Although we might suspect, with some reason, that those with a relatively privileged sense of law, custom and appropriate dealing would manipulate land transfer to their own advantage, it is also important to acknowledge that any excessive promotion of self-interest would fall foul of the expectations of the wider community. As we shall discuss a little later, it is clear that wealthy villagers were sometimes prepared to trade the censure and opprobrium of their poorer neighbours for the advantage that self-interested manipulation of their position brought them. However, in many cases, especially perhaps in open-field communities where a quasi-egalitarianism was depended upon for the collective functions of the community, the vast majority of villagers, possibly all, felt constrained by certain shared moral imperatives.[55] In such instances, charitable obligation towards the poorer villagers and the extension of small loans of cash and kind during moments of hardship may have saved poorer villagers from taking the unwelcome step of selling or leasing their land in order to raise capital. Charity and a sense of moral duty, capable of being enforced by the collective sanction of the community in any number of ways (for instance, through defamation and gossip, non-cooperation socially and economically, litigation, violence), became, in such a context, further restraints on a free market in land.

If all of the above – familial expectations, the claims of individuals, the obligations of community – were potential reasons why the tenantry may have felt compelled to constrain the transfer of land, they were, of course, also reasons for its encouragement. Just as families may have sought to hold on to land, they were also capable of dividing it amongst their members, either at death, through partible inheritance, or in life, as *pre-mortem* transfers to non-inheriting offspring.[56] It is also clear that families hived off small portions of their holdings in order to sustain themselves during crisis periods or in order to accommodate their landholding to the size of their families. The village community, through the extent to which it was prepared to reject custom when it stood in the way of ease of transfer and to support it when it promoted that ease, could also encourage land transfer. The community's role in countenancing and helping to generate an atmosphere where, for instance, a fluid land market was accepted as normal and appropriate is also important in this respect. The extent to which communities were prepared to tolerate, even to embrace, acquisitiveness matters here, especially in a period frequently characterised as one of transition from feudalism to capitalism. Further to this, individuals and families might see in the transfer of land opportunities for personal or dynastic aggrandisement. From at least the early to mid-thirteenth century, and with a varying chronology dependent upon, principally, regional patterns of husbandry and lordship, it is evident that sections of the tenantry sought to purchase land whilst other sections looked to sell. This redistribution was not, as much of this chapter has sought to illustrate, a simple function of changes in the size of the peasant family. Instead, there was a combination of factors, including, as we shall briefly now consider, the opportunism of sections of the peasantry.

Although it is clear that not all peasant involvement in land transfer was the product of self-interest, it is equally evident that certain peasants engaged in land transfer for reasons of commerce and speculation. As has already been discussed, by the late thirteenth century, lords in eastern England had capitalised on the burgeoning peasant land market there. In the late fourteenth and fifteenth centuries similar developments would be clearly observable elsewhere in England. This growing market in land was a product, as we have also seen, of a wide range of factors including patterns of landholding and inheritance practices, urban proximity, regional trade patterns, legal and political developments, but it was also encouraged by the desire of the peasants themselves. How we choose to categorise the nascent peasant land market of the high and late Middle Ages is dependent, to a considerable degree, upon our willingness to see in emergent capitalism a force which helped sustain the bonds of family and community or acted as a challenge to them.[57] There is, however, little doubt that certain members of the peasantry were not beyond placing self-advantage ahead of familial or communal obligation. In their early attempts at entrepreneurship they gave a significant boost to the land market. Uneven ratios of buyers and sellers on manors of the estates of Bury St Edmunds in the thirteenth and early fourteenth centuries are clear indication that some villagers were wealthier than their neighbours and bought from these poorer neighbours as opportunities presented themselves. That this advantage was reflected in other ways than through the land market can be seen from debt and trespass litigation recorded in manorial court rolls; that it created tension within the community is also revealed by this material.[58] That said, we should also acknowledge the possibility that individuals sometimes bought land not to compete with their fellow villagers but to support them; in particular, the extension of loans in difficult years was often guaranteed by leases of land by the impecunious to village creditors.[59] In this, we also need to recognise that self-interest came in a number of forms and actual motive could be hidden very deep indeed. Was the primary motive of the wealthy villager who bought land from his poorer neighbours simple economic advantage, charity, creation of a standing within the community? Or perhaps there was some other, even more obscure, motive. The purchase of land may, for instance, have been encouraged by external factors, as, for instance, when wealthier villagers reinvested moveable property in land in order to reduce their liability to pay lay subsidies.[60] Alternatively, the purchase of land, free or unfree, may have been a deliberate challenge to lordship and a claim for legal freedom, since alienation and the tenure of free land by the unfree were contrary to standards of common law villeinage.[61]

If individual peasants chose to buy land for a number of reasons, there were also various causes for the sale of land. We have very little information about the purchase price of unfree land although we do know more about the perceived value of free land. From entry fines paid in manor courts, however, we can gain some sense of demand. The size of entry fines varied enormously but they were at their highest in the decades around 1300 when population was at its highest levels and land was relatively scarce. In such conditions, the sale of land was, *prima facie*, attractive, realising a substantial sum of money. However, we have to acknowledge a range of variables that would have affected the value of land and the considerations of seller and buyer. If the seller owned substantial parcels of land, if he and his family worked the bulk of their land for their own subsistence, if the family farm brought in relatively little labour and was not heavily reliant on the market for food, and if the family holding was larger than was necessary to sustain the peasant family, then the sale of odd acres at times of land hunger was likely to be to the real advantage of the seller and his family. In such a scenario, we enter the world of Postan's 'natural sellers and buyers' where the size of the peasant family dictates the choice of the peasant to buy or to sell small parcels of land.[62] Undoubtedly, some members of the peasantry found themselves in such positions of relative comfort during our period. Widows, for example, might well find themselves relatively advantaged, with a surplus of land beyond their immediate needs.[63] However, in contrast to this scenario, peasant sellers of land in this period also included the severely disadvantaged. In this case, the transfer of land is less usefully perceived as one feature of the life-cycle of the peasant family. To reverse the criteria listed earlier, if the seller owned relatively small plots of land, if the produce of those plots was insufficient to sustain the seller's family, if the seller and his family were, as a result, partially or largely dependent upon the market, then the sale of odd parcels increased the market dependency and vulnerability of the seller and his family. Many examples of such a descent into market dependency exist, especially from the years of shortage and of land hunger in the late thirteenth and early fourteenth centuries.[64]

If smallholders in the thirteenth and early fourteenth centuries were obliged to sell off portions of their land in response to high prices and dearth, villagers by the fifteenth century faced a rather different set of incentives. In the later period, peasant sellers may have been responding to opportunity more than to shortage. With a substantially lowered population, low food prices, high wage rates and abundant wage-labour opportunities, market dependency was not the obvious curse that it had appeared in, for instance, the early decades of the four-teenth century. Although the actual value of land might be falling, as demand also fell, a feature revealed in declining rents and entry fines in the early and mid-fifteenth century, there were also villagers and non-peasants prepared to invest in land. These fifteenth-century investors in the peasant land market, keen to accumulate holdings and to establish substantial, if often short-lived, farms, also helped generate a seller's market in land. As in the thirteenth century and early fourteenth century, increased market dependency encouraged the sale of land but, by the fifteenth century, it was not scarcity of food which encouraged sales but the scarcity of labour (or, to put it another way, the relative abundance of food).[65]

Finally, as will already be evident, a potential problem clearly exists here if we elect to think of 'peasants' or 'tenants', even within the same community, as, in some way, a single group with common interests. As a number of studies have revealed, the medieval village was econom-ically stratified, that very stratification partially promoted by the trans-ference of land. The unconstrained transfer of land was, undoubtedly, more in the interests of certain sections of the peasantry than it was others. In the late thirteenth and early fourteenth centuries, for instance, during a period of intense harvest failure, the *inter-vivos* exchange of small parcels of land looks to have advantaged buyers who could capitalise on the misfortunes of their poorer neighbours. Athough such transfer worked to the benefit of those tenants with suf-ficient capital to invest in their neighbours' need, the transfer or market in land at such times clearly also met the immediate wants of those obliged to sell. When, towards the close of our period in the late fourteenth and fifteenth centuries, a renewed and intensified process of stratification created hitherto unknown polarisations of landholding within the medieval village, sections of the erstwhile tenantry on some manors were rendered effectively landless. In such circumstances, when, inevitably, rather different views of the efficacy of a free market in land are likely to have arisen, a unanimity of purpose within the village community could only be maintained if the wealthier members of the community were prepared to be constrained by their perceived social obligations to the poorer members. In contemplating such a precarious balancing act, it is easy to imagine the splintering of communities, divided along lines of vested interest, with the wealthy promoting an active market through their various machinations, including economic and political pressure exerted upon lord and village community alike, while the poor offered resistance in whatever form that presented itself. These are issues to which we shall need to return in later chapters when considering the political, commercial and moral world of the peasantry. Before we do so, we need to discuss what is often taken to be the mainstay of peasant society and economy: the family.

Part II

Family

The structure of the peasant family and of the peasant household serve as significant indicators of the nature of the peasant economy and its interaction with a wider economy. Discussion of changes in family and household structure across time also offer insights into the changing relationship between the peasantry and that wider economy. In particular, as Smith has pointed out, it is the identification of certain key variables in household type and formation that aid attempts to categorise the nature of the peasant economy.[1] Most importantly, historians need to grapple with and to explain the reasons why families and households increase and decrease in size during this period. Is the rise and fall of the peasant household simply a product of biology or the effect of other, additional and external factors, including, for example, the demands and opportunities of a commercial market which encourages peasant families to expand their enterprise and to buy-in additional household members as servants? In fact, as we shall see, the relative importance of purchased labour *vis-à-vis* family labour in the household economy and, as a consequence, the presence of servants in peasant households offer important indicators as to the workings of society and economy and of the degree to which the peasant family was an integrated element of such a broader society and economy.

In the following two chapters, an attempt will be made to describe, as far as possible, the nature and structure of the peasant family and household between 1200 and 1500. Important themes of this discussion will be the extent to which family and household changed over time as well as the variety of that development and the causes of it. As in Part I, on landholding, a central concern of this discussion is the extent to which such a fundamental element of peasant society as family was subject to a combination of influences.

5

FAMILY, HOUSEHOLD AND KIN

The relationship between peasant families and their land sits at the core of the majority of investigations of the peasantry. Family, as a preoccupation of peasant culture and life, is seen as of central importance and, for some historians, without evidence of this preoccupation the identification of a society as 'peasant' becomes problematic.[1] A simple model of peasant agriculture and everyday existence posits a collectivist enterprise in which each member of the peasant family neglects individual endeavour in favour of mutual responsibilities to the wider domestic group. In these 'true' peasantries, it is the family and not the individual that is significant. This close categorisation of the peasantry as family-centred has had implications for historians' preparedness to conceive of a peasantry operating within wider spheres. If the peasant thinks first and foremost of his or her responsibility to his or her relations, then his or her motives for interacting with the outside world are likely to be limited. Furthermore, since a linked assumption about such peasant activity is that the collective activity of the peasant family is primarily concerned with self-sustaining agriculture, it may also be presumed that the peasantry's focus of attention is almost wholly inward. The preoccupations of the peasantry, when seen as largely or exclusively familial, are likely then to have concerned the family's relationship with land – and, principally, how to keep it in the family and how to organise family labour upon it. In such a model, where the peasant and the peasant family interact with outside agencies, the peasantry is almost wholly passive and likely to be coerced, exploited, utilised: in other words, generally other than a free agent or one capable of independent, 'individualistic' action.

For such a model of peasant passivity and inward-looking to work in a historical reality, evidence of a few key elements needs to be presented. We would need to show that the peasantry was composed of individuals acting not for their own but for their families' best interests; the redistribution of land would have, for the most part, to be constrained by peasant and family custom; most land transfer – especially of family holdings – would necessarily be by inheritance. We would also need to find evidence that the bulk of labour in peasant agriculture was based upon the family and that the scale of that labour, along with the amount of family land available to be farmed, rose and declined according to family size. We would, therefore, necessarily expect to find reasonably complex or, at least, large households or wider family or kin groups where the majority of offspring remained in close proximity to the parental hearth, available to provide service for the family and anticipating some share of the family's bounty. Consequently, we might also expect to find a relatively low incidence of migration and we would tend to characterise the smaller family units as offshoots of neighbouring households rather than the products of in-migration. Furthermore, since the family in this model is largely self-sustaining, we should expect to find relatively little engagement with a wider market, apart, perhaps, from necessary expenditures and the sale of cash crops to provide money rents. Finally, in such a culture, the inward focus and preoccupation of familial activity would limit engagement with wider issues of society and politics.

As we have seen in earlier chapters, and as will become more evident, little of this model accords with the reality of peasant life in late medieval England. This is not to imply that there was no such thing as a peasant society in medieval England, but rather that a simplistic model of peasant society and its nature will not easily accommodate the complexity and variety of that society. If some of these elements can, in fact, be observed in different parts of the country at different moments in the late Middle Ages, they certainly can hardly be observed everywhere at all times and, in some places, they cannot be found at all. It is clear that medieval peasants looked to their families to meet many of their needs, education, health and charity, food and clothing, shelter, companionship and love, inheritance. All of these were more likely to issue from and be found within an individual's family than they were to be located elsewhere. Families were also recognised as units of account and reckoning by others who were not family members: servants sought employment in families, lords imposed obligations on families and divided their land sufficient for the sustenance of a family, taxation was levied on household units, and so on.[2] Undoubtedly, therefore, the family was, throughout this period, a central focus for many peasants but it did not, as many historians would now accept, define the peasantry's very existence. Instead, it may be best to view the peasant family not simply as a means for organising production for its own ends, but as a symptom of the stresses and forces which acted upon the English peasantry in this period. As such, the peasant family in late medieval England was in no way a static concept but, as with the peasant land market with which it was so inextricably entwined, was instead a barometer to wider developments, a point to which shall return in the next chapter. Consideration will be given there to the factors which may have promoted changes in family and household form, and this should provide an opportunity to re-address the issue with which we began this chapter – namely, the extent to which the peasant family and household were essentially insular or, alternatively, largely responsive to external factors. Before we engage with such issues, however, the basic form of the medieval peasant family and the household need to be established.

Family and Household, 1200–1500

Discussion of the peasant family and household in the later Middle Ages is not straightforward.[3] It should be already evident that the isolation of a 'typical' peasant family is a practical impossibility. Between 1200 and 1500 the demography of the peasantry underwent significant shifts which acted upon the nature of familial structure and which, as a consequence, make any temporally static statement regarding that structure problematic. Furthermore, the forces which combined to form the peasant family were not uniform throughout England and there are important distinctions between household and family form between regions. Finally, within any community there were significant differences in household form and structure which also need to be described and discussed.

The classic statement on the English peasant family remains that of G. C. Homans.[4] Homans argued that the tendency of the English peasant family, in central 'champion' England, was to produce a 'stem-family', in other words one in which a single male heir remained close to the hearth whilst his siblings sought opportunities elsewhere. He concluded, therefore, that the majority of English peasant families in champion England in the generations before the plague were relatively small, and predominantly two-generational, in other words, a nuclear family structure. Outside of champion England, according to Homans, a regime of partible inheritance produced 'joint-households', where all siblings remained within the household and worked the family holding jointly.[5]

Even if Homans's discussion of household formation systems has been modified in recent years, more recent research would also tend to stress the ubiquity of small, rather simple, 'nuclear', households, composed of parents and their children.[6] But, if the generality of household structure was nuclear, a feature hardly surprising in itself, it is also striking that not all peasants lived in nuclear households. In fact, it is the lesser proportion of complex households and the apparent fluctuations in that proportion that are particularly revealing of the varied and variable experience of the English peasant family in the late Middle Ages. In the following paragraphs, we will elaborate upon the ubiquity of the nuclear family, and the evidence for this, before turning our attention to the potential for the persistence and re-emergence of larger and more complex household formations. We will, for the most part, reserve consideration of the reasons for these variations until the next chapter. In reviewing the structure and size of the medieval peasant household, we will also need to describe the broader family, by considering the role and extent of associations of kinship.

Peasant Households: Size and Complexity

There is only very limited evidence for household structure in the late Middle Ages and even less that can count as direct evidence. There is, above all, no source which can serve as a census for the late Middle Ages, although the poll-tax returns from the late fourteenth century come closest and cover a large section of the population. 'Serf lists' from Spalding Priory also offer certain insights into household structure but, as Smith has shown, they are not easily interpreted. Court records and, by the end of our period, wills also permit observations of family structure, but no documents provide us with categorical information. In addition, archaeological evidence, especially evidence for peasant housing, encourages attempts to equate size of housing

with size of households while fifteenth-century funereal representa-
tions, especially brasses, of wool producers and clothiers of peasant
stock come closest (but not very close) to medieval depictions of families whose immediate ancestors were peasants, even if they were unlikely to have thought of themselves as such.

That the bulk of medieval households were small, conjugal units is
strongly suggested by the poll-taxes, especially those of 1379 and 1380
which record the names of all those liable to tax above the ages of
14 (1377) and 15 (1379/1380).[7] Russell's work on the 1377 poll-tax
encouraged him to estimate that there were approximtely 2.3 persons
per household over the age of 13 in the late fourteenth century.[8]
There is, further, evidence from the poll-tax returns and from other
nominative listings to indicate that certain individuals lived solitary
existences, a feature that would obviously reduce the mean size of
households. Although a feature more typical of towns than of the countryside, the presence of solitaries in the countryside in the second half
of the fourteenth century looks to be evidence of a highly mobile and
transient society rather than one founded upon associations of kinship.
This is further confirmed by the considerable presence of servants in
the poll-tax listings which, again, suggests a tendency for a proportion
of the young to move out of their own households into the households
of other families. Historians have applied the additional assumption
that these servants were 'life-cycle servants', who, once they had completed a period of service during their late teens and early twenties,
would establish their own households, either by returning to their
native villages or by settling in their place of employment or wherever
else opportunity presented itself. The important point here is that their
presence in our documents is indicative of a likelihood that many
households in the late fourteenth century would be small. Similar
observations can be made for earlier periods. The late thirteenth-
century Spalding serf lists, even allowing for the observations of Smith
who showed that, rather than listings of residential groups, they were
in fact genealogies, tend to indicate that households were generally
small.[9] Hallam, using this material, had calculated that the average size
of households on three manors in south Lincolnshire varied between
4.37 persons and 4.81 persons.[10] Although we cannot be confident of
these figures – and the likelihood, given Smith's comments on the
source, is that they overestimate family size on these manors – they do
accord with other calculations of late thirteenth-century family size.
Smith, using manorial court rolls, has estimated that the average family

size on the Bury St Edmunds manors of Redgrave and Rickinghall
(Suffolk) was 4.7 and 4.9 respectively, while, for central England, Razi
has produced the broadly comparable figure of 4.7 for peasant families
at Halesowen.[11] Howell, working on the Leicestershire manor of Kibworth Harcourt, has calculated that the mean household size there was
4.84 in the late thirteenth century but had fallen to 3.72 by the 1379.[12]

But not all peasant families or households within the high and late
medieval rural population were small. In the following chapter we will
return to explanations of the variety for household forms in the late
medieval countryside but, for the moment, it is sufficient to acknowledge that relative wealth and size of landholding did have important
implications for household size. In the central midlands, for example,
the wealthier tenants who, in the late thirteenth and fourteenth centuries, held 30 or 40 acres of land tended to have larger households
than did their poorer neighbours. The average household size of a
wealthier 'virgater' at Halesowen was significantly larger than that of
their poorer neighbours. Razi's comparison of numbers of children
amongst rich, middling and poor families indicates that, both in the
early and later fourteenth century, the average number of children in
wealthy peasant households could be between two and three times
as great as the number of children in poorer households. Although
household size declined in the second half of the century, Razi estimated that there were, on average, three children per rich household
compared with two children in middling households and 1.4 children
in poorer households; in the early fourteenth century, the respective
averages were rather higher at 5.1, 2.9 and 1.8.[13]

We might postulate, as a number of early modern historians have
been prone to do, a relative complexity for these wealthier households
also.[14] Thus, we might imagine that a large holding, perhaps a virgate
of 40 acres, would be inherited by an eldest son who could have suc-
ceeded to the holding in his late teens or early twenties. Succession
to the holding would be likely to have coincided with marriage which
could mean that a young wife would have had the best part of two
decades of child-rearing. Infant mortality would have been almost sure
to have taken its toll and breast-feeding by the mother would have
reduced opportunities for conception, but it is not unreasonable to
suppose that by the time the parents reached their early forties, they
could have six to eight surviving offspring between the ages of two and
twenty. At or near this point, they may have chosen to retire, hand-
ing over their land to their eldest male child. If they remained in the

household after this, then the complexity of the household was assured, with the likelihood of a three-generational household composed of parents, an inheriting son, his wife and their young offspring, and the siblings of the inheriting son. If there was room or need, the household might also have been made more complex by the addition of non-familial members, such as a servant. Examples of household formations similar to this can be found. At Weston (Lincolnshire), a three-generational household consisted of a widow, her four sons, and a grandson, as well, presumably, as the mother of the child.[15] Retirement contracts also suggest that, on occasion, the elderly or infirm remained within the household of their younger relatives. At Cranfield (Bedfordshire), in the late thirteenth century, a son agreed to house his retired mother and father

> on the chief messuage. And if it chance (which God forbid) that quarrels and discords arise in time to come between the parties, so that they cannot dwell together peaceably in one house, the aforesaid John will find . . . a house in his courtyard, with a curtilage, where they can honourably dwell[16]

Room was also, on occasion, found for non-inheriting siblings.[17] Servants also could be accommodated within the household, as the frequent payment of fines by villagers in manor courts for housing strangers and servants contrary to by-laws and labour legislation appear to indicate.[18] Documentary and archaeological evidence for house construction and design also suggest that house types existed which were capable of accommodating fairly large numbers of household members. Archaeological evidence from Houndtor in Dartmoor certainly suggests a complexity of housing that may have been a response to the need to accommodate relatives and servants within the family home.[19] The proportion and type of complexity is likely to have varied from one region to the next and to have altered over time but, lacking census-type sources, it is almost impossible to gain any accurate sense of the relative proportions. By the mid-fifteenth century, for example, notably in central and southern England, especially in areas where demesne farming had given way to leasing arrangements, peasants took advantage of lower rents and greater availability of land to accumulate large holdings. Such enterprises were often doomed from the start for lack of sufficient capital and family members to make them viable. However, some families like the appropriately named Dedrichs at Halesowen, as others in midland England, amassed tens and even

hundreds of acres which they worked for at least a couple of generations in the late fifteenth century, suggesting that they could call upon
a wide network of support, some of which may have been kin-based. In
particular, those peasants who became large-scale lessees of demesnes
in the fifteenth century may have been widely dependent on family
members to support their endeavours, in which case we might expect
to find complex households being created anew amongst the wealthier
fifteenth-century villagers.[20] Further, as was also the case in areas of pastoral husbandry, the accumulation of holdings reduced the number of
smaller holdings, and effectively rendered those who sold or were
obliged to sell, rather than bought, landless or near landless and in
search of employment. The wealthier, landholding villagers probably
relied as much on this newly available workforce as upon their own kin
and may well have accommodated servants within their own households. Certainly, surviving architectural evidence suggests these
wealthy tenants had the potential to do so since, in the late fourteenth
and fifteenth centuries, they constructed large houses for themselves.
The complexity of structure of the fifteenth-century wealden houses of
south-eastern England, with their central hall and two-storeyed gables,
may have been matched in household form. Separated rooms, as many
as five, clearly offered the potential to house aged relatives, unmarried
siblings and servants.[21] At all times, therefore, between 1200 and 1500,
peasant populations will have included complex households but their
proportion relative to the rest of the population will have varied. As we
have seen and shall consider in more detail in the next chapter, key
determinants of household size and structure included wealth,
economy and a range of demographic factors.[22]

Throughout most of the period and throughout most of England,
however, such complex household arrangements were relatively rare.
In the thirteenth century, on the Spalding Priory manors of Weston,
Moulton and Spalding, Hallam discovered only 4 (1.6 per cent)
three-generational households out of the 252 households which he
identified in the registers.[23] In fourteenth-century Halesowen (Worcestershire), where complex households were more common, Razi has
estimated that perhaps as many as 16 per cent of the households he
was able to reconstitute were composed of what he terms 'co-resident
extended families'.[24] For the greater part, large family groups tended
to fragment into smaller households, even if they retained a geographical proximity. Thus, as Razi has found at Halesowen, parents,
upon retirement, preferred to move out of the family home into

a smaller, neighbouring property (whilst retaining certain rights of access to the main domicile). Similarly, non-inheriting siblings did not linger close to the parental hearth. Instead, parents attempted to furnish them with small plots of land and dowries with which they could establish households of their own. Alternatively, at moments of land hunger, as in the early years of the fourteenth century, siblings moved out of the main home only to take up residence in separate but neighbouring houses which, often, were situated within the curtilage of the parental home. 'Thus on many holdings and the land adjacent to them', writes Razi, 'the main house was surrounded by cottages occupied by single as well as married relations of the tenant'; for instance, at the close of the thirteenth century, the Alwerd family holding at Halesowen was occupied by six households.[25] Razi contends that the amount of land held by any family was of vital consequence for the degree to which that family's kin remained in the vill; where some land was available upon which offspring could settle, the general pre-plague land hunger exerted a centripetal force, encouraging them to remain in the village rather than seek pastures new.[26] The opposite was the case for the poorer villagers, whose children could not be provided with land of their own; instead, the centrifugal tendencies of the land shortage drove them from Halesowen in a quest for land elsewhere.[27] But, amongst both rich and poor in the pre-plague countryside, even in areas where relatively large holdings existed and where the typical mode of transfer was inheritance, the general tendency was to form simple households. Whilst it is also possible, indeed probable, that a few wealthy villagers created newly complex households in the fifteenth century, it is also almost certain that, in an age of heightened mobility and polarisation of landholding, the majority of rural dwellers occupied small households lacking complexity.

Kinship

If household forms throughout much of England tended, then, with notable exceptions, to be simple rather than complex, and the size of one's immediate family to be small, there appears to have been much more variety in the relative importance of wider family groups, or kin. The previous discussion of household structure was concerned with the nature of the houseful, in other words, those living under the same roof. Thus, as happened at Halesowen, the households of the wealthy

peasants remained simple because aged parents and unmarried siblings were inclined to move out of the main household into separate
dwellings. But, as we have also seen, they did not necessarily move very
far, often remaining within the immediate proximity of the family
dwelling. Elsewhere, as in eastern England, as has also been discussed,
family members, when they moved out of family households, were
more likely, perhaps on account of a lack of resources, to move further
afield.

Such observations have prompted historians to suggest that, within
late medieval England, kinship was stronger in some parts of the
country than it was in others. In particular, Razi has suggested that
wealthy families in pre-plague Halesowen were what he has termed
functionally extended, enjoying high kin densities. Razi contrasts the
situation in the West Midlands (Halesowen) with that in East Anglia
(Redgrave, Suffolk) where, he suggests, the peasantry was far less 'kin-
oriented'.[28] Few individuals at Redgrave held large holdings and the
inheritance practice of partibility ensured that holdings remained
small; further, the land market at Redgrave in the late thirteenth and
early fourteenth centuries, apart from being more active, was also far
less intra-familial (46 per cent of land being transferred through the
family) than at Halesowen; finally, the population of the Suffolk manor
also seems to have been far more mobile. Taken together, these features encourage Razi to the view that 'kin density' there was much
lower than at Halesowen and he considers it unlikely that most villagers at Redgrave had relatives in the vicinity of their households.
Although, therefore, by the end of the thirteenth century, the same
pressures were coming to bear on the villagers of both Halesowen and
Redgrave (increased population, reduced availability of land), the tenurial situation at Redgrave prompted a different response than at
Halesowen; a burgeoning smallholder class meant that functionally
extended families were seldom viable and instead the nuclear family
predominated. What is more, as Razi has also suggested, even within
regions where networks of kinship appear to have been important, the
persistence and strength of bonds of kinship were dependent upon the
opportunities which existed for family members to remain closely resident. In other words, wealthy families were more likely to be well supported by kin than were their poorer neighbours who were, by
definition, more prone to transience and whose offspring were often
obliged to migrate out of the community in search of opportunities
elsewhere.

As well as regional and economic dimensions to the relative significance of kinship patterns, there is also an important temporal dimension which, again, Razi has been most active in exploring. For Halesowen, he has described an important shift in familial organisation either side of the Black Death, noting the alteration in family form from functionally extended to predominantly nuclear by the mid-fifteenth century but, thereby, stressing the persistence of the extended family group into the early fifteenth century.[29] Although the percentage of Halesowen tenants dying childless was greater in the late fourteenth century than in the fifty years and more before the arrival of plague, more than half of Halesowen families present in the late thirteenth century retained their hold on land until the end of the fourteenth century. Razi suggests that this phenomenon is to be explained by an influx of distant kin from neighbouring vills and manors who were permitted to pay cheaper rates than were complete strangers to take over vacant holdings of their deceased relatives. The attraction of such holdings for these immigrant kin also lay in the fact that that 'they gained relatives who could assist and co-operate with them'.[30] Thus, the functionally extended familial system persisted at Halesowen into the fifteenth century but not beyond; intra-familial transfers in the land market declined markedly in the 1430s and the surnames of old-established families disappeared from the records as tenants died without heirs. In the period 1431–1500, according to Razi, the majority of Halesowen peasants did not have resident kin beyond their own household and, consequently, the functionally extended familial system was no more; instead, the nuclear family predominated.

Given this variety of household and family size, as well as the relative importance of wider familial relations, it seems likely that the extent to which the collective of 'family' enjoyed the potential to meet the expectations of its members or to call upon those members to sustain it was dependent upon that size and proximity. These features were, in turn, the consequence of a range of factors which we will now need to consider.

6

PEASANT MARRIAGE AND HOUSEHOLD FORMATION: ISSUES AND INFLUENCES

The Demography of the English Peasantry: Factors in Household Formation

Important in our consideration of household formation, sense of family, and the strength of family and kinship bonds is the isolation of factors which will have affected these aspects of peasant life. A central issue here is the degree to which household formation and an individual's association with her or his family were influenced more by simple biological processes than by a range of other demographic and 'non-demographic' processes. Thus, the distinction is really between, on the one hand, the family cycle in which families naturally increase and decrease over time and where that rise and fall is explicable simply in terms of births and deaths, and, on the other, by a range of factors independent of these natural cycles. In this latter category we should therefore include factors which interfere with or disturb a process of family formation determined solely by vital events. Thus, a series of institutional, economic, social, political, religious and personal factors might have acted upon and helped determine household formation in the late Middle Ages. Importantly, also, the degree to which the peasantry relied upon family ties above other associations will have been influenced by the relative effect of such factors. A brief attempt to review these factors will allow us to assess the diversity of experience of the English peasant family and will also illustrate the inclusion of the peasant family within a number of separate spheres of influence. These spheres, as will be apparent, often overlapped, but we can isolate them artificially for the purposes of this discussion.

Demographic factors

We need to begin with a consideration of those demographic forces which, as independent or exogenous factors, operated wholly or almost wholly beyond human agency or control, and played upon household formation and, thereby, upon the strength of familial ties. Most obviously, demographic crises of some kind, such as the Black Death of 1348–50 or the Great Famines of the early fourteenth century, would have affected family and household structures, perhaps strengthening family ties by offering opportunities for survivors to marry earlier or weakening them by encouraging mobility and movement away from family to areas of new opportunity. As well as crises, though, the underlying effect of 'background mortality', the prevalence of a range of diseases and the general measure of health, will have impacted upon household structure and family formation in a number of ways. By the same token, levels of male and female fecundity, age of menarche, opportunities for women to conceive and carry children to term, the length of birth intervals, and so on, will all have played their separate and combined parts in the success or failure of the peasant household as a viable and sustained unit. Of course, it is largely unrealistic to think of all or any of these factors as truly exogenous – levels of mortality or of fertility are, at least in part, responses to a combination of influences both exogenous (climate change, for instance, or other environmental shifts, such as epizootics in native rodentine or bovine populations) and endogenous (for example, the availability of food or the institutional support for the young, the sick or the aged). Furthermore, perhaps needless to say, for much of these crucial demographic variables, the medieval sources are almost wholly silent and we are reliant upon comparisons with other preindustrial societies, including early modern England, from which relevant material survives.[1] However, there are opportunities to make some observations regarding late medieval mortality, morbidity and fertility before proceeding to consider the range of dependent factors.

Mortality
It is a standard of the literature on the medieval English peasantry that life was harsh and life expectancy likely to have been low.[2] Certainly, the peasantry did not escape the demographic crises of the period. Famine and plague were the amongst the realities of rural existence in the high and late Middle Ages. From the late twelfth century until

the middle of the fourteenth century, the English countryside was at frequent risk of famine and dearth. It has been estimated that there was real shortage in almost every decade from 1290 until the third quarter of the fourteenth century.[3] The spectre of famine continued to haunt the rural population after the dramatic fall in population of the mid-fourteenth century, although by the fifteenth century, famine would seem to have been mostly confined to certain regions, such as the far north-west of England.[4] In addition to famine, plague decimated town and countryside in its initial appearance in the mid-fourteenth century. Regular recurrence of plague in the late fourteenth and fifteenth centuries included severe national outbreaks, especially in the years before 1400, and there is reason to believe that plague remained a significant killer in the late medieval countryside. The demographic impact of these crises was extreme. The Great Famine of the early fourteenth century may have killed 10 per cent of the population while estimates of rural deaths from plague in 1348–50 suggest levels of mortality of between 45 and 50 per cent. Subsequent national outbreaks of plague in the 1360s, 1370s and 1390s may each have killed a further 10 per cent of the population. Campbell has estimated that, at Coltishall (Norfolk), recurrent plague reduced population by as much as 80 per cent from its pre-plague maximum.[5] Even if population, both rural and urban, was not slow to recover from the famines of the thirteenth and early fourteenth centuries, the staggering losses of the mid-fourteenth century were of a wholly different order. The national population was not restored to its pre-plague numbers until the eighteenth century.[6]

As well as the great demographic crises, disease and ill-health were likely to have been typical features of everyday existence throughout the period. Calculations of peasant life expectancy are problematic, to say the least, but those estimates which have been attempted accord with more substantial data for other late medieval social groups. Howell has calculated that, at Kibworth Harcourt (Leicestershire), the average age attained by landholders in the fourteenth century was between 50.7 and 54.9 years. Roughly, this would accord with a life expectancy at age 25 (e25) of approximately 27 years which, if correct, is rather better than that enjoyed by Benedictine monks in the fifteenth century, but still low by early modern standards.[7] Similar estimates have been made by a number of other historians and, as a rough measure, adults in the medieval countryside may have expected to live until their early 50s.[8] There is, in fact, every reason to suppose that the population of the countryside was pegged back by high levels of background mortality, which, in turn, were the creation of a combination of poor sanitation, limited and vulnerable food supplies, harsh and exacting labour conditions, environments favourable to the propagation of disease, and so on. The relative effect of these various elements would vary across time and between geographical areas, with certain of these confined to particular periods or places,[9] but it is striking that, by the fifteenth century, a time of generally improved living standards, adult mortality rates appear to have risen and life expectancy to have dipped.[10]

If adult life expectancy was relatively poor, it seems reasonable to assume that life expectancy at birth was much worse. Evidence for infant mortality in the medieval countryside is wholly lacking and comparative calculations from model life tables using estimates of contemporary adult life expectancy are likely to be as misleading as they are informative. That said, it is almost inconceivable that rates of infant mortality in the late Middle Ages were low and that life expectancy at birth (e_0) was less than 35 years, possibly less than 30 years.[11] The mortal dangers of childbirth and the attendant diseases of infancy must have taken a severe toll.[12] The likelihood is that infant mortality rates before the mid-fourteenth century were higher still, encouraging estimates of around 25 years for e_0.[13]

Fertility

As well as the death-rate, the birth-rate determined the demographic experience of the peasantry. There will be opportunity later in this chapter to consider the range of factors that affected fertility but, for the moment, consideration needs to be given to fecundity and biological constraints on childbirth. As with issues of infant and child mortality, there are, however, virtually no sources that shed light on the birth-rate or changing levels of male and female fecundity. Poos has exploited the only source which can offer information on birth-rates in the medieval countryside and has calculated that there were approximately 30 births per thousand of the population in the fifteenth-century parish of Walden (Essex), a low rate consistent with periods of demographic stagnation in the early modern period.[14] There are, however, good reasons for supposing that even if the birth-rate was low in fifteenth-century Essex, it was not necessarily low in all places and at all times between 1200 and 1500.

Indications in recent research are that, if the birth-rate was low in this period (or, more particularly, in the second half of this period), this is more likely to have been explicable in terms of responses to social and economic shifts than of male and/or female fecundity. However, comparison with the experience of modern societies, as well as preindustrial societies for which relevant historical material survives, makes it clear that periods of shortage and nutritional deficiency could reduce male and female fecundity as well as the potential for women to bear children to term.[15] Further, the age of menarche in girls will have some significance for household formation but only if young women married and started families soon after the onset of puberty, issues to which return will be made when discussing choices and pressures as regards household formation and the distinction between age at marriage as an exogenous or endogenous force. Unsurprisingly, there is no evidence for estimating age at menarche but, as with issues of conception and gestation, we might imagine that changing standards of living will have effected changes in the age at which girls entered puberty, so that it seems probable that puberty began earlier by the close of our period than it had two or three centuries earlier.[16]

If we cannot measure these key demographic variables, we can at least glean some sense of changing standards of living across the period from surviving records and, thereby, assess the likely impact of these on issues of mortality and fertility in the countryside. Research on standards of living amongst the medieval peasantry, principally contained within the writings of Dyer, has revealed that there exist a few sources which can be exploited to shed light on food availability both in terms of quantity and quality. Maintenance agreements or retirement contracts, made between outgoing and incoming tenants, sometimes include details of the food allocation for the retired tenant.[17] In addition, manorial accounts include not only details of payments and food renders to manorial servants, *famuli*, but also the details of provision for harvest worker payments. Where such records exist in reasonable series, it has proved possible to chart changes in diet over fairly long periods. In particular, Dyer's investigation of payments in kind to harvest workers at Sedgeford (Norfolk) is revealing.[18] It shows that over the period, and, in particular, either side of the mid-fourteenth century, there was a transition from a diet based almost exclusively on cereals to one in which protein featured much more prominently. Whilst the particular benefits of meat and fish consumption cannot be substantiated for this population, there is little doubt that the increased proteinous diet indicates that, in the second half of our period, the peasantry had more resources to expend on basic necessities. As a consequence, it seems reasonable to infer that child-bearing and -rearing opportunities are likely to have been poorer in the pre-plague countryside than they were later.

These, then, were the 'pure' demographic determinants which acted upon English peasants and which conditioned their lives and controlled the formation of their households. But this control was partial and against the impact of mortality and fertility we have now to review a range of additional factors which, either occasioned by the choices of the peasantry or forced upon them, helped mould the peasant family and household and their constituent parts.

Personal choices

In the often extreme demographic conditions of the period, the peasantry had little control over risks of mortality (with a possible exception being their preparedness to combine agriculture with high risk employment, such as mining).[19] There were, however, a number of choices which the peasantry could make which could impact upon fertility (what Malthus termed 'preventive checks') and, thereby, upon household formation. Of course, no choice was entirely 'free': each is likely to have been influenced by a number of other factors, including economic circumstance and social conventions, but there was in this, at least, an element of self-determination.[20]

Most evidently, age at marriage, an issue of fundamental significance for household formation, was controlled in part by the hopes and desires of individuals. In the medieval countryside, however, it seems reasonable to suppose – in the absence of any evidence – that the choice of when to marry was not one guided solely by physical attraction or emotion.[21] As we shall see, economic circumstance, custom, law and social convention all informed and constrained such choice but, for the moment, we should briefly consider its significance. In two important articles, J. Hajnal set the terms for a debate over age at marriage and its demographic significance. Hajnal distinguished between a European (or north-west European) and a non-European (southern European) marriage pattern. A European marriage pattern was, he argued, characterised by, *inter alia*, late marriage (mid–late twenties for men, early–mid twenties for women), a high incidence of life-cycle service, and a proportion of individuals who never married; by contrast, the features of a non-European marriage pattern were early marriage (late teens for women, early–mid twenties for men), low incidence of life-cycle service, with few, if any, examples of never-marrieds. Using late fourteenth-century poll-tax data, Hajnal concluded that late medieval England displayed a non- (or southern-) European marriage pattern. In the wake of Hajnal, demographic historians, notably Hallam, Razi, Smith and Poos, have attempted to test his characterisation and, although it would be inappropriate to suggest that a consensus has now been reached, the likelihood that different marriage patterns pertained at different moments, in different regions and amongst differing social sub-groups is now generally accepted. In other words, argument for the existence and persistence of a universal marriage pattern, even amongst one section of society, the peasantry, now seems highly tenuous.[22]

Changes in age at marriage will have fundamental significance for explanations of long-term shifts in population, but only if there is a close association between nuptiality and fertility. If sexual relations are delayed until marriage then changes in the age at marriage will impact upon the fertility of a population, earlier marriage prompting higher fertility, and vice versa. Discussion of the demographic regime pertaining in high and late medieval England has divided, in the broadest terms, between those who would argue for a high pressure regime of high mortality and high fertility, and a low pressure regime where both mortality and fertility were relatively low. Consequently, topics such as age at marriage, the extent of extra-marital sex and rate of illegitimacy, contraceptive practices, infanticide, and migration, which will be considered here as indices of the self-, or partially self-, determined role of the peasantry in household formation, have also been discussed as signifiant variables in determining population movements. Although, therefore, these factors will be discussed primarily as variables which contributed to the formation of the peasant household, their cumulative effect as vital engines of the late medieval population should not be overlooked.

Importantly, they also testify to the role which the peasantry, consciously or unconsciously, played in wider social and economic developments. Whereas it was once the view that the medieval village enjoyed a controlled demographic equilibrium, with the replacement of a dead tenant by his or her heir whilst the non-inheriting remained, unmarried, within the households as members of a stem-family, more recent work has rejected the largely internalised account of, above all, Homans, in which social convention and the institutions of land holding and transfer determine family formation and preserve the demographic regime in a reasonably passive state. It seems, instead, that the population of villages could, for instance, expand beyond available resources, a fact which would lead to demographic crises, widespread mortality and concomitant out-migration. Especially in the era before plague, Razi, for one, has portrayed the medieval village, in demographic terms, as a high pressure regime in which rates of both mortality and fertility were high. Smith, by contrast, has argued that, in addition to exogenous shocks, such as famine or plague, the endogenous effects of controlled fertility were instrumental in reining in population movements. Delayed marriages, economic opportunities beyond the village which encouraged out-migration, child-rearing practices, and so on, may all have slowed population growth and, subsequent to the plagues of the mid-fourteenth century, recovery. In other words, not only was the demographic experience of the peasantry determined by a range of developments beyond the manor and vill, as we shall see, but peasants, through their own life-choices, customary practices and institutions, helped effect broad demographic trends.

Aside from the importance of the study of age at marriage for our understanding and explanation of long-term trends in population movement, the age at marriage underpins the size and complexity of the peasant family and household. Half a century ago, G. C. Homans contended that peasant household formation was dependent upon marriage which, in turn, was dependent upon access to land. According to Homans, opportunities amongst the peasantry for land acquisition in thirteenth-century champion England were limited and predominantly a product of inheritance. Thus, niches which permitted household formation mostly appeared only upon the death of a relative. Opportunities for marriage were, therefore, relatively few and age at marriage tended to be late.[23] Razi, using material gathered in his extensive investigation of the manor of Halesowen, has argued the contrary case, suggesting that, amongst wealthy tenants at Halesowen, children of marriageable age were furnished with plots of land to establish their own households. He contends that the children of wealthy peasants could therefore marry and establish households at reasonably young ages and did not have to await the retirement or deaths of their parents before they married. Average marriage age amongst these wealthy peasants was, perhaps, between 18 and 22 years, a figure which increased with relative poverty since the parents of poorer villagers could not provide their offspring with plots of land and, thereby, the wherewithal to marry. Historians working on eastern

England have suggested that age at marriage in the countryside there was substantially later than that described by Razi for the West Midlands in this period. Hallam has estimated that the average age at marriage for men and women in Lincolnshire between the mid-thirteenth and later fifteenth centuries was 25.9 and 22.4 years respectively. After the mid-fourteenth century, the age at marriage for men fell slightly (0.6 years) whilst women's age at marriage increased by 3.2 years. Although generally seen as problematic in their calculation, Hallam's estimates of late marriage amongst the peasantry accord with recent work which suggests that peasants exercised considerable choice in their marriage plans and typically delayed marriage until economic circumstance permitted household formation.[24] Most obviously, there is some evidence to suggest that, especially in the post-plague England of the late fourteenth and fifteenth centuries, individuals took advantage of improved labour opportunities and opted to delay marriage until their mid- to late twenties. Where marriage was earlier, as at Halesowen, this has often been described in terms of relative wealth and opportunity: the wealthier peasantry tending to marry earlier than their poorer neighbours. We shall return later to consider the impact of, *inter alia*, wealth upon household formation; factors such as wealth were effectively constraints upon free choice. For the moment we should note that what now seems unclear, but was once held by historians to be entirely obvious, is the extent to which the peasantry, free of such constraints, would have opted for early marriage and large households. It may be that, amongst the wealthiest peasant families, especially in champion England, early marriage and the establishment of large and potentially complex households were conceived of as ideals throughout the period; the extent to which poorer peasant families failed to meet this ideal may, then, be testimony to the range of factors, additional to choice, which limited their ambitions. However, before we consider these we should briefly review some further elements which impacted upon family form.

Institutional, Religious and Political Factors

Inevitably, as we have already seen and as we will now explore in a little more detail, personal choice and independence of decision making, even as regards the most fundamental aspects of the lives of the peasantry, were limited and controlled by conventions and customs. A series of 'rules', generated by more than one institution or social group and not all of which were complementary, influenced household formation, most obviously by restricting opportunities for marriage but also by controlling distribution of property and the mobility of the peasantry. In considering these limits upon household formation and, broadly, individual choice, we can work outwards from those closest to the individual, his or her family and kin and, beyond them, the local community and the local lord, to the widest spheres of influence, the king and the national government and, further still, the church and Papacy.

Family

The degree to which marriage and, thereby, household formation were controlled by institutions, including the family, is an issue of real importance. To gain a sense of the factors which controlled peasant marriage and the consequent formation of peasant households is to begin to comprehend the forces that governed the lives of the peasantry. In the broadest terms, the distinction which matters most here is that between the domestic economy of the peasant household and the commercial economy: did peasants march to the beat of the market or did they regulate their lives according to rules established much closer to home? Evidence for the existence of significant familial, communal or feudal constraints upon peasant marriage in the high and late Middle Ages would encourage a view of a society according to which ultimate control of demographic and economic processes was vested in the peasant family. Familial conventions and alliances, guarded attitudes to marriage, preoccupations with the labour requirements of the family farm: such would be the motors that would drive social change or help maintain its stability. These determinants would stand in contrast to a range of other factors which may also have affected household formation and the decision to marry. Principal amongst these would be, for instance, an economy which offered opportunities beyond the family farm and the local community and which, therefore, encouraged migration and marriage beyond the aegis of the family (exogamy). Inevitably, certain sections of the peasantry will have operated closer to one sphere of influence than to another: we might expect, for instance, that the relatively poor will, of necessity, have been thrown onto the market and beyond the support

or control of family and kin whilst the lives of the wealthier members
of the peasantry, whose combined familial resources were more extensive, may have been more subject to the regulations of their families.
The role of alternative determinants, such as economic opportunity,
will be discussed in a later section of this chapter.[25] Here, we need
briefly to consider whether there is evidence for close familial control
of peasant marriage and household formation and to assess its significance, including the extent to which it differed between economic
sub-groups within the peasantry.

The underlying philosophy of medieval marriage, a philosophy constructed by the medieval church and developed in the early years of
our period, was that marriage was the creation of consent between,
and only between, the parties to the marriage.[26] A marriage could be
created between two legally entitled adults by exchange of words of
mutual consent: if the words were of present consent, the marriage
had immediate effect but if the words were of 'future consent', the contract could be annulled. However, words of future consent followed by
sexual intercourse ensured that the marriage was binding. The role of
the family or the lord in the creation of a marriage bond was therefore, at least in theory, minimal and has been described as 'secondary
and dispensable'.[27] The opportunities for unconstrained marriage
between adults therefore existed but, since, marriage brought entry
into a family and access to familial rights, especially rights to land, those
concerned to protect such rights, especially other family members but
also the lords of tenants, sought to contain and inform choice. At
Chalgrave (Bedfordshire), in 1299, for instance, a presentment in the
manor court recorded that Walter Sali had defamed his brother, John,
by saying 'many outrageous things' to the father of John's new wife, 'a
certain woman of the parish of Sharnbrook who John had married
against the will of Walter'.[28] Such efforts at constraint are likely to have
been most in evidence when a marriage would effect or threaten to
effect a significant transfer of landed or other rights, in other words,
when a substantial amount of property was involved. This is not to say
that families (but less likely lords) did not attempt to intervene in plans
for marriages for reasons other than those of the protection of property but issues of love and hatred, jealousy and fear, were not rights as
evidently protected or contested in the same fora as were inheritance
and dowry, although they might well appear quite clearly elsewhere.[29]

Explicit examples of familial control of the choice of marriage
partner amongst the medieval peasantry are elusive – although Poos

has offered some late fifteenth-century examples drawn from church courts which show parents opposing the offsprings' marriages to those they deemed unsuitable – but written agreements made between retiring parents and their offspring clearly indicate a measure of control over the timing of marriage on the part of parents.[30] Where household formation was dependent upon the inheritance of land or the donation of land by a relative – technically, a neolocal household formation system which, linked to vital events, has been described as homeostatic – marriage was essentially in the gift and under the control of the preceding generation. This could operate in a number of ways, as Clark's investigation of retirement arrangements has shown. Through an examination of the rolls of Norfolk manor courts, c.1300, she distinguishes three main ways in which parents exercised control over the marriages over their children: firstly, by promising their offspring the future use of land and thereby providing them with the security to contemplate marriage; secondly, by promising their offspring, once they had found a suitable future spouse, the future use of land; and, thirdly, by surrendering land to offspring and thus providing them with the immediate means to marry. In each of these agreements, the arrangements were explicit in their requirement that the children and marriage partners of the retiring parents assured the future security and sustenance of the parents.[31]

But parents could also, as Razi has shown, simply establish offspring with the necessary wherewithal to marry without choosing to impose particular clauses in order to protect their own self-interest. In such cases, it was the willingness or ability of the parent to provide for the establishment of a separate household for his or her children that controlled opportunities for marriage and household formation. In addition to leaving land to their progeny, parents could establish their children by providing them with small plots of land or giving them money or goods. Manorial records from this period abound with examples of parents providing land for their children, as a number of studies of the peasant land market have shown. Parents of unfree tenants also paid marriage fines (merchet) to the lord for permission for their daughters (and, on occasion, sons) to marry and provided their daughters with dowries. Ralf Odrich, a smallholder at Halesowen in the late thirteenth century, provided a small plot of land for his son and also paid a marriage fine for his daughter. At Redgrave (Suffolk), again in the late thirteenth century, wealthier tenants can also be seen providing for their offspring: Adam Jop gave two of his daughters dowries in the year of their marriage and helped a third daughter buy land. He also gave two of his sons substantial holdings which may also have provided them with the means to establish households.[32] Wills also show parents assisting in the marriages of their daughters. When John Thmelyn of Winslow died in 1428/9, he left, amongst a number of bequests, 40s. to his daughter, Agnes, as her dowry (*ad maritagium suum*) and instructed his son, William, who was one of his executors, to furnish her with an additional 20s.[33] Siblings could control access to land and, thereby, the resources which facilitated marriage. On the Crowland Abbey estates, a brother gave parcels of land to his two sisters 'in the more remote parts of the messuage'.[34]

Village community

The village community was also capable of exerting considerable pressure upon peasant household formation. It could achieve this indirectly by, for example, encouraging, or effectively insisting through collective moral pressure, that individuals and families channel resources, which might otherwise have been employed in establishing households, into communal projects and activities. Whether payments to support parish charity, the construction of chantry chapels, scot-ales and so on had a significantly deleterious effect upon the schemes for household formation amongst the peasantry is impossible to quantify. However, given the substantial sums which fifteenth-century wills show were paid to church and community, it does not seem wholly unreasonable to suppose that the expectant offspring of the peasantry were sometimes financially disappointed as a result of an elder family member's regard for his or her place within the community. That said, it is also, by the same token, the case that the community could help provide for the material needs of individuals both in order to establish households and to sustain them. Charity, in its various forms, reallocated resources which could be employed to give impetus to marriage plans and household formation. This is most explicitly evident in the case of bride-ales which, in the sixteenth century when we can best see them, served as opportunities to provide impecunious intending couples with the wherewithal to set up house. This activity included purchasing highly priced ale at communal feasts and providing the couple with utensils and money.[35]

But the community also enjoyed a more direct influence in peasant marriage and household formation. Two significant elements of communal impact were the collective censure and policing of marriage and choice of marriage partner and the manipulation of custom, particularly customary practices of inheritance. In both cases the community could exercise a profound influence upon the marriage and household formation plans of families and individuals.

The role of communities in helping to control the choice of marriage partner and restricting marriages to those between suitable individuals is not easily established. We might imagine that communities, mindful of the opportunities for advancement which marriage offered, would be chary of admitting undesirables into their midst. Consequently, we might also suspect that communities might have attempted to police and, possibly, to restrict the marriages of local men and, especially, women to strangers. In this, as we shall see, the interests of members of the community may have come near to those of their lord, whose expectations were also best served by the marriages of his or her tenants to those who were, in every way, suitable.[36] Certainly, statements by juries of the rights of particular parties in local court cases relating to claims to land may be more than a little tinged with regard for the well-being of the community itself. However, it is no simple matter to establish exactly what the community perceived as being in its best interests. In a case between two sisters from Little Dunmow (Essex) in the first half of the fourteenth century, a jury supported the one sister, Maud, in her claim for land held by the other, Denise. Maud asserted that Denise's tenure of the land was contrary to custom since Denise had married outside of the jurisdiction (homage) of the manor. Interestingly, a decade later the court, in responding to a plea initiated by Denise and her husband, reversed the judgment and returned the land to the claimant.[37] Where, however, we best see the community operating to control marriage and the choice of marriage partners is not in the context of choice of suitable tenants and fellow villagers but as watchdogs for the church and witnesses to the rules of consanguinuity.

Canon law encouraged scrutiny of the intending couple and made use of the community in this respect. From the early thirteenth century it had been a requirement of the church that parishioners policed marriages to ensure, at least in part, that prohibited degrees of marital union were not being breached. A public announcement of an intended marriage through the reading of banns in church on three successive Sundays or feast-days was intended to alert the community to the proposed union and to search the collective memory of that

community for likely impediments, such as degree of blood relationship or the marital status of the intending parties. It also served to
publish the marriage and, thereby, to make it secure.[38] Such expectations, placed upon the community by the church, offered an immediate opportunity for the community to interfere in the marriage
process. The marriage ceremony itself also developed its public nature
in this period. The transfer of dowry at the church door in the presence of priest and community was an established element of the marriage rites by the close of the twelfth century. While the priest enquired
into the intentions of the parties and the legality of their union under
canon law, the rite of marriage, undertaken in such a public forum,
passed into the collective memory of the village from where it
could subsequently resurface as evidence for rights pertaining to
marriage, such as inheritance and issues of legitimacy. The same could
also be said for the feasts and celebrations that could accompany
marriages.[39]

Marriages which were not publicised in this way were still valid
unions, as we have seen. A clandestine marriage, requiring only the
agreement and consummation of the couple – and therefore wholly
beyond the control of any additional element, be that familial, communal, seigneurial or ecclesiastical, – might still, at a later date, benefit
from some communal incursion. The eavesdroppers, night-stalkers,
loiterers and casual witnesses to unions and agreements between
putative spouses were vital witnesses when it came to challenging or
supporting alleged marriages in the church courts. In 1366/7, in the
village of Scamston (Yorkshire), a day-labourer and beggar, William
Bridsall, overheard an exchange of vows between Alice Redyng and
John de Boton, which took place just inside the doorway of a sheep-
cote (*bercaria*). He later gave evidence on behalf of Alice that she and
John had exchanged vows of marriage of present intent. John, in
return, attempted to extricate himself from the marriage by using
other members of the community as character witnesses to challenge
the mental health of the witness. In this case, as in numerous others,
the parties looked to the wider community to establish or to challenge the validity of their marriage and, in so doing, admitted the
community's own agendas, of which we are wholly unaware, into the
deliberative process.[40]

The community could also affect household formation and marriage
processes through its involvement in the transfer of property between
generations. Again, Homans has attempted to describe ways in which

the community might attempt to regulate sales of land and to veto sales to those perceived as undesirable.[41] As above, in a homeostatic household formation system, where marriage and household formation are dependent upon access to resources sufficient for the establishment of a household, any control over the ease and degree of land transfer will also exert a significant impact upon opportunities for household formation. Although it is possible that the medieval village community did exercise some restraint over the disposition of land between living parties, and enjoyed certain mechanisms for enforcing that control, such as a degree of influence in the setting of entry fines (sums payable to the lord by the incoming tenant), or through its willingness either to conceal or to report land transferred illegally, it was most palpably capable of directing the transmission of land through its manipulation of inheritance practices.[42] The transfer of free land at point of death (*post-mortem*), protected as it was by common law, was rather more immune from the interference of the local community than was the process of inheritance of customary or unfree land. The collective memory of a community might be called upon to support or to deny rival claims of both free and unfree tenants to land, but the community could also, in the case of customary land, challenge and subvert long-established practices of inheritance.

As in the case of clandestine marriage, the community served as witness to past events and was the effective arbiter in claims relating to succession to land. In that sense, the community acted as a store of genealogies, confirming or correcting familial rememberings of their own lines of succession. A manor court case from Brightwalton (Berkshire) in 1331 illustrates the community in operation as a repository of collective genealogical memory. A Walter de Herdewyk claimed a yardland presently held by William de Eversole. An inquest of the whole 'homage' inquired into the respective rights of the two men. The inquest found for Walter and ejected William because Walter was the 'nearer of blood', a fact established by a rehearsal of the line of succession to the holding over three generations.[43] Similarly, at Holne (Yorkshire), an inquest jury ruled that the current tenant had more right than the claimant, and supported their judgment with a detailed history of the holding which even included information on the hair-colour of previous tenants.[44] The community was also witness to more immediate events, such as an agreement between parties regarding a transfer of land other than by standard succession, as when, in 1483, at Great Waltham (Essex), John Artor the elder, languishing *in extremis*, in the presence of manorial officers and tenants, surrendered land for the benefit of his wife with reversions to his heir.[45]

As well as informing upon particular claims and rights, the community could alter custom and direct inheritance practice according to its memory or mismemory. Local custom, a maleable entity, was capable of being refashioned according to circumstance, and the role of the local community was a vital force in that refashioning. In such matters, the community found its voice in institutions such as the juries of the manor court and, as Poos and Bonfield have recently argued, reformulated custom in response to particular cases. The application of custom, a product of a decision of the community where it was not already enshrined in the written form of a custumal, had a direct bearing on the lives of those whose days were regulated by customary practices. In the case of customary practices of inheritance, the community's enunciation of, for instance, the rules of inheritance or of the rights of widows to hold tenements (free bench) had a direct influence upon household formation where access to land and opportunities for marriage were closely associated.[46] In a case from Barnet (Hertfordshire) in the early fourteenth century, an inquest jury in the manor court had to decide a succession to customary land where the father had left land to a youngest son, the son then dying without issue. At Barnet, it transpired, local custom was for the land, in such a case, to pass not to the eldest son or his issue but to the surviving brother who was closest to the deceased in order of birth. In other words, where the youngest of three brothers died without issue, his land would pass to the middle brother and not the eldest brother, a feature which, as the inquest jurors at Barnet acknowledged, was contrary to common law.[47] Here, as elsewhere, customary practice had implications of the most fundamental kind for landholding, the redistribution of property and the potential for individuals to establish families of their own. The role of the community in stating and formulating custom tended to weaken as the period progressed and as the authority of the written record came to supplant the collective voice of community. Although the peculiarities of a case might still require a ruling from jurors drawn from the local community even by the close of the period, increasingly the community and its representatives, the jurors of local courts, were called upon to attest to the facts of a case and not the customary law that may have underpinned it.[48]

A further significant element of custom in household formation, which was subject to communal control, related to widows and their remarriage. As in the case of inheritance, the rules relating to widows' rights in free land were established at common law: the widow of a free tenant could expect to receive a third of her husband's holding for life. Aside, therefore, from issues of fact, the community had little or no say in widows' rights in free land (known as free bench or widows' dower) but matters were rather different in the case of customary land. As with practices of inheritance, the form of widows' dower was dictated by custom and varied significantly between communities. On some manors, custom aped common law, the widow receiving a third of the holding for life; elsewhere, a widow's rights might be more extensive. At Islip (Oxfordshire), a Westminster Abbey manor, widows, after occupancy of the whole tenement for a full year after the death of their husbands, could choose between dower in a portion of the holding or occupancy of the full tenement for life. Similar conditions prevailed at the nearby manor of Launton (Oxfordshire), also a manor belonging to Westminster Abbey, but, at Launton, the widow, if she chose to take on all of the tenement, was expected to remarry as soon as possible. Upon remarriage, the holding would descend, in the first instance, to any offspring of this second marriage. The distinctions between, on the one hand, a local custom that insisted that a widow remarry within a year of her husband's death and, on the other, a custom which permitted a widow full occupancy for life were very real and will have affected both opportunities for and the nature of household formation. As the source and arbiter of custom, the local community clearly had a significant role to play in helping determine vital events in the life of the peasantry. In certain respects, the agenda of the community, if by village community we mean its elite members, its jurors, officers and memorialisers, was not wholly disassociated from that of lordship.

Lordship

Lords also were able to exercise a degree of control over the formation of the families and households of their tenants, both through a direct influence in marriage and property rights and through the regulation of other facets of rural life, such as rent, availability of labour and freedom of mobility. Discussion of the seigneurial impact upon the peasant family is also sure to direct our attention towards land and its availability as a determinant of household formation. Lords could and did influence the ways in which customary or unfree land was transferred and, as we have seen, different lordships adopted significantly different approaches to the alienability of land and its hereditability. In the intensity of their anxieties regarding peasant dealing in land, lords were also expressing, as we have also had cause to consider, their own concerns regarding the interpretation which common law would place on the behaviour of their tenantry.

As discussion of familial control of marriage has already shown, the right of a couple to marry was not in the gift of any other party. The high and late medieval lord of a manor could not, therefore, prohibit a marriage and had no legal sanction should the parties to a marriage be contrary to his choosing. Despite this, lords clearly attempted to direct their tenants to marry, especially in the first half of this period, when, for political and economic reasons, lords maintained a close interest in the marriages of their tenantry. Seigneurial insistence that tenants marry is no more than a forced aspect of neolocality, where the availability of land permits marriage and household formation. Lords were keen to ensure that tenements remained populated and that tenants were capable of meeting the obligations of their landholding. Instances survive, especially from the late thirteenth and fourteenth centuries, of lords insisting that tenants marry or remarry. On the manor of Horsham St Faith (Norfolk), the lord, the prior of St Faith, made strenuous efforts to ensure that his tenants were married. He employed members of the local community to find spouses for unmarried tenants and attempted to use the sanction of the manor court to force individuals into marriage. Those that refused and persisted in their singledom, seemingly the majority, were repeatedly fined. This artificial attempt at marriage and household formation, although often unsuccessful, clearly added a further element to the process of family formation and, if effective, would have served to reduce the mean age at marriage. What chance was there for the daughter of a tenant at North Elmham (Norfolk) to delay marriage when her parents had entered into a written agreement with their lord, the prior of Norwich, that his grant to them of 24 acres of customary land was conditional upon their daughter marrying one of his bondsmen within the year? If she failed to marry as instructed, the land would return to the prior and her parents would also owe a fine of 40s.[49]

A strong element of seigneurial control of marriage was most obvious in the case of widows of customary tenants. Where widows held substantial pieces of land, landlords sought to control the occupancy of the holding in order to ensure a return from rent, especially if the rent was paid in part as labour. Here, as in so many other aspects of their dealings with their tenantry, lords were constrained by custom. The discrete customary regulations regarding widow remarriage have been discussed above. Their promotion in the manor court, particularly in the form of pressure for widows to remarry, has been described as a product of both communal and seigneurial constraints.[50] Although, as Franklin reminds us, peasant widows may have been wholly capable of managing their holdings, independently of family members or servants, it is clear that lords and members of certain village communities preferred to oust widows or force them into remarriage. Such policies obviously presented opportunities to take up land for either the direct male heirs of the widow and her deceased husband or, where no such heir existed, the second husband of the widow. They may therefore have served the expectations of the village community as well as the lord.

In addition to pressure to remarry, there is also clear indication that lords encouraged their tenantry to retire once they reached an age or physical state that militated against successful management of their holdings. Whilst it is evident that retirement agreements were capable of taking form without the intervention and encouragement of landlords, it is also the case that lords were prepared to effect the ejection of elderly or incapable tenants should the need arise. On the estates of Glastonbury Abbey, for example, tenants not infrequently surrendered their holdings to the abbot on account of their poverty, impotence or old age.[51] Again, lordly intervention in order to force retirement was most likely to be evident where the retiree had occupied a substantial holding. It is not, therefore, entirely surprising to find more evidence of retirement contracts from the manors where landlords exercised a careful control over their tenants and expected to receive a proportion of rent as labour. This association of retirement with seigneurial pressure is also suggested by the apparent concentration of evidence for retirement – retirement contracts recorded in manorial court rolls – in the late thirteenth and early fourteenth centuries, a period of high farming and intensive management of manors and demesnes.[52] Futhermore, such action on the part of lords presented early opportunities for land acquisition and household formation for those capable of stepping into the shoes of the retired or ejected tenant. Such lordly policies may, in particular, have worked to the advantage of non-inheriting sons of wealthy villagers. On the

Westminster Abbey manor of Birdbrook in 1331, a tenant, Matilda Woderone, was obliged to surrender her holding of four acres to the lord. No was prepared to take on the holding, but in the next court Robert Leggard entered the holding on behalf of his son, who was a minor, paying a substantial entry fine (40s.) in order to do so. Here seigneurial policy appears to have provided an opportunity for land acquisition in anticipation of future household formation. It looks also to have diverted land into the hands of a different peasant family, but only because the previous tenant family had become exhausted.[53]

Less immediate, but also of vital importance in the seigneurial control of tenant marriage and household formation, was the imposition of fines related to marriage – merchet payments – in the manor courts. The payment of a fine for right to marry (merchet) had, by the thirteenth century, come to be closely associated with villeinage.[54] Payments, recorded in manorial court rolls and court books, vary considerably but were often fairly small, sometimes no more than a few pence. Occasionally, however, payments were large, sometimes as much as a pound.[55] Exaction by the lord of marriage fines of this magnitude will have affected the strategies for marriage and household formation, the distribution of family resources, and the choices of prospective marriage partners. Eleanor Searle has suggested that marriage fines were principally taxes upon property and a means of ensuring that the lord gained some financial benefit from the effective alienation of goods. She has also argued for a perceived need, on the part of landlords, to set financial hurdles for prospective tenants: in this context, the marriage fine can be seen as a test of the solvency of incoming tenants and stands alongside other financial barriers to entry into the tenant landholding, most obviously the fine paid on entry into villein land.[56] In considering merchet payments as fines upon the alienation of goods, she argues that the heaviest merchet payments were associated with female marriages to men living beyond the lord's jurisdiction, an attempt to ensure that the lord received some pecuniary recompense at the moment when property, in the form of dowry, passed beyond his or her control.[57] She also points out that the imposition and targeting of heavy marriage fines in this way may have served to restrict marriage to outsiders and have acted as a boost to endogamy.[58] Although Searle has not been without her critics, who have attempted to argue that the lord's involvement in marriage was less to do with property than it was with matters of personal status and/or the restriction of exogamy (marriage out of the community), her arguments regarding the specificity of marriage fines are compelling and suggest that lords saw the granting of licence to marry as an opportunity for profit and as a necessary moment to reassert control over land.[59]

In addition to its immediate impact upon marriage, lordship intervened in the mechanisms of the peasant family in a number of other ways. At moments of property transfer, the lord expected to receive some financial benefit, either from the incoming tenant as an entry fine or, in the case of inheritance, from the family of the deceased tenant, as a death duty or heriot. As in the case of merchet, the financial impositions of the landlord effected limits and restrictions upon freedom of choice and must have informed and helped determine strategies for household formation. Where landlords attempted to restrict *inter-vivos* dealing in customary land or prevented their unfree tenantry from acquiring additional plots of freeland, access to land was limited. In neolocal systems of household formation, this restriction on land availability would have controlled opportunities to establish families and households in the ways envisaged by Homans and described earlier.[60] Where, by contrast, lords permitted or even encouraged an active land market, then the implications for household formation may have been significantly different, as the work of Razi on the West Midlands and Smith on East Anglia looks to indicate.[61] There was similar determinative potential in lordly interference with customary practices of inheritance. Where, as at Gressenhall, lords deliberately intervened to alter forms of inheritance, the implications for landholding, the availability of resources and marriage opportunities were considerable.[62]

The lord's rule was most evident in the regulation and control of mobility. Villein tenants of the lord were not permitted to leave the lord's domain without her or his licence. Those villeins intending to leave the manor were expected to pay the lord a fine – *chevage* – for permission to do so; where villeins fled the manor without the lord's permission, the lord could attempt to return them and would employ the common law to pursue them. There is a marked chronology to control of villein mobility as well as an evident social and economic specificity to its application, a point that will be discussed a little later.[63] Attempts to restrain mobility are particularly notable in the immediate post-plague period when, at a time of rising prices and wage levels, lords looked to maximise profits through the employment of their unfree labour force to provide cheap labour on their demesnes. A period which combined reintensified seigneurial exaction with new opportunities for labourers and wage-earners prompted a wave of illicit villein migration from the manors of landlords who sought to use labour services. There is also evidence for considerable attempts at control of mobility in the pre-plague period. In both the pre- and post-plague periods, it was the villein tenants of customary standard holdings (broadly, those owing labour services) who, as we shall discuss in a little more detail below, came in for the particular attention of their lords, but all unfree tenants might expect to pay chevage if they wanted to quit the manor. In addition, lords attempted to tax poorer in-migrants, those entering the vill in search of seasonal work or other labour.[64]

Any attempts at restriction of mobility had obvious implications for landholding and access to land. In communities and amongst those sections of the peasantry where the availability of land and the opportunities for marriage were closely associated, landlords' efforts to curtail the mobility of their tenants would reduce opportunities within their own manors as well, of course, as reducing competition from outsiders elsewhere. Whilst it would be inappropriate to overstate the demographic and social-structural implications of lordly attempts to curb mobility, the particular attempts to control the mobility of wealthier tenants, which included recapture of runaway villeins, may, as we shall see, have added an additional factor which helped determine the household formation regime peculiar to this sub-group of the peasantry. It seems less likely that chevage payments, which were not especially large, would have reduced levels of migration sufficiently to alter the patterns of household formation amongst the majority of the peasantry, although they will, as certainly, have entered into the calculations of those planning marriage beyond the community.

For the most part, these impacts were economic more than they were symbolic or political (if these elements can be disassociated). They also reflect the possibilities and practicalities of lordly power: landlords were more able to insist on performance of obligations at times of relative hardship (for instance, c.1300) than they were at moments of relative tenant prosperity (the fifteenth century). Further, as in the consideration of lordship and its impact upon peasant marriage, the lord's influence was mediated by local custom and the role of the village community. A lord's rights to claim fines (gersuma) from a tenant intending to sell land or from one entering land, to demand a death duty from the family of a recently deceased tenant (heriot) and a fine from the heir hoping to enter, all of these impositions were effected, at least in part, by the local community. It was the local community that established whether the incoming tenant could pay an entry fine or whether the dead tenant's family had livestock sufficient to afford a heriot. It was also that community which informed the lord if attempts had been made to transfer land illegally, that is, without registration in the manor court and without the payment of an entry fine.[65]

It is also not surprising to find that the incidence of obligations declined as seigneurial interest in direct management of their estates and tenantry also declined. During the first thirty years after the plagues of the mid-fourteenth century, lords continued to exact payments, such as merchet, which were likely to impact significantly upon the peasant household and its formation. Often these exactions, at a time of reinvigorated lordly exactions, were as heavy as they had ever been but, by the fifteenth century, lords were less inclined and, possibly, less able to make such demands of their tenants.[66] Despite this general decline, the determinative role of lordship as a force in peasant household formation, even in the later Middle Ages, should not be dismissed. It has recently been suggested that, as late as the mid-fifteenth century, it was flight from serfdom that eroded functionally extended families at Halesown.[67]

Crown

The expectations of government also had a significant impact on the formation of peasant households. The exactions of the state, notably through direct taxation, reduced the resources of the peasantry in the same way as did the demands of lordship or the church.[68] Labour legislation from the mid-fourteenth century, such as the Ordinance of Labourers (1349) and Statute of Labourers (1351), also had potentially significant effects on both the resources of the peasantry and their freedom of mobility. By attempting to maintain conservative wage rates and, in subsequent legislation (Statute of Cambridge, 1388), to restrict mobility, the legislators of the mid- and later fourteenth century, curtailed opportunities to find employment, to enter into flexible contracts, and to maximise labour opportunities. The demographic and social-structural consequences of such initiatives may well have been considerable, although commentators are divided on their overall effect, not least because evasion of such legislation seems to have been commonplace.[69] It also seems evident that the potential effects of such legislation were not uniform. If we assume that labour legislation was reasonably effective, it is conceivable that it slowed capital accumulation and, thereby, delayed household formation. But it is also possible that such legislation, again energetically administered, would have reduced employment opportunities and discouraged 'speculation' in the labour market. A consequence of such 'speculation', it has been argued, was the surge of female employment in the labour market of the late fourteenth century which, in turn, delayed marriage and household formation; anything which inhibited 'speculation' was likely to have had the contrary effect.[70] More obviously, attempts to control life-cycle service and employment within households had obvious consequences for membership of those households whilst also affecting the financial resources of the individual employed, as well, perhaps, as the household from which that individual originated. When Eleanor, the daughter of Adam le Smyth, was presented before the Suffolk Justices of the Peace for receiving wages of 10 s. from John Deye at Hoo during the year 1363/4, we can only guess at the consequences.[71] They may have been minimal but they may also have precipitated a *volte-face* in Eleanor's life-course.

With less immediacy but no less force, developments at common law also had potentially significant consequences for household formation. The growth of a common law of villeinage intensified the demands which lords made of their unfree tenantry and made lords chary of tenant activity that might be considered 'free', that is, consistent with implied manumission. As has already been discussed, this turned certain obligations into important mainstays of the seigneurial economy and also, on some estates, helped contain an active market in peasant land. Ironically, however, other developments in common law had a much less constraining effect on the peasantry, both free and unfree. For unfree tenants on those estates and manors where landlords were less chary of the general alienability of customary land, the absorption of common law devices into manorial courts provided a range of protections for certain sections of the tenantry. In particular, widows of unfree tenants in the late thirteenth and early fourteenth century enjoyed the advantages which came from the adoption of common law actions for the recovery of land alienated by husbands without the wife's consent (*cui in vita sua*) whilst jointures, a further borrowing from common law, also afforded a degree of protection to female tenants.[72] Similarly, common law rulings on the validity of wills

and the role of executors also served to protect the interests of bene-
ficiaries.[73] For those peasants who held freely, the developments in
common law conveyancing and the protections extended to freehold
land were even more immediate. In particular, the increased support
which the common law extended to the concept of the alienability of
freehold helped bolster a market in free land. Essentially, all of these
developments and borrowings influenced the ways in which land and
other resources could be transferred. As we have already seen, where
marriage was dependent upon the prior acquisition of such resources,
and principally land, then any such shifts in the ways in which land or
resources were both held and conveyed had likely consequences for
processes of household formation.

Church

Finally, the church must also feature in this consideration of the institutional factors capable of influencing peasant household formation.
We have already considered ways in which the community was
employed as an agent of the church's bidding in the effective policing
of marriage but we should also give some attention to the direct role
of the church in such matters. The regulation of marriage by the
church, which had increased significantly by the early thirteenth
century, controlled and limited marriage patterns and household formation. Priests were expected to ensure that an intended union was
appropriate. Rules of consanguinity and restrictions upon endogamy
were developed and revised in the twelfth century. Pope Alexander II
had, in the eleventh century, forbidden marriage between blood relatives to the seventh degree, where the number of degrees is calculated
by the distance in blood relations of the more remote party to a
common ancestor. Thus, a couple who could identify a common great-
great-grandparent would be separated by four degrees of consanguinity and would thereby fall within the prohibited degree. The
extent to which relatives within the seventh degree of consanguinity
avoided marriage is not altogether clear but it is evident that, by the
close of the twelfth century, the church recognised such an extensive
prohibition as virtually unworkable. If individuals had paid too close
a regard to the church's rulings on consanguinity, the pool of available spouses within local communities would have been extremely
limited, even non-existent, especially given that marriage was also prohibited between parties where there existed certain relations other

than those of blood: affinity or a state consistent with consanguinuity was established through sexual intercourse as well as through legal ties, such as godparenthood or indirect relationship through marriage.[74] Consequently, in the early thirteenth century, the Fourth Lateran Council reduced the degree of prohibition to the fourth degree of blood relationship, a move which appears to have been in line with the schemes of national councils of the church.

The publication of these prohibitions appears to have had some effect and priests and local communities combined to ensure that inappropriate unions did not take place.[75] At Broomhill (Kent), in the later thirteenth century, an intended marriage foundered because the man, John of Gateberghe, had previously enjoyed sexual relations with the cousin of his intended bride, Petronilla Faron. Since it transpired that both parties were aware of this impediment, they were sentenced to be whipped, both through the local market and around the parish church. Proceedings within the ecclesiastical court of the archdeaconry of Sudbury, also in the late thirteenth century, illustrate local awareness and concern regarding marriage and its permissible degrees of kinship, as well as the role of the church and local community in attempting to ensure that these limits were not breached. A number of entries in the court detail relationships within the prohibited degrees, as was the case in the incestuous relationship of Peter de Hertherst and Mabel de Melleford, who were related to each other within the third degree. Degrees of consanguinuity were not always easy to establish however. When William Sorel and Alice le Chapmanes were accused of an incestuous relationship, seven jurors failed to confirm that this was the case, since they were 'unsure of the degree of consanguinuity' existing between the parties.[76]

Alongside this careful if not always realisable regard for affinity, the church promoted the morality of marriage and attacked acts which deviated from its central message. A process of moral education, provided by the clergy, served to promote the institution of marriage at the expense of alternative, extra-marital, unions. Confessors' handbooks, priests' manuals and sermons aimed, increasingly from the thirteenth century, at encouraging a sense of the value of marriage. Episcopal statutes from the early thirteenth century promoted the institution of marriage while church courts, as we have seen in the earlier discussion of consanguinuity, reinforced the message and, with the support of the local community whose members acted as inform-ants and witnesses, censured deviance.[77] Closely associated with issues of endogamy, the church made real efforts to contain incest and, as part of its efforts in this regard, priests attempted to direct their parishioners in matters of household organisation and living and sleeping arrangements.[78] Priests used the moment of baptism to ensure that parents were married. If couples refused to marry, pressures were brought to bear which might occasion their separation.[79] By the same token, bigamy, concubinage, adultery and fornication were matters which the medieval church sought to censure and, ideally, to prohibit.

The church's opposition to sexual intercourse beyond marriage had, as we have already discussed, significant demographic potential. If, as Smith, has argued, a moral culture, encouraged by the exhortations of the church, developed which was antagonistic to pre- and extra-marital sex, then there may have been, in the later Middle Ages, a fairly close association between nuptiality and fertility. Factors which delayed marriage therefore delayed household formation and reduced the number of births.[80] As importantly, the church's instruction on marriage and the limits of appropriate unions may have also encouraged an outward-looking mentality amongst the peasantry. If the church's preachings on the perils of endogamy found root in the religious and moral convictions of the peasantry, then we should not wholly reject the possibility that the church had a role to play in encouraging out-migration and marriage beyond the farmstead, manor or village. The church's promotion of marriage as a valid and independent act may have reduced the number of non-marital unions. As we have already discussed, explicit in the church's message on marriage was the independence of the couple entering into marriage. It was their mutual consent which established the marriage. Although the church preached against clandestine marriages and suggested that marriages should be solemnised by a priest in a public ceremony, a verbal agreement was sufficient to create the marriage. Clandestine or otherwise, the marriage as an act of independence distanced the couple from their families, their communities, their lord and even their church. As we have seen, each of these groups or individuals could affect the decision to marry but there was no actual expectation that they should. In that sense, the act of marriage and of household formation underlined the potential for independent self-reliance. The degree to which such self-reliance could be sustained or even acknowledged was partly determined by the relationship of the couple to the range of institutional factors discussed above.

Beyond direct concern with morality within and beyond marriage, the church censured infanticide and offered guidance regarding the care and upbringing of infants. Whilst the degree of infanticide in medieval villages has been the subject of some debate, there is little or no conclusive evidence and certainly no clear way of gauging the effectiveness of clerical attempts to contain such enormities.[81] Of further consequence for household formation amongst the peasantry, as amongst other sections of society, was the church's willingness to hive off portions of lay property for its own use. In a neolocal household formation system, any redistribution of property has consequences for marriage and household formation. Regular payments made to the church as tithe or obits were a further drain upon resources, payments which can be set alongside rental payments to the lord and taxation paid to the state. Payments linked to marriage and death also reduced family income and, as with the equivalent secular payments of merchet and heriot, may have had significant impact upon marriage plans. When, in 1279, at Tebworth (Bedfordshire), Reginald son of Thomas Hiberd, a bondman of Peter de Loreng and a vagrant, died, he left in his will a surcoat to the vicar, Walter, and a cow to his sister, Juliana, who was a leper. Walter and Peter, the respective vicar and lord of the dead Reginald, then fell to squabbling over the cow, the one claiming it as mortuary, the other as heriot. The beast was taken from Juliana and, eventually, awarded to Peter, the lord, as heriot. Juliana's potential impediments as a future bride clearly did not stop at the lack of a cow, but the loss of this single resource, subsequently valued at 12 s., cannot have helped.[82]

Further, pious benefactions to the church, also capable of being seen as responses to and affirmation of communal membership,[83] also made demands upon the income of the peasant family.[84] Rules regarding the transmission of land at point of death were also adjusted in significant ways by the church so that land did not necessarily devolve to heirs (but could rest elsewhere, including, of course, in the eager hands of the church).[85]

The 'institutional' factors which have been discussed so far in this chapter did not have a general consequence but fell unevenly. In considering their impact, as well as the more general 'demographic' and 'personal' determinants described earlier, we need also to make some fairly crude distinctions between 'rich' and 'poor' peasants.

Exogenous/Economic Factors: Wealth and Opportunity

Although it is generally accepted that the decision to marry and the formation of peasant households were both dependent upon the accumulation of sufficient resources to permit these events to occur, the means by which the necessary resources were accumulated is less clear. A previous generation of historians, as we have seen, explained household formation principally in terms of the occupation of a vacated niche, where limited resources passed from one generation to the next. In this 'peasant' or 'niche' model of peasant household formation, death and inheritance occasioned opportunities for the next generation but only those who were heirs. Non-inheriting siblings were frequently destined to lives as bachelors and spinsters within the households of their more favoured brothers.[86] This view has been modified more recently by those who have suggested that other opportunities existed amongst the peasantry for land acquisition, either through a market in land (which permitted parents to furnish their offspring with small plots of land) or through opportunities presented when other tenants died heirless.[87] All of these explanations are based upon a homeostatic model, where opportunities for marriage, and family and household formation, are dependent upon vital events, especially, but not exclusively, death. Even discussion of the land market, as we have seen, has tended to be couched in terms of the life-cycle of the peasant family.[88]

Most recently, however, historians have taken to emphasising the role of external, commercial factors in the lives of the peasantry. The market, as we shall see in a later chapter, played a significant part in the lives of the medieval peasantry and, as our earlier discussion of the peasant land market will also have shown, the redistribution of land (as indeed was the case with other resources) was not solely occasioned by marriages and deaths. Individuals were able, where opportunity for capital accumulation existed and where institutional restraints, especially seigneurial policy, did not prevent it, to buy land or the other resources necessary to establish households. Where such conditions existed, the restraints of family, community and lordship may have featured less in determining an individual's life-chances than did the forces of supply and demand. Opportunities for labour, wage-rates, the price of land, and so on: these will have been the factors that mattered as much or more to those operating beyond the 'peasant' or 'niche' model of household formation.

As Poos has suggested, there is good reason for supposing that this alternative model, sometimes referred to as a 'proletarian' or 'real wages' model, could co-exist with the 'peasant' or 'niche' model.[89] In particular, we might suppose that a broad distinction can be drawn, at certain moments during our period, between sections of the peasantry, typically the wealthier peasants working substantial holdings and paying part of their rent in labour, who tended to operate in ways more consistent with the homeostatic 'peasant' or 'niche' model and a probable majority of peasants whose lives were played out in a manner which conformed more closely to a 'real wages' or 'proletarian' model. Even within families, we might also imagine that differing mechanisms for household formation existed. The life-cycle of an heir was likely to have been rather different from that of non-inheriting younger sons or daughters who may have been obliged to look beyond the family, community or lordship for the opportunities which would allow them to establish households of their own. In that sense, the poorer peasants may have avoided some of the institutional restraints which existed for their wealthier neighbours but were, as a consequence, more vulnerable to the vagaries of the market. Furthermore, the institutions of family, community and lordship, whilst restraints, were also cushions which could afford the wealthier peasantry greater protection than they did the poorer.

In order to separate the factors which may have been significant in the marriage and household formation plans of the peasantry, we should briefly consider the differing experiences of rich and poor peasants in the medieval countryside. We can then proceed to consider, for those of the peasantry – the vast majority – who were not isolated from the market and from exogenous economic shifts, the range of variables which affected their lives.

Wealthy peasants were provided with opportunities which did not exist for their poorer peers. Essentially, these opportunities can be reduced to land, resources and family support. Each of these elements affected the choices which members of wealthy peasant families made in terms of marriage and household formation. Heirs anticipated the death or retirement of older relatives and stayed close to the family hearth as a consequence. The ready availability of land, as Razi's research on the manor of Halesowen has shown, also made it possible for the non-inheriting to establish their households within the vill. We have also seen how peasants in other parts of the country provided for their siblings and other dependents.[90] The likelihood is that the existence of an established 'estate' of land provided the wealthier peasants with opportunities to marry earlier than poorer peasants who would have needed to accumulate sufficient resources before they could contemplate household formation.

The resources which a family could command also materially affected the condition and, ultimately, the structure of the family and the household. As with land, financial resources presented opportunities for marriage: the healthy dowries of young women or the future riches of heirs established them in the marriage market as eminently desirable. Decisions to employ servants, midwives and wet-nurses were, of course, predicated upon financial resources. The employment of a household servant obviously had an immediate effect on the structure of the household, whilst money spent on midwives, supplements to the diet (such as fish and meat) and basic health care may have had real benefits for mothers and infants. Wet-nursing increased the fertility of the wealthy peasantry by allowing mothers to conceive sooner than they would have done had they continued to breast-feed their own offspring. While we have little or no information on the relativities of child-care, retirement or maintenance agreements made between elderly tenants and, typically, their offspring illustrate the disparity in resources and the advantages which the wealthier tenantry enjoyed. To quote one especially detailed example of this close assocation between resources and familial support/dependency, in October 1281, Agnes, the widow of Thomas Brid of Rugacre in Hales (Worcestershire), through a retirement agreement, handed her whole tenement over to her eldest son, also called Thomas. In return for the holding, Thomas was to provide his widowed mother with 'all necessities' and these were listed in some detail. During the year, at various stated intervals, Agnes was to receive from her son four quarters of wheat, four quarters of oats, two bushels of peas, and five cart-loads of sea-coal. Further to this, Thomas was to build a house for his mother, '30 feet in length and 14 feet in width within the walls, of timber, with three new doors and two windows'.[91] This was a huge provision, far beyond the individual consumption requirements of Agnes and substantially larger than the average allocation in agreements of this kind.[92] Such levels of support must have been far beyond the capacity of the majority of the thirteenth-century peasantry.

Finally, the superfluity of land and resources enjoyed by the wealthier peasants ensured that their households were likely to be large and relatively complex. They were also less likely to seek their opportunity beyond the manor or vill but were, instead, more inclined to expect advantage close to home. As a consequence, the wealthy peasantry also enjoyed the support of wide kin networks and, as Razi has termed it, 'functionally extended families'. It must also have been the case that there existed, amongst the wealthy peasant families, a culture of mutual dependency and of obligation which, as an ideal, would have been less realisable amongst poorer peasants. In addition, the resources of the wealthy tenantry were 'protected' by lordship which, as we have seen, imposed restrictions upon the exportation of resources beyond the vill and also resisted the division of family holdings. Lords, it has also been suggested, sought to tax the household formation schemes of the relatively wealthy and, as Searle has argued, marriage fines exacted by lords acted as an encouragement to endogamy.[93] Further to this, lords were especially keen to constrain the mobility of the tenants or potential tenants of customary standard holdings, that is, those holdings which might owe labour services. In other words, seigneurial concern over the migration of their tenantry was likely to have been focused upon a solvent and able workforce. Only the church amongst the institutions discussed above, through its attempts to control incestuous relationships, encouraged the wealthy peasantry to marry beyond the vill, but it is impossible to ascertain the effectiveness of prohibitions which ran counter to so many other demands upon members of wealthy families. In most other respects, by promoting marriage, parenthood and godparenthood and by resisting non-marital unions, the church reinforced the solidarity of the peasant family.

By contrast, poorer peasants had less land, fewer resources, and were less likely to enjoy the wider support of family and kin. The families and households of poorer peasants tended to be smaller than those of their wealthier neighbours, a fact consequent upon a range of demographic and non-demographic factors which were more likely to be associated with the poorer peasantry. The smaller landholdings of the poorer peasantry meant that there was less opportunity for offspring to inherit sustainable holdings or for parents to provide for their children through retirement contracts, gifts and bequests. Lacking in land or the local opportunity to acquire land, the offspring of poorer peasants were, therefore, more inclined to seek opportunity beyond the vill. Limited financial resources will have had the same outmigratory effect as well as preventing poorer peasants from investing in their families by providing them with the basic foodstuffs and basic medical support, such as midwifery. The period between conceptions may have been extended for poorer peasant mothers but their infants may have suffered a degree of neglect if, as is sometimes suggested, women with infants sought paid employment as wet-nurses. In either case, the effect was to limit the family size of the poorer peasantry as may have been the consequence of contraception which, Biller has claimed, was the resort of the poor more than it was of the wealthy.[94] In apparent contradiction to the previous statments, it is also suggested that poverty led to greater rates of illegitimacy in the medieval village.[95]

In terms of the institutional factors discussed earlier, poorer peasants were, perhaps, subject to lesser control than were their wealthier counterparts. The preoccupation of lords in a manorial economy will have been directed towards the tenants of the more sub-stantial holdings owing the larger rents. The constraints which, as we have seen, lords imposed upon their tenantry look to have reflected seigneurial concerns over property. Efforts to restrain or to recover the poorer refugee tenants, who did not hold and were incapable of holding substantial customary holdings, were unlikely to have been so intensive, especially given that such efforts were also fuelled by a desire on the part of lords to stem any flow of moveable goods from the manor. In the 150 years before the plague, there were also attempts to limit villein mobility but, in this period of land hunger and limited opportunity, lords enjoyed the whip-hand and those hoping to work standard customary holdings are unlikely to have fled. Instead, it was non-inheriting sons and the poorer members of the village community who must have made up the majority of out-migrants. Lords were more concerned with taxing this mobility than they were in wholly con-taining it. Landlords did, however, aim to 'tax' their poorer tenantry in ways appropriate to the everyday lives of these poorer tenants: fines for fornication, bearing children out of wedlock, and for regrating have all been described as fines aimed particularly at the poor. Most recently, Harold Fox has shown that lords also sought to draw finan-cial benefit from landless labourers resident on their manors by extracting small financial payments as a form of chevage.[96] If though, generally, the lord was less concerned with his poorer tenants and vil-lagers, the village community was likely to show them greater regard, serving both as surrogate family but also as a constraint upon freedom of action. The community extended charity to its poorer fellows and, on occasion, saved them from the fines and amercements of the lord by failing to report infractions in the manor courts. But the community also expected rich and poor to meet their communal obligations and may have placed a particular weight of expectation upon its poorer tenants. The community may have resisted marriages to unwelcome outsiders and could have employed gossip and the church courts to force the unwanted from their midst.

As to issues of familial responsibility, the plans of poorer peasants were less likely to be influenced by concerns over family property, the rights of succession, and duties towards the elderly. Of course, even the meanest peasant may have wished to prevent an unwelcome marriage for his or her daughter or son, and for no other reasons than a sense of parental duty and love, but the lack of resources obliged poorer peasants to look beyond their families for employment and sustenance. Further, lower life expectancy and later marriage amongst these poorer peasant sub-groups will certainly have ensured a smaller pool of elderly dependents and, thereby, removed duties of care. It is likely, therefore, that, amongst the relatively poor, a culture of mutual dependency and obligation did not extend beyond the immediate families.

Essentially then, the forces which played upon the poorer peasants were distinct from those that affected the lives of their wealthier neighbours. With reduced opportunities close to the family hearth, limited support of family and kin and fewer institutional constraints, the poorer peasants were far more subject to centrifugal forces than were the wealthier tenantry.[97] If the poorer or less advantaged peasantry had to seek out opportunities beyond local networks of family, community or lordship, what opportunities existed for them and how did these affect marriage processes and household formation? As above, if we assume that marriage and household formation were dependent upon the accumulation of sufficient capital or resources, the poorer peasants, as the wealthier, needed to present themselves with the opportunities to acquire land and/or capital. We should deal with each in turn. To begin, what opportunities, beyond family and inheritance, existed for the relatively poor or disadvantaged to acquire land?

As we have seen, on certain manors and under certain lordships, the land market was capable of meeting the needs of the poorer tenantry.[98] On manors where there had been opportunities for late colonisation of the waste or where there were large numbers of plots of free land, sufficient niches existed for the middling and poorer peasantry to acquire small parcels of land. On many manors there may also have been opportunities to sub-let holdings or parcels of holdings. However, such conditions did not prevail universally. Aggressive lordship, an active land market dominated by the wealthier peasantry, and limited supplies of small plots of land all restricted opportunities for land acquisition. In such cases, poorer peasants will have been obliged to seek opportunities for land acquisition elsewhere. In the thirteenth and early fourteenth centuries, opportunities to acquire land were generally limited and prices for land were sure to have been higher than those which the poorer peasantry could afford. Manors on which colonisation of the waste remained a possibility may have attracted more than their share of in-migrants, although research into assarting in early fourteenth-century west Yorkshire discourages any view of such colonisation as a universal benefit.[99] In the post-plague period, when land prices look to have fallen and the oppressions of lordships to have eventually relaxed, opportunities for poorer in-migrants to acquire land improved. However, by the fifteenth century, a combination of acquisitiveness by a growing class of extremely wealthy peasants, the ancestors of a Tudor yeomanry, and investment in peasant holdings by entrepreneurs once again removed possibilities for landholding from the grasp of the poorer and middling peasantry.

Where the potential for landholding was limited, poorer members of the peasantry and the non-inheriting offspring of wealthier peasants were obliged to look to paid employment in order to gather together sufficient capital to contemplate marriage and the establishment of households of their own. Opportunities for paid labour existed in the medieval village throughout the period but the proportion of the rural population largely or wholly reliant upon such employment increased between 1200 and 1500. Employment amongst the peasantry can be divided between wage- or day-labour and long-term service. Opportunities for both existed within the village. Both the lord and the wealthier villagers employed casual and occasional labour to support their endeavours whilst the households of wealthy peasants also included servants. Counted amongst these servants were the children of poorer neighbours and the non-inheriting children of the wealthy. In the late fourteenth and fifteenth centuries, as landholding polarised, an increasing proportion of the peasantry must have relied upon employment by their wealthier peers as the mainstay of their domestic economies. Employment opportunities within villages attracted outsiders. Certain regions and communities presented greater prospects for employment than did others. In areas of moorland and pastoral husbandry on the fringes of the highland zone, such as the south-west or the far north-west, there is evidence that the households of wealthy peasants offered employment to landless labourers. The wealthier peasants of Ashwater, it has been suggested, employed significant numbers of live-in servants. Situated in pastoral countryside between the edge of Dartmoor and the Atlantic coast of north Devon, Ashwater was, in the fifteenth century, quite remote. There were few towns within its close orbit and, instead, its cattle were driven fairly large distances to market. Holdings were large and, by the end of the Middle Ages, there does not appear to have been any land held by poorer peasants.[100] Areas of proto-industry in the countryside, such as the cloth-producing centres of the south-west, southern and eastern England, offered employment both to the local peasantry and to in-migrants. Large numbers of the peasantry were also drawn to towns and cities in search of employment. At the same time, local industry and nearby urban centres eroded landholding opportunities for the poorer peasantry as wealthy outsiders competed to buy up surpluses of land, a feature of the rural economy especially evident in the fifteenth century but also familiar in certain parts of the country much earlier. In Cornwall, in the fourteenth century, administrators and tin-dealers purchased huge tracts of arable.

Importantly, labour opportunities existed for the poorer landless or near-landless peasantry throughout the period and increased as the period progressed. The economic and demographic forces which combined to force large sections of the peasantry to seek wage-labour or service changed over the period, but it is clear that, by the close of the period, a concentration of land in the hands of fewer peasants and non-peasants obliged a greater proportion of the peasantry to seek their living through employment. This 'proletarianisation' of the countryside had significant consequences for the demography of the peasantry. Whilst occasional wage-labour may not have affected the demographic processes of the countryside significantly, as Bailey has recently argued, a demographic regime dominated by waged labour and service in husbandry is likely to have had a significant delaying effect upon marriage and household formation, as we have already discussed.[101] Here we need only note that features of such a regime would include high levels of mobility and delayed marriage as the young accumulated sufficient resources to marry. Late marriage would also reduce family sizes whilst migration in search of labour would serve to weaken or to sever bonds of family and kinship. Amongst the poorer peasantry, therefore, nuclear families ill-supported by wider kin networks were more likely to have been the norm and, at least in certain parts of the country, their numbers relative to those of larger, more complex peasant households will have increased over the period.

Irrespective of the relative wealth of individual families, it is evident that something as potentially insular as the peasant family could not be isolated from external factors. The influence of 'exogenous' factors, including disease and climate, but also the 'endogenous' forces of church, state, lord and neighbour, had each, in varying measure, significant consequences for peasant household formation and the subsequent success of that household. The role of the peasant as individual and as family member in responding to these influences needs now to be addressed.

Part III

Worlds Beyond: Market, Crown and Church

In the first two sections of this book, an attempt has been made to show how the basic 'elements' of peasant life in the Middle Ages – land, lord-ship, community and family – were in no way divorced from outside influences. It was, as we have seen, in the various combinations of those influences that the diverse experience of the English peasantry in the high and late Middle Ages is to be explained. Having explored that diversity and considered the range of factors which could and did play upon the medieval peasantry, it will now be useful to describe in more detail peasant interaction with some of the most important of these external factors.

Clearly, some of these factors were beyond the control of the peas-antry: earlier processes of settlement and colonisation, for instance, or demographic crises and climatic change could act upon the peasantry but left peasants little in the way of response. Others, however, were capable of affecting the lives of peasants, as we have, in part, already seen, and of being influenced by peasants who could engage with them as active agents. In attempting to consider peasant engagement with such influences, we can divide our investigation into three sub-categories: the market, politics and the church. Each of these, as we have already seen, effected important developments in the individual and collective lives of the peasantry. Interaction with the market, that is to say with sources of supply and demand which were external to the individual peasant and his immediate family, was, as we have seen, an important element in determining levels of rent, size of landholding and land use. The market was also an influence on peasant household formation, providing, in some instances, the wherewithal for families to stay together while in others it offered employment opportunities which pulled peasant families apart. 'Politics' also, by which is meant here interaction of a kind that was neither overtly commercial or religious between groups or individuals who held distinct interests and agendas, had a significant effect on fundamental aspects of peasant life. The performance of lordship, the tenure of land and the exploitation of a tenantry were, by definition, 'political' acts. Just as these had singularly important roles to play in peasant landholding, so also, as we have seen, did the authority of the state. The rule of law and the levy of national taxation, for instance, altered peasant landholding in significant ways while the demands of the state might also materially affect household economies and life-cycle strategies. Even more obviously, extreme expressions of politics and government, most especially warfare, also had dramatic consequences for peasant society and economy. In this context, we should also acknowledge that 'politics' has a wider application than that of state and the instruments of government. Individual schemes and strategies within the peasant household or village community were also charged with consequences and these could generate their own 'political' tensions. Finally, the church and religious belief cannot, as we have seen, be omitted from discussion of the peasant family and economy. The role of the church, for instance, in influencing choice of marriage partner and the regulation of the peasant household again illustrates the extent to which the English peasantry was subject to influences situated well beyond the confines of farmstead, manor and village.

As already noted, it is not solely as passive objects, acted upon but in no way acting, that we should describe the medieval peasantry. The following chapters are an attempt to illustrate further the ways in which peasants were subject to a multiplicity of influences but were also active agents in medieval society and economy.

7

PEASANTS AND THE MARKET

This chapter examines how peasants used markets. It is also about assessing the extent to which peasants were dependent upon the market or, alternatively, tended to produce for themselves. Some concept of the evolution of the market and its relevance to the everyday lives of medieval villagers is vital in discussing the form of the economy of the countryside; in particular, historians have distinguished, to a greater or lesser extent, between the natural economy of the self-sustaining enclosed community, notably the manor and its smaller constituent parts, the demesne and the tenant holdings, and the monetary economy, exemplified by market-dependent smallholders and the landless, including, of course, those who lived in towns. However, research has shown that it would clearly be inappropriate to talk in terms of a linear progression from a natural economy to a market economy in medieval England; as we shall see, not only was there no steady and continuous drift towards market dependency over time but, spatially, the experience of regions was quite distinct. Overall, there is a strong sense that, throughout the Middle Ages, the population was, to a varying extent, integrated into the market and that it is the question of the degree of market involvement rather than whether that integration existed that has dominated recent historical discussion.[1]

Any discussion of peasant involvement in the market has, of course, to take account of changes in the distribution and function of the market in medieval England. The availability of markets was not constant over time, and the fluctuation needs to be explained both in terms of demand and supply. The question of demand obviously relates to population density but also, as population fell and remained low after the first plague outbreak, to changing standards of living and heightened consumer choice. Supply, on the other hand, would also be influenced by changing patterns of consumption, notably a drift towards regional specialisation which could make local markets into centres for the distribution of essentials brought from further afield to provide for a population less directly involved in producing its own foodstuffs. In either case, and obviously the two are not mutually exclusive, the peasantry's relationship to its markets was likely to alter over the three hundred years between 1200 and 1500.

Britnell has established a chronology of market foundation in England in the Middle Ages, identifying a good deal of market foundation by 1200, an accelerated increase in the next 75 years and, after a further glut of foundations in the first quarter of the fourteenth century, some stagnation in the 25 years before the Black Death.[2] It has been observed that, by the eve of the Black Death, 'most people . . . had reasonably convenient access to a market and not infrequently to more than one.'[3] This growth in the number of markets has been explained in terms of dramatic population increase from the late twelfth through to the early fourteenth century; as the English population perhaps doubled or even trebled to near 6 million c.1300, the clamour for land to support the swelling numbers also increased.[4] Holdings were divided to accommodate the additional families and more strenuous efforts, notably increased rates of seeding and cropping, were made to improve the land's productivity. Despite these injections of labour and capital, the increase in the number of smallholdings meant that the majority of tenants in thirteenth-century England could not expect to sustain themselves from their own land and had to look to alternative sources of employment to supplement, if not to replace, the produce from their holdings.[5] Only a minority of the peasantry in the highly manorialised manors of, for instance, Cambridgeshire or the West Midlands were tenants of large, labour service-owing holdings; on manors where customary tenants could each hold virgates of, for instance, 30 acres, there would also be smallholders and cottagers, some holding by free tenure, others in villeinage, who could not expect to glean all of their family's requirements from their smaller plots of land.[6] It has been argued that anything less than a quarter-virgate, roughly 10 acres, would be insufficient land to support a peasant family, so that more than half of all holdings in late thirteenth-century central England were incapable of providing a subsistence.[7] Kosminsky's analysis of the 1279 hundred rolls showed that, simply in terms of frequency of holding size, the concept of the self-supporting family farm was an atypical phenomenon in late thirteenth-century England; his examination of over 20,000 peasant holdings in the belt of central and eastern counties girdling England from Warwickshire in the west to Cambridgeshire in the east, illustrated the high proportion of smallholdings, less than 5 acres, relative to virgates and half-virgates of between 20 and 40 acres.[8]

As a consequence, smallholders were drawn increasingly into market dependency, producing goods for sale, developing specialist crafts and skills, or labouring for wages, all in order to purchase their basic requirements from the market. The reduction in market growth in the quarter-century before 1349 and the arrival of plague may indicate either that a point of market saturation had been reached or that population had, as some have argued, already begun to fall in the wake of famine in the 1310s. Whatever, the 150 years from 1350 to 1500, when the population in England, reduced by the initial outbreak of plague by perhaps as much as 50 per cent, remained at less than 3 million, saw a decline in markets which has also been explained in terms of population movement. By the sixteenth century, the 1002 markets located in 21 counties throughout pre-plague England, had declined to 426. Hardest hit were the village markets, a feature which David Farmer explained in terms of a halving of the number of mouths to feed in the countryside. The increased availability of land meant that those who lived on the land were less dependent upon the market to supply their needs and that, as a result, rural markets tended only to survive where they could also serve nearby towns.[9] That said, the decline in the number of markets was not the death-knell for an integrated market network in late medieval England. By the early modern period there were, for example, 124 market towns in Lancashire and Yorkshire, a structure of marketing unknown before the thirteenth century.[10]

This general view of the number of markets rising and falling along with the population also needs to be modified in order to admit a regional and, to a lesser extent, a seigneurial dimension. The importance of the market, in terms of exchange between town and countryside, varied according to region; most importantly, geographical remoteness from centres of trade, poor arable husbandry, and/or early specialisation had made and continued to make some regions more market dependent than others and, whilst throughout the country the availability of markets for the villager altered over time, in some regions the role of the market was of far greater consequence than elsewhere.[11]

The concentration of local periodic markets in East Anglia, for example, has been described in terms of the dense population of that region and, thereby, its market dependency.[12] A combination of factors already described in earlier chapters intensified market integration. It is clear that in eastern England, as in areas of free or less onerous unfree tenure such as Kent and Lincolnshire,[13] where lordship was relatively weak or had abandoned early any pretensions to exact labour services and had, as a consequence, rejected the concomitant need for a carefully regulated tenantry, an extremely active land market and an inheritance regime which favoured partibility thrived. Holdings were, consequently, small, frequently too small in fact to support the tenantry that lived upon them, and the peasantry's links to the market were strong. Villagers supplemented the income from their holdings with that earned from by-employments or wage-labour; in this they contrasted with the customary tenants from other parts of the country. As well as those villagers who only engaged in proto-industry as an addition to the mainstay of their agricultural existence, there were others who were wholly or largely absorbed in non-agrarian employment. In areas such as the Breckland, where a good proportion of those living in the countryside were involved in a variety of non-agrarian occupations, including the various occupations associated with cloth production, the need for surrounding areas to provide consumables was manifest. There was, therefore, a 'reciprocal trade' with specialist goods of the region travelling out in exchange for the 'import' of foodstuffs, notably cereals.[14] This relatively local trade in consumables was vital if industry in the countryside was to survive; low yields and a burgeoning population meant that the areas of relatively high division of labour, such as the Breckland but also, for instance, the textile-manufacturing areas of south Suffolk and north Essex, the lead-mining centres of Derbyshire, or the tin-mining regions of central and west Cornwall, were dependent to the point of vulnerability. The increased immersion of livestock producers from highland zones into market networks and the concomitant establishment of specialist livestock production also left such communities vulnerable to the vagaries of the market, a feature especially evident in the dearth years of the late sixteenth century.[15] In high grain-price years, when demand for durables declined, it must have been the cottagers, labourers and smallholders in such areas who were most at risk.[16] In all years, the involvement of such groups in marketing at the local level and, indirectly but not infrequently, at a longer distance, was intensive.

This view of the English 'peasantry', as one maintaining close links with the market whilst gleaning what it could from small plots of land often incapable of providing as much as a meagre subsistence, contrasts with that of the traditional peasant economy once advanced as characteristic of the medieval English countryside. The 'traditional' medieval peasant farm during the century before the arrival of plague, in other words the large villein holding in an open-field manor, comes closest to the 'ideal' of a self-supporting system, that is, one without recourse to the market. The peasant family, in such a state, would produce for its own needs from its own holding whilst any surplus in kind or in labour would be paid as rents, which were fixed according to custom, or stored against short-falls in the coming year. Any exchange, especially of land, according to this model, would be generated by vital events, especially changes in family size; a closely regulated land market with small odd acres transferring from one family to another to accommodate their particular requirements was the nearest thing to a market. Consequently, it is to areas of 'strong' lordship and direct management of the demesne, such as those of the larger lay and ecclesiastical estates of the midlands, southern England, or the north-east, that we might look in order to find elements of a self-sufficient peasantry of the type described.[17] As we have seen, in certain areas, such as parts of the midlands, and under particular lordships, typically those that continued to exact labour services and who resisted attempts at fragmentation of holdings through insistence on monogeniture and control of the land market, the peasant farm retained its size and potential to support a peasant family, even into the post-Black Death period.[18] The concept of the *terra unius familie*, land sufficient to support the family that survived upon it, was artificially extended by certain landlords in the late Middle Ages.[19] A product of estate policy, their survival has been equated with the last throes of non-monetary feudalism and a 'natural' economy.[20] On the estates of Westminster Abbey in the fourteenth century, for example, the monks attempted to ensure that their tenants' holdings remained intact and that a structure of self-supporting, relatively enclosed manorialism continued.[21]

Even tenants of the largest holdings on these estates were unlikely to be wholly isolated from the market; total isolation would only exist if the peasant holding produced sufficient for the needs of those living upon it, with a surplus to pay rent in kind. This would be an extreme example at one end of the natural–monetary economy spectrum; most of the wealthiest villein tenants in late medieval England would have had cause to engage with the market, as producers as well as consumers, selling their surplus on the market, extending credit to their less wealthy neighbours, purchasing those goods that they could not produce themselves, or hiring labour either to supplement their own family's labour on their holding or to perform labour services for the lord in their stead. They would also have to pay non-manorial dues in kind but also in cash, notably taxation which would have affected them greatly in the late thirteenth and early fourteenth centuries. Christopher Dyer's theoretical budget for a virgater, Robert le Kyng, of Bishop's Cleeve, Gloucestershire c.1300, offers a good example of a tenant able in most years to produce sufficient for the needs of his family and, in addition, a saleable surplus.[22] Although produce from the holding could feed his family, other impositions would have forced Kyng into the market at the very least to convert some of his crop into cash so that he was also market dependent.

Similarly, the tenantry of the moors and uplands was not permitted a total self-sufficiency. Beyond champion England, the more isolated communities of the highland zone might indeed contain pockets of relative self-sufficiency, geographically insulated, as they must have been, from an effective market integration. In particular, it is from the more remote farmsteads that we gain the strongest sense of a foraging culture, making best use of all that the surrounding environment had to offer rather than trusting to the market. High on the southern Pennines, for instance, holly was used as a substitute winter fodder for livestock.[23] However, intelligent use of natural resources may have been – was almost certainly – but one element in the rural economy of even the relatively remote locales in high and late medieval England. As tenants and as taxpayers, albeit often in the northern marches infrequent ones, rural dwellers in these more distant environments were integrated into 'political economies' whilst their produce, especially livestock, drew them into market economies. Cottagers, fishing the lakes and streams of medieval Cumbria, were exploiting the resource not just to feed themselves but to meet market demand.[24] Further, peasants, while they might expect, in 'normal' conditions, to survive through the employment of, for the greater part, local resources which were at their disposal, could be left vulnerable through changing circumstance. Even a relatively minor ecological shift, resulting in the failure of an acorn crop or the depletion of fish shoals, or an imbalance in other local conditions, such as the over-capitalisation of a neighbour, could have dramatic consequences for a way of life and, in particular, drive individuals and communities into greater market dependency.

What form did the market take? The market could, of course, operate at any level: between neighbours, between villagers, and beyond the village.[25] A distinction needs to be drawn here between local markets and distant markets, towns, and fairs, the latter tending to be held at fairly long intervals and at some considerable distance from each other, whereas the former were closely integrated both spatially and temporally.[26] Fairs tended to operate for and on behalf of traders; most markets, on the other hand, existed to satisfy local consumption, acting as a point of redistribution for predominantly local produce.[27] Although peasants could, indirectly, be involved in long-distance trade (for instance, as labourers in the wool and cloth trades), it is essentially the local market and regional trade with which they were most likely to be involved on an everyday basis.[28] There is then an important distinction to be made between the local redistribution of locally produced consumables, either as sales or in the form of rent, and specialised production for more distant markets. We should attempt to investigate this range and, in order to do so, can begin with some observations regarding exchange at the local level, between family and neighbours.

At the simplest level, exchange occurred between family members and members of villager communities in an atmosphere that cannot easily be defined as 'commercial'. The reciprocal sharing of resources must have been an important part of family and village life, so important, in fact, and so everyday that, in one of history's oft-repeated paradoxes, we have little or no information regarding it. The exchange of petty items of household economy or the short, interest-free, loans of livestock, cereal or small sums of money largely go unrecorded, but we can, however, glean some sense of them from legal records. An attempt by a Chalgrave (Bedfordshire) villager, William Yngeleys, to recover 'a certain cat', which had been unjustly detained by John Saly and Cristina his wife, is possibly reflective of this low-level exchange.[29] Debt litigation in manor courts for relatively small loans, such as the fairly small debts of 6d., 10d. and 11d. recorded in three cases at Cuxham (Oxfordshire) in 1304, also hint at even smaller exchanges for which individuals may have chosen not to go to law.[30] Other exchanges to which society might wish to attach a value, such as advice and education, were also capable of being given freely within the village.[31] Clearly, some or all of this low-level exchange was conditioned by influences other than that of the market. In particular, some sense of social obligation, itself informed by the teaching of the religious, may well have been the spur to acts of charity and the giving of gifts or the extension of loans to poorer villagers.[32] Whether, exchange under such circumstances is solely to the benefit of the receiver is, of course, a moot point – medieval charity was, after all, as much about the giver's spiritual expectations as it was the receiver's material wants – but such interactions, if we are prepared to accept our characterisation of the circumstances, were the closest that medieval villagers may have come to non-commercial exchanges. Application of the same principle underpins assumptions regarding land exchange where the presumed motive force is life-cycle and not acquisitiveness, a point discussed in an earlier chapter. In other words, the *inter-vivos* transfer of land between villagers, be they related or not, can be characterised in such circumstances as a simple and mutually convenient redistribution according to immediate needs.

It is, however, also evident that systems of exchange in the medieval village were not necessarily altruistic or even especially reciprocal; there were, in fact, plenty of situations in which exchange occurred for reasons other than those of mutual reciprocity and advantage. To begin, once again, with the peasant family, transactions between family members could be motivated by the self-interest of individual family members. Although, as we have seen, bonds of mutual dependency may have been important in determining familial relationships, there is also evidence to suggest that commercial regard also played no small part in such relationships. This is most evident *in extremis*, as, for example, in the early fourteenth century, during the Great Famine, when wealthier family members bought land from their poorer relatives, transactions that, it has been argued, reveal an effective reduction of support in time of crisis. Faced with real hardship and uncertainty themselves, better-off family members were prepared to offer limited support only in return for security, hence the transfer of land between kin.[33]

In ordinary years, family members could be engaged in commercial transactions as part of their everyday dealings. Parents employed their offspring as labourers and servants, wives and husbands contested each others' rights to property and its employment, siblings negotiated inheritances between each other with an eye to their own advantage, and the elderly bargained with younger family members over retirement arrangements.[34] All of these interactions had economic causes and consequences. The employment of children as family labour, whether, for instance, as carers for their younger siblings, foragers or herds, had an economic worth, not least in the replacement cost of that labour with a purchased alternative.

If transactions between kin could be imbued with 'commercial' considerations, it goes without saying that dealings between non-kin were also capable of being 'economic' in character. Village society was equal neither in the resources which each villager or peasant household possessed nor in the particular benefits which the individual or peasant family brought to the community or hoped to receive from that community. Records of taxation assessments and levies, inventories of goods, and wills all reveal the disparities of wealth in the medieval village. Raftis has recently reminded us that peasants, even on southern and midlands manors c.1300, where a degree of uniformity of holding size might be expected, still paid markedly different amounts in terms of lay subsidies, that is, taxation on moveable goods, and that, therefore, some customary tenants were clearly much wealthier than others. Masschaele makes a similar observation based upon his use of purveyance records. Historians of the peasant land market in eastern England have also described an inconsistency of holding size, a feature reflected in the uneven lay subsidy assessments.[35]

This basic inequality in economic status, a product, it seems, of commercial enterprise, was perpetuated by economic sub-groups within the village. In other contexts we have already seen, and will discuss further, how wealthier villagers could sustain their position through office and the control of important administrative and legal frameworks.[36] This position of advantage was also maintained through mutual support, a dependency which went beyond ties of family and neighbourliness and is, perhaps, better classified as economic in its motive. Examination of arrangements for mutual support, such as the extension of pledges by one villager to guarantee performance of a particular task by another, look to indicate that villagers operated within well-established economic contexts.[37] The existence of economic 'interest groups' heightens the sense that the village community was not a level playing-field but one that could be composed of winners and losers. How did this difference reveal itself?

The range of commercial dealing within the medieval village was extensive and reflected the economic inequalities which existed there. Those with a surplus of capital were able to employ that surplus in ways that were beyond the means of the poorer villagers; the relatively poor, by contrast, sought out employment opportunities which met the expectations of the wealthy by acting as their servants and labourers. In the simple provision of services, inequalities of capital determined commercial opportunities so that poorer villagers could provide only basic services whilst their wealthier peers were capable of investing in more elaborate enterprises. As we have already seen, transfer of land amongst the peasantry can, in certain circumstances, be described as a market, with wealthier individuals apparently speculating in that market to the disadvantage of their poorer neighbours.[38] Whilst the wealthy buyers could employ their surplus to buy land, the poorer villagers could only sell; in other words, the asset of the poor was under-capitalised and economically passive, a prey to those with surplus capital. In eastern England, where such aggressive land market activity has been most closely studied for the late thirteenth and early fourteenth centuries, ratios of buyers to sellers illustrate the dominant role which a few wealthy villagers could play in the peasant land market. Similar observations could be made for the mid- and late fifteenth century when a process of accumulation of peasant land-holding was also exacerbated by the invasion of the rural land market by wealthy outsiders.[39] If dealing in land offers the strongest indication of the commercial potential in exchanges between villagers, there are others.

Evidence for the provision of services also reveals distinct economic roles within the village. Most obviously, individuals provided their neighbours with a variety of services, provision that was dependent upon individual and familial resources. Opportunities for poorer villagers to enter into economic relations with other villagers were limited and were essentially restricted either to the basic services which they could provide, predominantly physical labour of some kind, or to the few resources which they could sell or use as security. Employment as servants within peasant households or as occasional wage labourers offered employment opportunities, as did similar work in the lord's household or on the manorial demesne. Goldberg has estimated that, in rural Rutland in the second half of the fourteenth century, one-sixth of households contained servants. He tells a similar story for the West Riding of Yorkshire and concludes that, in the countryside, most families relied on their own children, especially girls, to provide services which might elsewhere (the towns) be performed by servants. Crafts in the countryside, such as weaving, did afford employment for servants but, according to Goldberg, this tended to favour adult males more than it did young women and children, with unmarried women more likely than their male counterparts to remain in the parental home.[40] At the more extreme limits of physical employment, prostitution was a further form of wage-labour to which poorer villagers might turn.[41] Aside from their own labour, poorer villagers had very few moveable or immoveable, that is, landed, resources with which they could support economic endeavours. As we have also seen, the families of poorer villagers tended to be relatively small so that they also lacked the physical resources which could, in other more fortuitous circumstances, have permitted the accumulation of a capital surplus through employment. Some poorer villagers acted as regraters, selling on goods, such as bread and ale, for a modest profit, an example of limited capital expenditure which would be unlikely to realise a significant return. Faced with such limits, poorer villagers were at a clear economic disadvantage and, as a consequence, their meagre resources could be vulnerable to the ambitions of their wealthier neighbours.[42]

By contrast, middling and wealthy villagers, those with a surplus of capital or physical resources, could enter into economic relationships with a greater confidence and with a stronger sense of their own volition. Wealthier villagers were, as has already been discussed, less likely than the poorest villagers to be wholly dependent upon the market, but their economic ventures were still capable of being directed at market opportunities. In the first place, peasants on larger holdings produced substantial amounts of cereals and livestock which found their way into the market. Masschaele's recent discussion of peasant producers identifies numbers of substantial peasants whose large surplus of cereals the state was eager to tax. Six virgaters on the Ramsey Abbey manor of Elton (Huntingdonshire), for instance, each supplied one quarter of wheat and one quarter of malt to the king's purveyors in the early fourteenth century. Surpluses such as this – a quarter weighed nearly 400 pounds and could have provided an individual's principal food intake for a year – not only found their way into the royal finances but also onto the market. Similarly large quantities of livestock were also produced as surplus. At Coney Weston (Suffolk), in the very early fourteenth century, 44 villeins held between them 60 horses, 51 pigs, 117 head of cattle and 342 sheep. At nearby Walsham le Willows, tenants in the early fourteenth century folded large numbers of sheep. One tenant, William of Cranmer, paid a 2s. fine for folding 72 sheep when his entitlement was only 40. Such surplus encourages Masschaele to estimate that the peasantry before the mid-fourteenth century produced somewhere in the region of two-thirds of the country's marketable commodities.[43] A good deal of this surplus went to markets beyond the immediate vicinity, as we shall see, but wealthier villagers also sold to their neighbours. Debt litigation in manorial court rolls offers valuable insights into local sales of produce; from these we gain a sense of who sold what to whom. Some of these transactions involved only small sums, perhaps often accumulated over a number of years. At Walsham le Willows in 1329, in an entry that is interesting for a number of reasons including the evidence for the commercial independence of a woman before marriage, Alice Spileman pleaded debts from William Kembald which included 1 bushel of wheat worth 10d., ale worth 14d., as well as small pieces of ironmongery, casks, vats and bowls.[44] Others were clearly the product of large deals intended to service husbandry as well as the by-employments and small-scale industries of the countryside. At Downham (Cambridgeshire), in 1316, John de Wyrham [Wereham] acknowledged that he owed Roger le Clerk a quarter of brewing barley while, on the manor of Wakefield in the same year, William Marjori-man sought recovery from William Wytbelt of ten and a half quarters of rye, a very large amount of grain indeed.[45] Livestock was also sold and leased within the village. Draught animals, horses and oxen, were lent to neighbours, as at Writtle, where John Pawlyn sued for recovery of the sum of 4d. owed for the lease of a horse to Thomas Elkyn 'to labour in the fulfillment of the same Thomas' husbandry' for two days; similarly, the produce of livestock, milk, eggs, hides, wool, meat, all were traded.[46]

It was not only cereals and livestock, the chief raw products of the countryside, that were sold within the village. An energetic market in a range of finished produce and services can also be observed in the village community. Villagers' surnames and the occupational tags often given to them further indicate the range of employment within the village community with brewers, bakers and butchers amongst the more obvious providers of particular services.[47] In market villages, such as Botesdale (Suffolk), in a region of intensified market integration, the list of crafts and trades is longer still; as well as the ubiquitous carpenters, cooks and food suppliers, thatchers, smiths, and coopers, there were also practitioners of medicine (*leches*) and teachers (*magistri*).[48] By the close of our period, village inns and hostelries were establishing themselves as permanent features of the countryside.[49] Long before the fifteenth century professional village brewers, identifiable by their regular appearances as such in lists of breachers of the assize of ale, provided local communities with ale that could be purchased.[50] Robert Oldman, at early fourteenth-century Cuxham (Oxfordshire), for instance, brewed more than any other villager, his trade in ale but one part of a substantial body of interests which, during his life, allowed him to accumulate horses, a flock of sheep, cattle, and an array of household goods.[51] Similarly, bakers and butchers also serviced the community with their wares. As well as consumables, durables could also be bought and sold within the village. The village carpenter found employment, both with his lord and his neighbours, constructing domestic as well as agricultural buildings while smiths were called upon to forge and maintain metalwork, including ploughshares and sundry items such as nails and latches. By the late Middle Ages, peasants were prepared to pay substantial sums to craftsmen, as is indicated by the quality of carpentry in surviving fifteenth-century rural housing.[52] Earlier than this, we gain a sense, especially from manorial accounts which include details of individuals employed on the manorial demesne, that certain villagers were prized for their particular skills. At Birdbrook (Essex) in the late fourteenth century, John Parkgate was regularly employed on the demesne as a carpenter whilst other villagers worked year in, year out in other specialist tasks, such as leatherwork and harness repair.[53] Such know-how could also be imparted. That young men entered apprenticeships to established craftsmen is also clearly shown by the information of manorial accounts, with the cost of an apprentice's education paid in labour. Within the village there were also, potentially, individuals skilled in notarial practices and possessing some degree of literacy. These skills could be bought and sold like any other.[54]

There also existed those particularly advantaged villagers with a simple surplus of land or labour which they could also sell or lease to their fellow villagers. Villagers who held substantial parcels of land might look to sell off parts of their property through the land market, as we have seen. Unlike poorer villagers, wealthier tenants, in so far as they were not constrained by the various elements outlined above,[55] could hope to speculate in such a market, selling at times of peak demand. Whittle's analysis of rare and very detailed payment

agreements for customary land on the Norfolk manor of Hevingham
Bishops in the fifteenth and sixteenth centuries illustrates most effectively these fluctuations in demand and the consequent rise and fall of
land prices. The acceleration of the market and of prices in the last
decades of the fifteenth century suggests that sellers were prepared to
meet demand, but only at a suitable price.[56] At Hevingham Bishops,
holdings less than 4 acres in extent showed a substantial increase in
price per acre between the mid-fifteenth century and the middle years
of the sixteenth century, a fact which has been explained in terms
of the significant and, by the late-fifteenth/early-sixteenth century,
growing demand for small plots of land.[57] Tenants of larger holdings
could also grant part of their holding as a lease or use the land as
security for a loan. Edmund Bisshop, a tenant of at least 30 acres at
Hevingham Bishops in the late fifteenth century, surrendered a small
plot of his land – two acres and one rod called 'Puppysclos' – to a
London merchant, Thomas Kesyng, 'in the name of a mortgage'. If
Edmund paid, actually repaid, five marks to Thomas by June of the
next year, the surrender would be void and Edmund would recover
Puppysclos.[58]

In not dissimilar ways, villagers with larger families could also put
their biological advantage to good use, hiring out family members for
short- or long-term employment. In such circumstances, where the
peasant family from which the labour originated was relatively wealthy,
the hiring out of labour may have been judged according to the expectations of that family and not the hirer. It might, for instance, be to the
advantage of the family to hire out some of its labour if the family's
own needs for labour were presently limited or because there was a
heightened demand for labour in the wider community. In both cases,
that is, where land was sold or leased by wealthier villages or where
the same villagers hired out labour, the situation can be contrasted with
similar behaviour by poorer villagers. While, as we have seen, prominent amongst the recorded behaviour of poorer villagers was the sale
or lease of land and the hiring out of their own labour, such activity
tended to be based less upon choice and a response to favourable
market conditions but rather more upon necessity.

The most explicit indication of the relative advantage of some villagers and rural dwellers over their peers was, of course, money. The
previous discussion has shown that there were some villagers who
owned more of certain things than did their neighbours, be that advantage to be counted in land, grain, livestock, chattels, labour (family

members or servants), learning or skill, or, simply, available time. The villager with a surplus could invest it in the needs of his or her neighbours and thereby gain some material or social benefit. In many cases, the benefit was financial. Some villagers chose to maximise that benefit not by reconverting money into whatever asset had produced such an advantage in the first place but by employing money as a resource in itself. Loans of cash were common in the medieval village. As we have already discussed, such loans, along with loans of basic foodstuffs, could be short-term and reciprocal, the mutually beneficent interchanges of everyday living. But loans could also be commercial. Although the charging of interest was prohibited by canon law, interest-bearing loans could be disguised in numerous ways, as, for instance, sales at false prices or in leases of property for more than their market value.[59] That those who lent money were not infrequently engaged in the business of money-lending rather than offering support for their less advantaged neighbours is confirmed by litigation recorded in manor courts. Creditor plaintiffs sued debtors for recovery of money and goods lent, while debtors responded by resisting such claims and offering counter-claims, not in debt but in trespass. In May 1327, on the bishop of Ely's manor of Downham (Cambridgeshire), John Hayt attempted to recover 6s. 6½d. from Simon Cardinal. Simon claimed that he owed only 10d. An inquest jury subsequently found that John was in fact owed 4s. 2½d. by Simon, which sum he was awarded plus 3d. in damages. But John was also amerced 2d. for a false claim, since he had originally pleaded for more than the actual debt. In a subsequent plea of trespass in the same court, and one presumably generated by the previous plea of debt, the irked Simon claimed that John had caused him damage by draining water from his fishpond so that Simon's fish had died. The plea was summarily dismissed by the jurors of the manor court.[60] Tension between creditors and debtors could also spill over into defamation and acts of violence.[61] The commerciality of such credit relationships is further indicated by the security offered by debtors and the preparedness of creditors to seize such security if repayments lapsed. Some, perhaps many, of the inter-peasant leases, for which licences were frequently recorded in the court rolls, should be counted as securities for debts, or gages. At Hinderclay (Suffolk), for instance, in the late thirteenth century, those villagers who acted as creditors also appeared as lessees or buyers of land whilst debtors almost exclusively appeared as lessors or sellers.[62] A similar situation has been observed at Halesowen (Worcestershire), where, in the problem years of the late thirteenth and early fourteenth century, smallholders 'had to sub-let and to sell land . . . to remit debts'.[63] The considerable increase in land market activity in dearth years, for example, could, in part be explained by foreclosure on mortgages or the evolution of the gage into a hereditable interest on the failure of the debtor.[64] In later periods, conditional surrenders of land were not infrequently actual mortgages and remortgages of property, as was clearly the case at Hevingham Bishops (Norfolk) in the fifteenth and sixteenth centuries.[65]

Competitiveness and economic dealing within the village were not sustained solely with an eye to the village and its internal mechanisms. Nor was such dealing only driven by those same internal mechanisms, such as the life-cycle of peasant household or of the individual peasant. Although individuals might wander through a range of employment opportunities during their life-cycle, with, for instance, young women taking employment as servants, and widows finding themselves with sufficient surplus to act as creditors in their later years, they did not all pass through the same range.[66] The economic differentiation within the village community was not purely a consequence of such developments but, as we have already seen, of a range of factors of which the market was but one. Those villagers, for example, who were able to speculate in the land market did not always do so solely to dominate landholding in their community nor to provide for their offspring. The villager capable of speculating and profiteering in this way had more than half an eye on markets beyond the manor and village. His or her commercial activities within the village helped sustain transactions beyond the village. By the same token, such external activities enhanced commercial enterprises within the home community. This leads us to consider the markets and trading opportunities of the peasantry beyond the immediate nexi of family and local community.

A growing number of studies of marketing in medieval England has allowed historians to gain a clearer sense of the relationship between the countryside and marketing centres.[67] It is now evident that peasants did not confine their economic activity to their own communities but sought opportunities in a range of markets beyond their villages and hamlets. We can organise our brief consideration of these opportunities by describing the peasant's economic world in terms of concentric rings, centred on the individual and his family, then moving out through various levels of trade: neighbours, the local community, nearby villages, including market villages, market towns, more distant markets and fairs, and so on. We have already considered economic exchange at the local level. If we now turn our attention to the next level, neighbouring villages, market villages and small town markets, in other words places with no more than 500 to 1000 souls, we find a wealth of trading outlets for the medieval peasantry.

Local periodic markets were an important part of the peasantry's economic world. Although each village or hamlet might not contain a market of its own, there were in many parts of the country, by the close of the thirteenth century, well-established market networks which afforded country-dwellers access to marketing centres.[68] In areas of dense population and heavy market dependency, such as Suffolk (where there were just short of ten markets for every 100 square miles in the mid-fourteenth century), a villager might find himself within a few miles of a number of markets, each of which might be held on a different day of the week. At Botesdale, a local market in northern Suffolk, the market was held on Thursdays; within a few miles in any direction there were markets held in neighbouring villages on Mondays, Tuesdays, Fridays and Sundays. In other words, Botesdale was part of an integrated network of local markets. Elsewhere, typically where population density was lower, this integration might not be so intense and market dependency less pronounced. In the West Riding of Yorkshire, an area of relatively low population density, there were just over two markets per 100 square miles in the mid-fourteenth century and marketing opportunities were obviously reduced, although they may still have met the needs of the local population and economy.

What did a local market provide that the local community did not? Whilst it was once suggested that the principal role of external markets in the peasant economy was to facilitate the conversion of cash crops into money in order to met the pecuniary demands of lords, it is now more generally argued that such markets provided peasants with the diversity that could not be obtained in their own communities.[69] Peasants operated in such markets as producers and as consumers. As producers, the markets in villages and small towns offered outlets for the surplus that locals generated, and they did so in ways that lowered the transaction costs of such sales. Villagers could sell their produce through middlemen or through their own small outlets. At Botesdale, as Smith has shown, local peasants hired booths or stalls from which they could sell their produce. Adam Jop, a substantial villager from the nearby manor of Redgrave, rented stalls at Botesdale market,

presumably to sell the surpluses generated by his large landholdings.[70]
These products could include the raw produce already discussed but
also finished goods, including consumables such as bread and ale,
butchered meat, and more durable goods, such as cloth. Where production was specialised, in areas of quarrying or of forest, local markets
presented immediate opportunities to sell speciality goods and ware.
At Brill (Buckinghamshire), where clay was extracted in the late
Middle Ages and where pottery production thrived, the local market
provided a focus for sales of local specialist ware.[71] As within their own
villages, individuals also sought out other commercial opportunities in
local markets: they offered their services there and may have perceived
market centres as better places to find employment. They also
extended credit in these markets and loaned their money at interest,
a point to which we can return a little later.

Of course, local men and women came to these rural markets also
as consumers. Essentially, local markets furnished individuals with the
products that they could not obtain closer to home. Specialist goods,
pottery, metalwork, higher quality cloth were available in such markets
but, importantly, it is also probable that, especially in areas characterised by high population density, a proliferation of smallholdings,
low kin density, and intense market dependency, local periodic markets
were also meeting some of the more basic demands of consumers.
Grain and livestock, bread and ale, meat and poultry, these were the
common fare of local markets. Villagers also came as consumers of
labour and capital. Agreements to hire labour or livestock might be
struck at local markets while markets also provided the commercial
atmosphere and a superfluity of cognisant witnesses conducive to the
creation of contracts, especially of loans and sales on credit. In the
manor court at Walsham le Willows, a Thomas Kyng impleaded one
Ralph Wybert for a debt of 13s. owed on the purchase of an ox at
Botesdale two years previously.[72]

It is clear that such markets met the expectations of significant
numbers of the peasantry. The movement of peasants in search of
work or even, as we not infrequently see in the late fourteenth
century, fleeing lords and manors for new opportunities elsewhere,
often took them no more than half a dozen to a dozen miles from their
home villages.[73] However, these small markets, although 'lightly
urbanised' if we restrict ourselves to a definition of 'urban' which was
dependent upon size and burghal status, almost certainly offered sig-

nificant marketing opportunities.[74] If the geographical horizons of some villagers were reasonably limited, this does not mean, of course, that their contacts were also few. Local markets did not just sell to local consumers and nor did they only deal in local produce. Traders from beyond the locality came to buy and to sell at these markets, just as they also came to village and farmstead, as well as to the manorial curia.

So far, we have mostly been discussing local production for local consumption; this has not taken us a great distance from the village and the family farm. When we attempt to examine peasant involvement in this longer-distance trade, including that of fairs, we are forcing the peasant from the world of the local economy into the regional, national and international market.[75] This broader economy was extensive and varied. We can include within it the regional marketing centres of the larger county towns and, of course, cities. Fairs also provided regular but less frequent marketing opportunities for rural dwellers.[76] Larger towns and fairs also brought the peasantry into contact with traders and dealers from beyond the locality, including foreign merchants; further, merchants and other traders were not beyond travelling into the countryside both to sell and to buy. In considering the engagement of the peasantry with traders and markets beyond their locales, we will divide our discussion between production and consumption, beginning with the former.

Production

The inter-dependence not just of regions but also of countries is a well-attested feature of late medieval Europe; parts of the Low Countries, southern France and the Baltic, for example, were engaged in varying levels of reciprocal trade with England; grain shipped from England supported their own specialisms;[77] peasant production for this export trade should certainly not be discounted. Although we might not be entirely confident with Masschaele's overall estimates of the number of tenants holding virgates in early fourteenth-century England (Masschaele estimates around 12 such tenants per settlement which seems on the high side) and hence be inclined to reduce his estimates of peasant commercial productivity of grain, there seems no real reason to question his basic thesis that the peasantry, both large- and smallholders, provided a significant share of the gross domestic product of medieval England. Whether that share was as high as two-thirds is, generally speaking, anyone's guess, and Masschaele has cautiously suggested reasons why peasant productivity may not have matched their share of landholding.[78] Similar observations could be made for livestock production. There is plentiful evidence to suggest that peasants produced livestock for long-distance trade. In some cases, such as, for instance, rabbit production in the Brecklands, this met the needs of specialist markets whilst, in others, long-distance trade met the demands of large urban centres.[79] Cattle-droving from the Welsh Marches to London was not solely the preserve of landlords.[80] A good deal of peasant involvement in longer-distance trade would have been indirect, selling their produce, be it grain or wool or cloth, to middlemen, such as cornmongers, woolmongers or clothiers, who would actually deal in the produce themselves and who possessed sufficient capital to cover transport and transaction costs. As well as supplies of grain reaching London from the demesnes of large estates, small-scale traders toured the Home Counties making very small purchases, presumably from peasants, and returning to the capital with their purchases. A single cart-load of grain was characteristic of these endeavours.[81]

It was not just in the production of cereals and livestock for consumption that the peasantry had a vital role. Although peasant and small-landholder involvement in the supply of long-distance and overseas trade in wool varied over time, their overall impact was more than considerable. Again, Masschaele has offered some recent and valuable comment and, writing of wool exports, has estimated that the peasantry was responsible for more than half of all exports in the early fourteenth century. He further concludes that at this time the peasantry controlled two-thirds of wool production in the country.[82] His figures offer a statistical basis to a feature of the countryside that historians have long recognised. Earlier economic historians, notably Power and Postan, both noted the significant amounts of wool purchased from rural producers.[83] Although this part-time trade may have given way to the merchants with increased specialisation in the years of high wool exports and growing cloth production in the late fourteenth and early fifteenth centuries, by the mid-fifteenth century, however, there is evidence of small-scale purchases supporting the overseas trade in wool and cloth. In a Common's Petition of 1455, complaints were expressed regarding the activities of alien merchants in the wool and cloth trades, which

marchaunt straungers Italyans . . . have custumably used to ryde aboute for
to bye Wollen Clothes, Wolle, Wolfelles and Tynne, in every partie of the
same Reame, by the sufferaunce wherof the said Merchaunts have know-
eleche . . . of the poverte of your peple, as of theire penurye. Wheche
poverte and penurye the said Marchaunds percevynge, have redie Money
and therewith at the ferst hande bye Wollen Clothes, Wolle, Wollefelles and
Tynne, of such indygent persones as sell hit at their grete myschief
and losse.[84]

This petition was presented during a period of depression, when a
good deal of both local and overseas trade was experiencing a slump,
and both merchants and landowners struggled to make ends meet;
although, therefore, 'indygent persones' might conceivably include the
larger lay and ecclesiastical landlords who were feeling the pinch, the
likelihood is that the alien merchants were buying at lowered prices
from the poorer groups of wool producers, including the peasantry.[85]
It is clear that by the mid-fifteenth century, in addition to the leasing
of some of the larger demesnes which had left peasants and small
traders in direct management of large tracts of land, there had been
an accumulation of land in the hands of certain peasant families, particularly in the midlands and southern England, and, along with this,
there had been limited investment in wool production through a concentration on sheep grazing.[86] The Goddard family of Aldbourne in
Wiltshire had passed from being tenants of free and customary land
in the late fourteenth century to lessees of whole demesnes by the
fifteenth, a position they maintained and strengthened during the
century; when one of their number, John Goddard, died in 1501, he
left 1100 sheep in three flocks.[87] If overseas traders were able to buy
directly from growers in the mid-fifteenth century, they were as likely
to find themselves dealing at the farm-gate with the wealthy peasant
landholder, or gentleman-farmer as he was fast becoming, as 150 years
earlier they would have done business with the reeve of a monastic
estate, such as that of the abbot of Meaux.[88]
If a proportion of reasonably well-to-do peasants were able to
produce a sufficient surplus to help satisfy the demands of local and
long-distance trade for raw materials, there were others living in villages who were dependent on the same raw materials to produce finished goods. It is well known that the manufacturing industries were
not confined to towns; extractive industries were not, of course, based
on urban centres. In particular, textile production was an important

feature of the countryside, especially in the later Middle Ages. The increase in cloth production in the late fourteenth and fifteenth centuries and the enhanced role in production played by those living in the countryside caused signficant developments within certain regions. Especially, but not exclusively, in parts of Somerset, Berkshire and the Suffolk–Essex border, the concentration of the industry transformed villages, both through the labouring opportunities that were created and the injections of capital that were encouraged.[89]

Consumption

If peasant production for distant markets was substantial, what did peasants expect to gain from markets beyond their immediate *pays*? As we have already seen, most of the consumption needs of peasants were likely to be met by local marketing networks, but some produce needed, inevitably, to come from further afield. Consumer durables, such as pottery, found their way into local markets, suggesting that traders and longer-distance ware were more likely to come to the rural dwellers than they were to travel to them. At Westbury (Buckinghamshire), pottery finds suggest that significant amounts of medieval pot came from the relatively local kilns at Potterspury; a few sherds, however, came from further afield, from Brill and from Oxford, indicating there was a trade in 'exotic imports'.[90] Consumables, such as salt-fish, also found their way far inland. At Wharram Percy (Yorkshire), around thirty miles from the North Sea coast at Bridlington, oyster shells and the bones of cod have been unearthed.[91] The merchants, denizen and alien, who purchased from the peasantry, may have brought goods with them but there were also important supply networks, maintained by a largely efficient road and river network. Long-distance trade did not just involve bulk produce. On a small scale, hucksters, chapmen and peddlars must have serviced the peasantry with occasional fripperies and a thousand and one minor specialist items, while barber surgeons travelled the countryside in search of victims. An unusual archaeological record of an itinerant barber surgeon looks to survive from Avebury (Wiltshire), where the skeleton of an adult male was discovered beneath a toppled sarsen stone. A leather purse containing early fourteenth-century coin, as well as scissors and a probe or lance, suggest that the man may well have been a wandering surgeon who made the fateful and incautious decision to join with the pious villagers of Avebury in felling their standing stones.[92]

Transaction and transportation costs must have made distant trade prohibitively expensive for the majority of the peasantry but it is clear that there were some peasants who did travel to more distant market centres. In the first place, labour for the lord could involve carrying and carting services to quite distant locations, including ports and major urban centres. Villeins at Little Downham (Cambridgeshire), for instance, had to accompany the manor bailiff on livestock-buying expeditions to the market towns at Bury St Edmunds, Wisbech or St Ives.[93] Such visits presented opportunities to engage with distant markets. The expectations of the state, such as attendance as jurors at eyres and other assemblies, would also bring peasants into major regional capitals and at times when traders would look to make best advantage of the court's presence. Peasants also visited important centres of trade of their own volition. Examination of borough court records, for instance, reveals villagers visiting towns to make purchases and to take out loans. The wealthiest villagers may also have seen more distant trade as an opportunity to trade on a scale not open to them at the local level. In December 1321 John Baude of Ipswich pursued William Wodebite, a villein of the manor of Walsham (Suffolk), in a plea of debt. William was attached to respond to John. The jurors agreed with John that he had delivered 12 marks of silver to William in 1319 at Ipswich 'to trade and profit for John's benefit, and William was required to render faithfully a true account thereof quarterly, in accordance with the Law Merchant and by a certain written agreement'.[94] Quite what security William had presented to secure such a huge loan is unclear but this case indicates a number of the advantages which a particular sort of peasant might hope to gain from longer-distance commercial activity. The first is clearly capital: such substantial sums of money (in this case enough to employ two men at a more than moderate wage for a year) could be reinvested in a local credit-market, land or produce within the local community, or employed in more remote markets. Transactions such as this brought other advantages: an education in the law and an awareness of business efficacy. Since, for instance, a good deal of trade was conducted through credit, villagers could not rely on credit in their dealings beyond their immediate locality unless they imitated the practice of merchants and traders and used negotiable credit instruments, such as bonds.[95] An awareness of the wider context of trade could also be employed in local transactions, as on the manor of Wakefield in August 1317 where Christina of Nottone sued Thomas Monik 5s. 'for a quarter of oats bought from her on [11 November 1315], according to the higher rate at which oats were sold between Martinmas and Michaelmas, during which period they were sold for 7s. Thomas paid 2s. and withholds 5s'.[96] Of course, such transactions also brought risks: the failure of significant business ventures could redound to the injury not only of the individual concerned but those of his smaller business contacts and dependants in local markets and the village community.

For others amongst the peasantry, it was not the larger commercial opportunity that was sought in more distant markets but employment. Towns, it has long been recognised, exacted a considerable pull on the countryside throughout the period. Most of the information regarding servants survives from the late-fourteenth and fifteenth centuries, notably the poll-taxes of the late 1370s and 1380 which cast light on numbers of live-in servants, and the church court records which become more abundant in the fifteenth century and inform us, *inter alia*, about relations between servant and master or mistress and conditions of service. As we have seen, from fairly young ages, children in villages might be employed as servants in the households of neighbours. But, where villagers did employ servants, they did not look only to their neighbours for employable youth. Manorial records are replete with cases of individuals housing strangers contrary to village by-laws, or of young males who had entered the village within the past year and had yet to be admitted to a tithing group. At Chalgrave (Bedfordshire) in 1303, villagers harboured strangers from the nearby town of Dunstable and clearly employed these, contrary to the village by-law (*contra statutum*) as collectors of grain.[97] In other words, peasants, especially the young, were quite likely to seek their opportunities in neighbouring villages or even further afield.[98] As well as travelling to villages in search of employment, villagers also travelled, in their late teens and early twenties, to towns, where they could be employed on yearly contracts in urban households.

In the towns, the proportion of households containing servants was greater than in the countryside, with perhaps twice as many householders employing servants. Although, of course, a proportion of these servants were themselves townspeople, it is also clear that a significant element were rural migrants.[99] In the thirteenth and early fourteenth centuries, towns may have provided opportunities, or been perceived as places of opportunity, for the children of peasants, especially the poorer peasantry. There is evidence that migration to towns increased markedly in the late thirteenth and early fourteenth centuries, at times of severe economic distress. The population of certain districts within Norwich increased considerably in the early years of the fourteenth century, possibly as a result of in-migration from a beleaguered countryside while, at Halesowen, the borough court records suggest a dramatic increase of in-migrants before the Black Death.[100] In the period of population decline and stagnation after the plagues of the mid-fourteenth century, there appears to have been a further wave of migration into towns. It has been suggested that a significant proportion of these new migrants were young women who moved into towns in the hope of taking advantage of improved labour conditions at a time when the workforce was greatly reduced. By the late fourteenth and fifteenth centuries, when alternative opportunities for female employment, notably as occasional wage labourers in agriculture, appear to have subsided, it seems likely that young women from the countryside were frequently employed in urban households as live-in servants. Church court depositions from late medieval York certainly indicate that young men and women did take opportunities to move into towns, but seldom travelled more than a single day's journey to their new place of employment.[101]

The implications of this broad range of market activity are, as has been already discussed to a certain degree in earlier sections of this study, considerable. We have seen how integration with the market helped promote polarisations of wealth in the village community, influenced the policy of landlords, altered the social fabric in communities and permitted forms of behaviour that might, in other contexts be deemed inappropriate.[102] The pull of distant markets could draw on communities while the established commercial and industrial opportunities within a locale could bring new blood into villages. The market also intensified an awareness of the outside world, bringing with it information, education and a familiarity with new mechanisms, both legal and social. Such experiences were, as we shall see, features of the peasantry's interaction with politics and religion and, of course, none of these influences on the peasant world acted in isolation or was independent of the other. Commercial networks and market integration facilitated the spread of political and religious ideas while the market was both a political and a religious issue for all sections of society, including the peasantry. Finally, the interaction of peasants with the market made them substantial figures in the economic life of the country, both as producers and providers of capital.[103] That economic importance also mattered when we come to consider their role in politics.

8

PEASANTS AND POLITICS

The recent historical emphasis upon commercialisation, elements of which have been outlined in the previous chapter, threatens to alter fundamentally our view of the late medieval peasantry and tensions within the medieval village. Discussion of the burdens imposed upon late medieval villagers has, traditionally, been couched in terms of lord and tenant relations and has an illustrious historiography, with Marxist historians, notably R. H. Hilton, at the forefront.[1] Central to this discussion of peasant resistance to the lord is a class-based view of the peasantry; implicit in the work of Hilton and those who have followed him is the contention that, at its essence, peasant society operated as one against lordship.[2] Although Hilton has, throughout his career, been alive to the tensions existing within peasant society and the fact that the late medieval village was clearly not egalitarian, there is an assumption that the enemy and the driving force for resistance and mutual co-operation was the lord of the manor.[3]

In recent years, this assumption has been challenged by the alternative hypothesis that the prime mover was not the lord but the market. In other words, a view of the late medieval economy which emphasises class has, to some extent, given way to one in which capital has come to dominate.[4] The medieval villager is now seen more as an individual animal, taking opportunity as it best presents itself to him or her. That opportunity could knock in this way came about because the everyday life of the villager was not constrained by the boundaries of the manor and the tenant's relation with his lord but, instead, was determined, to a considerable but variable degree, by the external forces of market demand, the lure of towns, national taxation, and the like. The location of high levels of mobility in the decades before the Black Death, delayed marriage, the growth in the number of markets and evidence for considerable demand of peasant surplus and so on, have all encouraged historians to cast the peasant producer more in the role of entrepreneur than rebel leader.[5] This, in turn, has had significant impact upon historians' view of the medieval village where tensions between peasants have assumed a new importance. Increasingly, discussion has refocused upon stratification in the medieval village. Once a major theme of the work of the so-called 'Toronto school' of historians, there is again a burgeoning awareness of the opportunities which the market presents for some villagers to advance at the expense of their peers.[6] Further, this rediscovery of the market has also meant that historians have not been obliged to await the redistributive forces of the Black Death to explain stratification, nor do they have to explain it solely in terms of tenure and the availability of holdings; instead, at least in some parts of the country, notably eastern England, and at least from the mid-thirteenth century, the land market can be shown to have been driven as much by aggressive forces of supply and demand influenced by the desire to accumulate and speculate, as by some rather more passive Chayanovian impulse.[7]

Concurrent with but largely independent of these historical explorations of commercialisation is recent work by political historians that has sought to challenge a view of the peasantry as largely isolated from the political events of the period. The research of historians such as Maddicott and Carpenter has done much to test concepts of political communities and, for the most part, to extend membership to lowlier sections of society, including the peasantry.[8] Earlier work had also shown that, even if not always as active agents, the peasantry was far from isolated from the politics of their day. Historians have long recognised peasants as the passive recipients and sufferers of national and international politics as, for example, the over-taxed source of revenue for foreign wars or as the local administrators of the medieval state.[9]

In what follows, the variety of ways in which the peasantry could be 'politicised' will be discussed. The chapter will divide into two broad sections. Beginning with local politics, both between lord and peasant and between peasant, the chapter will then proceed to investigate the role of peasants in politics beyond their local communities both as recipients and as active agents. There is a clear overlap between these sections. Shared assumptions, perhaps gained in acquaintance with the mechanisms of the state, such as the common law, could, for instance, inform peasant relations with local lords whilst, similarly, the passive experience of the peasantry, as taxpayers or as tenants, for example, clearly did promote direct action on the part of the peasantry, most obviously in the form of open revolt. Whilst therefore separating out these elements has the merit of convenience of argument, it should not disguise the variety of influences that could combine in shaping the political mentality of the peasant. Furthermore, in discussing the politicisation of the peasantry, we should conceive of 'politics' in the broadest sense, as a dynamic in which the individual takes a particular stance, a stance informed by his or her sense of right or wrong and informed by his or her own or shared experience. The politics of the family or of the local community is as central to this discussion as the politics of the state or the community of the realm.

Local Politics

Relations between lord and tenant offer the most obvious starting point for discussion of a politicised peasantry. The struggle over the exaction of rent was not only an inevitable source of tension and dispute but also, given that the historical record of the medieval peasantry is principally the product of seigneurial administration, one of which historians are particularly likely to be aware. If resistance sits at the centre of most historical discussion of lord–tenant relations in this period, it is also important to recognise that the expectations of lordship also honed the political consciousness of the peasantry. The demands of lordship may have furnished sections of the peasantry with a collective identity in their opposition to their lord, but it is also the case that, in order to meet those same demands, some amongst the peasantry, notably the more important villeins, were obliged to develop the skills of the local administrator, to acquaint themselves with documents, accounts and the law, and to travel.[10] In such ways, sections of the peasantry were partially admitted into a rather different community, the community of the realm, and were thereby able, even if they were not always inclined, to invite their peers and neighbours to join them. Further, it was not only disagreement over rent that promoted clashes between lords and their tenants: the insecurities and uncertainties of servile tenure were increasingly contested by peasants who operated in an economic and social environment in which such impediments challenged opportunity as much as they did fundamental entitlements.

We will begin with lord–tenant relations before turning to this associated aspect.

The expectations of lordship, basic elements of which have described
in Chapter 2, created a range of responses in the medieval peasantry
which ranged from mild indifference to violent hostility. For some
tenants, both free and unfree, the burden of rent relative to the other
incomes and expenses of their lives was likely to have been reasonably
comfortable, whilst for others the pressure of exactions was intense.
The famous example of the fifteenth-century villein, William Heyne at
Castle Combe, whose family paid their lord, Sir John Fastolf, a total of
almost £200, a sum predominantly arising from burdens additional to
rent, over a period of almost thirty years, indicates the extent to which
lords could and did exploit their tenantry.[11] Earlier examples of similar
heavy-handedness abound, as the huge entry fines claimed by the abbot
of Halesowen in the late thirteenth century illustrate.[12] Even where the
exactions were not so extreme, rent could still carry a social stigma.
When, by the late fourteenth century, the archbishop of Canterbury still
insisted that his unfree tenants perform carrying services, the tenants
attempted to do so secretly, ashamed by the base nature of their
obligation.[13] A century earlier, in an incident that has attracted the
attention of historians as much for its atypicality as for its general appli-
cability, a tenant of the earl of Gloucester drowned himself in the River
Severn rather than hold land as a serf.[14] The type of obligation, as we
have seen, carried legal import, a fact that also induced distinct
approaches to exaction and performance during the period.

The combination of economic weight and socio-legal penalties encouraged tenants to resist seigneurial exactions. In their resistance, the
most immediate tactic was some form of passive non-cooperation.
Manorial records are replete with examples of poor perfomance of
labour services, the withholding of money rent, non-attendance at
court and failure to act as suitors. Although the extent to which such
intransigence suggests indifference and disregard for obligations
rather than a concerted response to the demands of lordship is uncertain, there is some clear indication that rent-strikes and premeditated
'feet-dragging' were political gestures by tenants. In a pioneering arti-
cle, Hilton cites numerous examples of 'deliberate non-performance
of labour service'. To quote but one example, he finds that, on the
abbot of Ramsey's estates, there were 146 cases of non-performance
presented in the manor court in the decades either side of 1300.
Recently, Franklin has identified an even more substantial example of

collective 'rent-strike' at Thornbury (Gloucestershire), where 759 examples of poor or non-performance of labour services were recorded in the manor court rolls during the second quarter of the fourteenth century.[15] Non-performance has been seen, though not with universal acceptance, as part of a policy aimed at reducing the lord's advantage. At Thornbury, according to Franklin, rent-strikes, 'a kind of economic guerilla warfare', were one part of a concerted and ongoing campaign against the excesses of the lay lord there, whilst Hilton saw these 'obscure local clashes' as giving coherence to peasant enterprises that would see more formal expression in appeals to common law.[16]

If 'rent-strikes' were indeed part of the peasant's armoury of resistance to rapacious lordship in this period, they were certainly not the only weapons available. Faced with intransigent lords, tenants could turn to deliberate acts of negligence, clandestine dealing and violence. In the relatively minor acts of violence, of negligence and of subterfuge frequently reported in the manor court rolls, we see action but are seldom given a glimpse of motive. What, for instance, past act or grievance lay behind the actions of the tenants of Isabel, widow of Hugh Bardolph at Addington (Surrey), when, in February 1314, they 'maliciously tied together the feet of the Lady's swine'?[17] Whether such petty trespasses, which could also include hedge-breaking, allowing livestock to wander into the lord's crops, and similar malfeasances, generally constituted political acts in opposition to lordship is mootable and the same could be said of acts of waste, allowing holdings to fall into ruin. Uncertainties also surround the instances of attack on manorial officials which can be found in some number in manorial court rolls: were they as much the product of rivalry within peasant communities as they were assaults on the authority of the lord?[18] How also are we to interpret the clandestine sales of unfree land, leases without licence, and the recurrent failure to report offences, all of which appeared repeatedly as presentments in manor courts during this period?[19] Clearly some of these acts were likely to have been motivated by an intense animosity towards lordship or the product of oppressive demands which made a necessity of such actions. Others, however, may have been rather more calculated, examples of pragmatic risk-taking.

Certainly all such actions, wittingly or not, challenged lordship and, since rent and dues were, as we have seen, tests of the status of tenants *vis-à-vis* lords and the state, as embodied in the common law, it was refusal or unwillingness to render such dues to the lord that offered the most significant challenges. In the case of unfree tenants, attempts to purchase free land, or to avoid payment of marriage fines (merchet), tallage, chevage, heriot or fines for the education of offspring, not only offered potential harm to the coffers of lords but also to their legal authority. If such actions went unchecked, then the unfree tenant might throw off the taint of servility. The same was also true with the most extreme example of non-compliance: flight from the demands of lordship. Unlicensed departure of villeins from their lords' manors appears to have increased in the second half of the fourteenth century, as population decline, increased land availability on amenable terms and improved wage-labour opportunities lured villeins from their home manors. Villeins, if in fewer numbers, had taken similar opportunities to leave their manors in earlier decades also and, in all such cases and whatever the actual motive, the lord was compromised in ways that were more than strictly financial. In that sense, therefore, all activity between lord and tenant, since it was conditioned by ideas of tenure, legal status and obligation, was charged 'politically'.[20] It was, no doubt, in recognition of the importance of the issues at stake that lords attempted to stamp down with real force on those who challenged their authority in such ways. Amercements ('fines' in the modern sense of the word) imposed for such acts of malfeasance were, not unusually, much larger than the norm. Failure to pay merchet or tallage, to sell without licence or to implead villeins in courts other than the lords' could result in amercements of shillings and pounds. In 1301, a villein tenant of the Abbey of Bury St Edmunds was amerced the extraordinary sum of £4 because he had, in part, used a common law writ of trespass against others of the lord's villeins.[21] Lords could be even more stringent in their response. When, in the aftermath of the Black Death, a minor rebellion on the part of villein tenants of the Abbey of Meaux at Beforth (Yorkshire) was quelled, the cowed and defeated tenants were held in fetters in a grange at Wawne until they acknowledged their villeinage.[22] The return of runaway villeins was also more than a matter of principle, as the real efforts of lords to recapture their unfree tenants illustrate.[23] Finally, lords could be equally intolerant of land transfers which either threatened the integrity of the manorial economy or brought into question the unfree status of their tenantry. The lords' confiscation of free land purchased by villeins and its subsequent regranting as 'new rents' offers one further indication of the potential of lords to impose themselves upon their tenantry and, most importantly, of the way in which everyday

exchanges were imbued with legal and political meaning.[24] That peasants might, therefore, need more powerful forms of resistance is
evident in the way that lords were prepared to treat with contempt
such informal resistance.

Less open to questions of motive are the specific attempts to challenge the authority of lordship, either in direct petition to the lord or
through common law plea. Petitions to lords were made by individuals, small groups of tenants and whole communities. In the case of the
king's own tenants, recourse to legal action has something about it of
the tenant's petition to his lord but, for the majority of tenants, petition to their lord was an extra-curial affair. Although examples of such
petitions are quite rare, enough information survives to encourage
the belief that tenants had the confidence and the degree of awareness
to approach their lord with demands. On the Eynsham Abbey of
Woodeaton (Oxfordshire), the few tenants who had survived the first
outbreak of plague insisted that the lord alter the burden of their
tenures.[25] Most famously, in the early fourteenth century the tenants
of the prior of Canterbury's manor at Bocking (Essex) petitioned their
lord over the behaviour of his steward.[26] Such petitions could be a stage
in the initiation of more formal action, in the way that Hilton also suggests may have been the case for the withholding of rent.

As well as petitions directed to their lords, tenants were prepared
to challenge seigneurial authority at law. Most obviously, individuals
contested their status with their lord both to free themselves from
serfdom and its obligations and to avail themselves of the particular
advantages of free status.[27] Collectively, villagers combined to enquire
into the rights of their lord to make impositions of them. The development of the concept of ancient demesne and the advantages
attached to it in the thirteenth century prompted numerous attempts
by communities to prove their own association with the crown. Such
claims were founded on the belief or, at least, contention that, at the
time of Domesday, the manor on which the claimants were presently
tenants had been in the hands of the king. The tenants of the Abbey
of Bury St Edmunds at Mildenhall made such a claim by common law
writ in the early fourteenth century. Their leader, Roger Hervy, by the
Abbot's view a villein of the Abbey but by his own 'a man of the Abbot',
insisted that Mildenhall was 'ancient demesne of the Crown of England
and this is verified by Domesday Book'.[28] Pleas such as this increased
in number in the thirteenth century, during the period of high
farming, as, according to Hilton, the demands of lords also intensified.

There was also a flourish of such litigation in the third quarter of the fourteenth century, a point to which we shall need to return.[29] Not all collective action was aimed at proving ancient demesne status. In some cases, tenants simply claimed they were not unfree or, rather, that they were free. In 1279, three tenants at Garthorpe (Leicestershire) attempted to plead that their lord had increased their dues.[30] When pleas such as these came to nothing, as they frequently did, lords were not always decorous in the celebration of their triumph.[31]

While petition and rent-strike may have presented peasants with the cohesion that permitted them to proceed to collective litigation, by the same token petition and litigation may have been routes which, if they proved fruitless, led to more extreme acts of violence and open revolt. The concept of legitimate ejection of the misruler was already familiar to political theorists by the end of the thirteenth century and something broadly similar may have been in the minds of villagers during this period.[32] But there was also in the violence directed at lords (and lordly violence against their tenants), the sense of process in which violence was but one part of dispute resolution. In the occasional and seemingly *ad hoc* risings against lords in the thirteenth and early fourteenth centuries, the impetus appears to have come from long-standing tensions between lord and tenant, as is illustrated at Halesowen, where seemingly petty incidents presaged the greater struggle that was to come between the abbot and his tenants.[33] The trigger for risings was sometimes an incident on the estate or a moment of more general civil disruption or upheaval. The supposed failure of the tenants of Mildenhall to secure their status as tenants of ancient demesne helps explain, it has been suggested, their violence towards the Abbey of Bury St Edmunds in later decades of the fourteenth century. Dyer notes that the villagers of Mildenhall were in the vanguard of the rising in Suffolk in 1381.[34] Earlier, in 1327, Mildenhall men appear to have joined the townspeople of Bury and peasants from surrounding villages in attacking the Abbey and imprisoning some of the monks.[35] The response of the tenants of the abbot of Halesowen to the excessive demands and brutal tactics of their lord was a programme of petty acts of violence and destruction which eventually, in the late fourteenth century, spilled over into something closer to full-scale revolt.[36]

Ultimately, disputes between lord and tenant could turn into full-scale revolt. The Peasants' Revolt or English Rising of 1381, whilst it encompassed numerous agendas and was the product of manifold antagonisms, had issues of serfdom and seigneurial obligation at its heart. That opposition to lordship was a crucial component of the Peasants' Revolt is given foundation by the evidence of attacks on the property and person of lords by their tenants during the course of the revolt. The well-known assaults on the Abbeys of Bury and of St Albans during the revolt included symbolic acts which harped back to ancient disputes. At St Albans, the rebels tore up a paving constructed from mill-stones which had been confiscated from the abbey's tenants. The confiscation of the mill-stones had obliged the tenants to use the abbey's mill and to pay a customary rent to do so. The destruction of the pavement was probably a long-cherished notion.[37] Further symbols of lordship were also identified for destruction during the revolt. As well as the manor houses and other property of lords, seigneurial documents, such as manorial court rolls, where they could be found, were destroyed. Timber on estates was cut down and livestock driven onto the lords' demesnes. Violence did not stop at property. In Suffolk, the prior of Bury and a chief justice were killed by the rebels. The death of the former appears to have been either at the hands of or with the considerable support of Bury's tenants at Mildenhall.[38]

In these more extreme acts of the peasantry, it is difficult to identify a clear agenda. There appears to be something terminal in such action but that would be to misread events. The destruction of records of tenure and the killing of lords and their men may have the feel of desperate acts but the irony is that, by the time of these most violent outpourings in 1381, the condition of most men and women in the countryside was improving. The further irony is that the leaders of the revolt were not the poorest villagers but the village elite.[39] The Peasants' Revolt and other more extreme manifestations of the tenant–lord dispute were, in that sense, spectacular episodes in a continuum in which, from the thirteenth century, we repeatedly witness complaint and dispute generated not by the hopelessly oppressed but by those who sought to shake off the shackles of lordship because they were aware of real opportunities elsewhere. The villagers who collectively sued their lords at common law were typically the wealthier members of their communities, as were the villagers who provided the impetus for the Peasants' Revolt.[40] These were the same villagers who, in other contexts, might be most inclined to identify their interests with those of their lord.[41] An awareness of such economic and social distinctions within the ranks of the peasantry and the agendas which they could generate should also, therefore, encourage us to consider the internal politics of the village.

In discussing tenant–lord disputes in this period, historians have, to varying degrees, presented the peasantry as a force, group or class, combined in its opposition to lordship. These combinations, it is also recognised, were not amorphous lumps espousing a single interest but were composed of distinct sections of the peasantry. Economic distinctions within the community created, as has already been discussed, tensions and rivalries. Not only did individuals vie with each other as equals in competitive markets but success or failure in such dealings helped to create the sub-groups and stratified society conducive to social and economic exclusion.[42] Social tension within the medieval village community is revealed, for example, in the violence displayed by wealthier villagers to their poorer neighbours, in the various incidents of housebreaking and illegal distraint, and in the occasional attacks meted on individuals or their property by fellow villagers supported by armed gangs which had presumably been organised for the purpose.[43] In a similar way to that of tenants' relations with their lords, the tensions between villagers could revolve around issues of status, obligation and expectation. Debt and trespass litigation recorded in manorial court rolls illustrates the sorts of contractual and tortious relationships which could exist between neighbours in the village community. Issues of service, of loans, of leases, as well as of unneighbourliness and recklessness (encroachment, poor maintenance of ditches, and similar acts of nuisance) provide us with some sense of the normative behaviour deemed appropriate within such communities and of the attitude of the community to those who breached agreed bounds of behaviour.[44]

Campaigns of gossip and the reporting of inappropriate behaviour within the village, as well as more formal mechanisms, encouraged good or, at least, normal behaviour. Especially in areas of open-field husbandry, by-laws regulated the access to and use of the arable and pasture and controlled movement within and beyond the village. Restriction of carting by night, penalties for housing strangers during the harvest, the setting of times for entering the common fields, and the control of the marketing of produce all limited personal freedom, even if they did not necessarily represent the collective will of the community.[45] Office-holders also oversaw appropriate standards of behaviour and were influential in regulating the community. The lord's officials resident within the village – reeves, bailiffs and haywards – ensured that the manorial economy functioned according to the expectations of the lord.[46] Jurors in the manor court, whether they ruled according to substantive legal principles or factual equities, still expressed an elite view through their findings and their judgments.[47] In the regulation of the vill, that is the geographical unit rather than the legal entity that was the manor, a range of officials, whose ranks typically included the same men who were important manorial officers, were responsible for the standard of general behaviour in the village. The smallest units of criminal and quasi-criminal policing, such as the ancient frankpledge system, through which males over 12 were divided into groups or 'tithings' where their behaviour was overseen by chief pledges, and the constable of the vill, presented upon and were obliged to ensure the good behaviour of those within their charge.[48] Such systems of mutual responsibility also found their expression in legal institutions such as the hue and cry, which required that individuals call forth the community against malefactors and through which the role of peacekeeper was extended beyond the office-holders and the worthies of village society to include all villagers. Finally, parish officials such as churchwardens and guild officers also oversaw the more practical aspects of pious expression and, by the fifteenth century, provided a further check on the excess of the wayward.[49]

The role of officers rather than that of the whole community in determining the limits of normative behaviour looks to have increased during the period. The concept of the whole community of the vill as law-giver in manor courts, most evident during the thirteenth century when plaintiffs and the lord both looked to the wider community for their law, gave way to smaller units of jurisdiction, such as the jury of presentment in the early fourteenth century.[50] The policing function of the tithing group had diminished by the early fourteenth century and the use of hue and cry to apprehend malefactors also declined after $c.1350$.[51] By the fifteenth century, there is also indication that officers and the wealthier villagers, those most conversant with the institutions of law and church, were increasingly assiduous in their attempts to impose these learned norms.[52] That said, throughout the period, village communities contained a sub-group of upper and middling villagers whose role as mouth-pieces and self-appointed consciences of the community was really quite pronounced.[53] The maintenance of community and the control or ejection of those who threatened the security of local communities were, in themselves, political acts which were encouraged not just by the natural justice of the village and countryside but were informed by external institutions, including the law and the church. The imposition of such standards might, in itself, have been a cause of tension and a stimulant to 'anti-social behaviour'. Teenage violence and the apparent correlation of extra-marital sexual relations and illegitimacy with the non-elites of the village, both observed for the medieval village, could be considered acts of social discontent and rebellion against communal norms of behaviour.[54]

If differences over communal agendas and attempts to impose normative behaviour by village elites might act as stimuli to intra-village tension, the day-to-day approach of these elites to their role in the community and to their office were also potential sources of friction. It was clearly the case that individual villagers might perceive their interest to lie not in the support of their community but in adherence to some other, and better, benefit, such as the market or the lord. In the advantage which accrued to one villager and the consequent cost to another, the seeds of dispute and feud could be planted. Where the advantage fell to those who were perceived as leaders of a community, then the tenor of debate shifted from one of individual rivalry to that of collective censure. While, therefore, disputes within the village had much to do with economic opportunities and the degree to which individuals felt able to avail themselves of them, disputes between self-serving office-holders and other villagers also became overtly political in the sense that judgement was made on such matters as the performance of office, and appropriate modes of dealing. In other words, the community could employ the failure of the office-holder to re-emphasise its own criteria of action for the common good and to remind others, should the need arise.

The abuse of office, an essentially political act, could work to the advantage or to the disadvantage of the community of the vill. In an earlier chapter, we considered ways in which manorial officers might respond to communal pressure in concealing offences. Village office-holders, such as affeerors (who established the level of penalties in manorial courts), reeves, bailiffs, chief pledges and manor court jurors, could and did work to the advantage of their peers and to the detriment of their lord.[55] The concealment of offences and the latitude extended to labourers reveal that, as Justice has recently argued, manorial officials, as tenants, owed a *trewþe* to each other which surpassed any obligation to their lord.[56] There was, however, also the possibility for certain wealthy villagers, holding such office as reeve, to side with the lord rather than their fellows. At Elton (Huntingdonshire) famously, in the late thirteenth century, the reeve extorted money from tenants with threats to change their conditions of tenure.[57] That through such action, officers and members of the village elite could, to follow Justice's line, be deemed *untrewe* by their fellow villagers is suggested by the occasional glimpses in manorial court rolls which illustrate ways in which the community could turn on those who were deemed to have betrayed it: accusations of the misappropriation of goods, concerted resistance to the demands of individual office-holders, acts of violence and the forced recovery of distrained property could be construed as political gestures, undermining the administration of the manor and bringing into question the rightfulness of the lord's jurisdiction. The community could go further and employ the misdeeds of the officials to improve its own standing. By petitioning those with authority over recalcitrant officials, the village community was presented with an opportunity to lay claim to rights and to appeal to ancient precedent. At Bocking, the heavy-handedness of the steward of the prior of Canterbury provided a chance for the prior's tenants to remind the prior of their rights with regard to such important matters as the transfer of free land, suit of court, frankpledge jurisdiction, and the level of rents.[58]

As we have already had cause to note, tension and dispute between lord and tenant and amongst villagers was not an internalised affair. Recent work by historians has shown how villagers employed frames of reference and agendas gleaned from external sources.[59] Thus, instruction in Christian morality and charity, as we shall see in the next chapter, informed behaviour in the village, an awareness of law and its possibilities encouraged villagers against their lords, and a grasp of external market opportunities loosened the bonds that tied one villager to another. Some of these influences were sought out by villagers, who read or listened to improving texts or sermons, who gained elements of education in law and who took an interest in the matters of high politics. Others, however, were imposed, heedless of the will of the villager. We now need to consider more fully the points of political contact between the peasantry and the world beyond.

Peasants and External 'Politics'

Peasants as passive recipients

Aside from the most extreme expressions of active peasant engagement with politics, an aspect that will be discussed later in this chapter, consideration of peasants and politics beyond the manor and vill has tended to concentrate on the relative passivity of rural dwellers. Peasants are seen as society's payers and natural victims.[60] It was the peasant population that, without its consent, supported the initiatives of medieval government through taxation, provided for its armies with men and with kind, and suffered the depradations of national and civil strife. It was also from the peasant ranks that the lower rungs of administrators were drawn to help maintain peace in the countryside, serve as jurors, tax-assessors and collectors, witnesses, suitors and so on.

The peasantry could suffer the depradations of high politics in the most immediate of ways. In particular, the endemic warfare of the high and late Middle Ages could have devastating consequences for the peasantry. In the north of England, the campaigns of English armies against the Scots and the frequent raids deep into England by the Scots themselves led to the destruction or theft of crops and livestock and the slaughter of the peasantry.[61] As the chronicler Trokelowe wrote, for the year 1315,

> Meanwhile the Scots, with their forces, moved throughout the whole of Northumberland and the Western parts, from Carlisle to York, slaughtering and looting without any opposition, and destroying with sword and flame whatever crossed their path. And it is known that there remained in those parts nowhere where the English could be safe, unless it was within the town of Carlisle or the borough of Newcastle Upon Tyne or the Priory of Tynemouth or in other castles throughout Northumbria, which were guarded with tiresome effort and a huge amount of supplies. To these few places fled the people from the countryside, together with those who did not have sufficient means with which to pay the Scots tribute, as they had been accustomed to do on many occasions previously in order to save their wretched lives.[62]

For a shorter period during the high and late Middle Ages, and possibly to a lesser degree, those living in the Welsh Marches also suffered from the conflict between English and Welsh.[63] Whilst the south and east were relatively isolated from such predations, villagers, especially in the southern counties, did not entirely escape first-hand experience of raiding. French attacks on the south coast, especially in the 1370s, and the tendency of English troops embarking for the campaigns of the Hundred Years War to run amok, both caused considerable suffering amongst the rural population.[64] Internecine warfare and the clashes of baronial gangs and overmighty subjects also, undoubtedly, affected the lives of peasants and their communities from time to time. The random consequence of being the tenant of the 'wrong' lord or simply living in the way of a marauding force could have disastrous consequences. During the events which led to civil war in 1322, the opponents of Edward II and his favourites attacked the estates of the Despensers and destroyed whatever they could find.[65] Rivalry between retainers or the general lawlessness of the overmighty, disillusioned or downright rebellious, could all redound to the severe disadvantage of the peasantry. During the Wars of the Roses, in 1463–4, a period of Lancastrian control in Norhamshire in the north-east of England, the lands and tenements of tenants of the prior of Durham returned reduced rents 'because of the [civil?] war (*guerra*) and the invasions of the Scots and on account of the waste created by the rebels against the lord king Edward [IV]'.[66] Aside from violent conflict, everyday disputes between the lords of tenants could have adverse effects on villagers, as lordly plaintiffs distrained the goods of their neighbours. To quote one example: a dispute over land between the Abbey of Meaux and a local knight, Sayer of Sutton, in the middle years of the thirteenth century, resulted in the death of one of Sayer's unfree tenants.[67]

Beside these more extreme encounters, in the relatively ordinary everyday running of government in later medieval England, the peasantry was likely to encounter the machinery of the state through three main avenues: taxation, military levies, and the law. In each case, the villager's experience might simply be an inert one, as the payer of a subsidy, or as the guilty criminal, but it is also possible that he, but not she, would be called upon to act in some capacity which facilitated the operation of either system. Hence, at law, the villager might appear in criminal cases at the assizes, as a juror for his village, or as the person responsible for producing a malefactor apprehended within his vill; in terms of taxation, the state was heavily reliant on local men for the assessment and collection of goods and money, as it was also reliant on these men to respond to summons for military levies.

To begin with taxation, the incidence of taxation showed a general increase in this period. While taxation by the crown in England pre-dates the twelfth century, the form of taxation and its extent underwent significant development in the thirteenth century. As older forms of levy, mostly those arising from the obligations of the more elevated free tenures or impositions on the crown lands, fell into abeyance, they came to be replaced by an array of taxes that were levied on goods more than they were on land. From the reign of Edward I, the

employment of taxes on a percentage of moveable goods, the lay subsidies, took centre stage as a source of revenue. There were other
developments in the late thirteenth century, such as the establishment
of the customs duties on exports while purveyance and prises
(arbitrary and *ad hoc* seizures of foodstuffs) provided for the royal
household or supported military levies. Military levies were also a
source of revenue: while those who campaigned with the English army
or undertook some other military function, such as coast-guard, paid
with part or all of their lives, members of their communities were
increasingly expected to pay for their attendance. The form of taxation continued to undergo developments after the thirteenth century.
Before the middle of the fourteenth century, the individual assessment
of lay subsidy payers had been replaced by single sums from each
township. In order to finance the early stages of the Hundred Years'
War, Edward III also attempted novel levies on wool production and
export, such as a ninth of all sheaves, fleeces and lambs for two years
from 1340. In the second half of the fourteenth century, in the wake
of the ravages of plague, further innovations were attempted, including the introduction of a parish tax in 1371 and, most famously, the
poll-taxes of the late 1370s and 1380. In the fifteenth century, direct
taxation of the mass of the laity diminished, to be partially replaced
by taxation of baronial income, but lay subsidies in particular persisted, if, relative to the decades either side of 1300, muted in their
incidence.[68]

The general effect of these developments was to pass the burden
increasingly to the poorer members of society and reduce the burden
of the wealthiest. Even under an earlier and apparently less onerous
revenue-raising system, one which was more closely linked to the landholding of substantial tenants, the potential for those who were
expected to pay to pass the burden on to their poorer tenants should
not be overlooked.[69] With the development of the lay subsidy and, in
the late thirteenth and early fourteenth century, an energetic employment of purveyance and prise, the burden of direct taxation fell on
the peasantry to an unheralded degree. Between 1290 and 1337,
during the period of intense employment of the lay subsidy, levies on
moveables were collected on four or five occasions per decade, with
the exception of the 1320s when, during the period of Edward II's
'tyranny' between 1322 and 1326, direct taxation was replaced with
other, more direct, money-raising tactics.[70] The inequity of the lay
subsidy came in its basis of assessment. An assessment based on move-

ables penalised less those whose chief income came from rents than it did the non-rentier sections of society. To quote Maddicott, 'Tenants . . . who needed to produce both to maintain themselves and to find the money for rents and dues demanded by their lords, were bound to be caught within the net of the subsidy'.[71] Although a threshold was established for taxes on moveables, this was set at fairly low levels so that, on average, the upper third of villagers in any community might be expected to contribute directly.[72] Even those who did not contribute directly suffered as the burden of the tax was frequently passed to the poorer members of the community. This was achieved in various ways, as, for instance, when local assessors extorted bribes from the poorer villagers in order to avoid adverse assessments. After 1334, when individual assessment was abandoned in favour of a lump sum payment by the community, it has been suggested that the wealthier payers of direct taxation were even more inclined to pass the burden onto their poorer neighbours.[73] Purveyance was at least as onerous. An inability to afford the substantial bribes that could deflect the attention of the king's purveyors made the peasantry especially vulnerable. The incidence of purveyance, unlike the taxes on moveables, was geographically limited, reflecting the productivity and infrastructure of regions. Thus, the East Midlands and East Anglia, grain-yielding areas with good transport networks to the north, bore the brunt of purveyance in the later thirteenth and early fourteenth centuries during a time of frequent campaigning against the Scots.[74] The seizure of goods not only removed livestock and grain from the countryside but also pushed up the price of the grain that remained. Even where the immediate costs of purveyance were met by the relatively wealthy, the effective incidence of purveyance could still be passed on to the peasantry, as at Crowland in 1314 where the lord increased one element of the customary rent in order to compensate for the expenses of purveyance.[75] Lords could also transmit the effects of taxation such as purveyance to individual tenants. On the Durham Priory manor of Kirke-Merington (Co. Durham), in 1296, a plea was brought against a bond tenant, Gilbert Pape, because he was unable to perform carriage-service to Durham on account of the illness of his horses; in the absence of Pape's horse a priory official, William Serjeant of Merrington, had been obliged to use one of the prior's mares to cart the produce to Durham where it was seized by the king's officers to carry goods to northern parts, presumably for the war against the Scots, from whence it did not return.[76]

The same transmission of the burden of taxation almost certainly occurred in relation to more remote forms of taxation, notably the custom duties, and could still have a deleterious effect on peasant producers, causing prices to fall as merchants, especially wool merchants, attempted to pass some of the burden onto the growers.[77] Later developments in direct taxation, responses to changing demographic, economic and political circumstance, also placed pressures on rural dwellers. That, for instance, the poll-taxes of the late fourteenth century were deemed excessive is evident both in their initial evasion and the eventual concomitant violent reaction. The poll-taxes of 1377, 1379 and 1380 were described by one contemporary chronicler as 'new and almost unbearable burdens which appeared to be endless and without remedy'.[78] Hyperbole, certainly, but payment of the first poll-tax in 1377 did produce a substantial yield. The yield was not matched in subsequent exactions, even though the later versions of the poll-tax were less regressive than that of 1377.[79] The taxes themselves may have been less a spark to revolt in 1381 than were the unwelcome administrative innovations of the later Edwardian government, including the appointment of commissioners to enforce payment of the 1380 poll-tax, a point to which we will return below, and taxation does not feature prominently in the stated grievances of the rebels in London.[80]

In ways broadly reminiscent of developments in direct taxation, the raising of armies underwent significant modification during this period and added to the demands faced by the peasantry in this period. Most especially, the weight of the obligation to provide forces for the campaigns of the crown shifted from the major tenants of the crown, the great lords and the lesser nobility, to the townships of England. The obligation for men of each community to be armed for defence and the effective policing of their communities was an ancient one but was re-enacted by the Statute of Winchester (1285). Villagers, theoretically practised in the use of arms, served as a pool of soldiery for English armies and were systematically used as such from the thirteenth century while English kings also experimented with ways of deflecting the additional costs of provisioning to local communities. The Lincoln Parliament of 1316 provides an early example of this new system in its injunction that

> the men of the township shall provide the arms of the foot-soldiers [i.e. 'one able-bodied foot-soldier from every township in England', saving royal demesne] at their own expense, and the expenses of the soldiers on the way

to the place to which the king shall summon his army for his war, and their wages after his arrival, for sixty days at most, while waiting there or proceeding on the king's service, at the rate of fourpence a day for each infantryman.[81]

At the same time, the size of armies, the expense of arms and armour, and the frequency of campaigns had all increased in this period; again, it has been suggested that the overall effect of such developments was to make additional impositions upon the finances of the peasantry.[82] Whilst the campaigns of the late thirteenth and early fourteenth centuries were the largest of the period, warfare continued to be conducted by the English crown on a number of fronts throughout the fourteenth and fifteenth centuries. Although the English armies employed in France were smaller than those arrayed in England for the wars against the Welsh and the Scots, Edward III and Henry V both took armies of 15,000 men to France, and the majority of these came from hamlets, villages and small townships. Although, as has been noted by more than one historian, the economic effects of these levies were unlikely to have been devastating for regions, in terms either of manpower recruited or the associated costs, the military levies, frequently acting in combination with other impositions, could be significant indeed.[83]

Taxation was a mainstay of government in the Middle Ages. It helped provide government with form and identity: issues of revenue – how it should be raised, with whose consent and to what purpose – underpinned debates over the nature of power and the degree to which various elements of society had a determinative role. The administration of taxation, although issuing from the centre of government through the king, his council, and, increasingly from the mid-fourteenth century, parliament, was dependent upon local men. Individuals in each township or village were expected to oversee the assessment of taxation on an individual basis and to organise its collection.[84] That there existed men in the countryside sufficiently attuned to the workings of government that they could meet its expectations was principally a product of law.[85]

Individual villagers might, of course, fall foul of law as defendants in civil cases or as the accused in criminal trials, and thereby gain a first-hand acquaintance of legal process. Increasingly, also, government sought to regulate the lives and labour of individuals and looked to law to enforce that regulation. The establishment of labour legislation in 1349 and 1351 with the Ordinance and Statute of Labourers and their subsequent re-enactments meant that illegal movement of labourers, the taking or giving of excessive wages, and breaches of contract fell within the jurisdiction of criminal sessions.[86] Earlier attempts to fix prices, such as the Ordinance of 1315, illustrate the potential for law to invade and contain the everyday dealings of men and women, in town and countryside, but in this case no means of enforcement was established and the experiment was quickly abandoned.[87] The encounter with law could be almost as immediate for those who failed to meet legal requirements in other ways: by the end of the thirteenth century, failure by communities to bring criminals to book meant a financial penalty for members of the community concerned.

In addition to these forced impositions of law, important sections of rural society below the level of the gentry acquired their understanding of law as practitioners of it. Hyams remarks that English peasants in the thirteenth century made their first acquaintance with law 'at their father's knee' and that, in the medieval village, legal consciousness was 'an aspect of general culture'.[88] In terms of matters criminal, this meant that villagers gained an early sense of the structures of law, locally, as well as its expectations. The system of frankpledge, which required all males over the age of twelve to be members of tithings [*decennae*], was an early imposition of law upon the villager. Others followed: general obligations of pursuit of criminals were bolstered by more particular requirements. The Statute of Winchester (1285), as already mentioned above in the context of military levies, required

> that every man have in his house arms for keeping the peace in accordance with the ancient assize [of arms]; that is to say, every man between fifteen years of age and sixty years, shall be assessed and sworn to armour according to the quantity of their lands and goods.[89]

Law also required that these policing institutions were reviewed. The requirements of the Statute of Winchester were to be ensured by the scrutiny of constables who were to make the 'view of arms' whilst the tithing system was overseen by a bi-annual 'view of frankpledge', where the right to hold the view was held privately, or, in the case of royal jurisdiction, the sheriff's tourn. Minor criminal or semi-criminal matters could be dealt with in the private jurisdiction of a lord but, increasingly, legal redress for the more significant crimes, felonies, became the prerogative of the crown.[90] The minor crimes, trespasses, might proceed no further than the view of frankpledge or the sheriff's tourn, where local men, in their capacity as suitors, tithingmen and representatives of their lords, had important roles to play. It was here that petty criminals were presented and the collectivity of the suitors or their representatives responded to the articles of the tourn or view of frankpledge, a list of misdemeanours against which they not only reviewed the affairs of the last year but were reminded, as if by rote, of the basic elements of neighbourliness and law-abiding behaviour.[91] Trespasses also found their way to the county court and here also came the same men of the village. As well as the great of the county, many lesser figures would also have attended, including suitors owing attendance on account of their tenure, jurors, witnesses and, in civil actions, litigants.[92] Even the county courts could not deal with felonies, such as treason, arson or murder. Instead, the apprehended criminal had to await the itinerant justices of the central courts. The eyre of the high Middle Ages, the assizes and the commissions of gaol delivery, trailbaston, oyer and terminer, which toured the shire courts and dealt there with the more serious crimes, were also dependent for their function upon local men.[93] From the early fourteenth century, the central court of King's Bench was sent into the localities to inquire into cases of lawlessness, a development that gained a degree of permanence in the fourteenth century and was not unlike the earlier commissions.[94] The presence of the itinerant justices within a county would not have escaped the attention of its residents since all other business, including the work of local courts, was suspended for the duration of their visit.

The articles of the eyre, following the precedent of the Assize of Clarendon (1166), were the basis of inquiry of jurors from local administrative units, including the private jurisdictions of the hundred and the manor.[95] This meant that villagers were expected to attend, and not always to their advantage. During his attendance at eyres at Cattishall (1287) and at Norwich (1286), Nicholas Wodeward, a villein of the Abbey of Bury St Edmunds, had been cuckolded by another villager, Robert the son of Adam, who had come to his house and commenced an affair with his wife.[96] Whilst jurors were typically freemen, and must therefore have included smaller freeholders, including peasants, there is some indication that villeins might serve as jurors. In Lincolnshire in the late thirteenth century, a local administrator, the hundred-bailiff, extorted 4s. from John Parys of South Witham, villein, so that he should not have to attend the assize nor serve as juror.[97] Such tactics were commonplace in the thirteenth century, and although attempt had been made to control them by the Statute of Westminster II (1285), it was only to limited effect. Attendance as suitor and juror was an imposition which added to the burdens of the peasantry.[98] Coroners also expected that local jurors would present to them on suspicious deaths.[99]

Increasingly, however, during the fourteenth century, the role of the villager within the workings of criminal law was diminished, a consequence of the rise of the justices of the peace and the disappearance of the eyre and, subsequently, the commissions. The appointment of local gentry and magnates as justices of the peace was perhaps the most important development, in terms both of changes in legal apparatus and the common experience of legal process, in the late Middle Ages. Justices held sessions relating to felony and trespass which were very similar to the earlier sessions of eyres and of commissions. Articles of inquiry were established and local jurors attended in order to respond to them. The difference from earlier practice came in personnel; where once the justices had come from the central courts, these justices of the peace were local men. Any relief that villagers may have experienced by a decline in duties as jurors was tempered by a certain loss of leverage within the county community, as the authority of the county court declined, a point to which we shall need to return. There was also the sense that the same men who were local landlords and employers also had legal authority which could be abused, an impression that was given focus from the second half of the fourteenth century when justices of the peace took over responsibility for the enforcement of labour legislation.

Villagers had similar roles within the operation of civil jurisdiction. The structure of courts was essentially the same as that operating for felonies, trespasses and acts of petty criminality. At the most local level of the manor, lords established their own courts, courts baron, which, in addition to facilitating the regulation of the manor and the village community, including the conveyance of customary land, provided fora for personal actions, that is, litigation between villagers. For these courts to operate, an array of officers, drawn from local men, needed to be employed. As we have already seem, an expectation in the thirteenth century was that all tenants owed suit, or attendance, at these manor courts and that they, as the 'whole homage' or 'whole court', could be called upon to judge the rights and wrongs of particular cases. Increasingly, juries of presentment replaced these more general bodies whilst personal actions, following developments in common law, also increasingly relied upon inquest juries rather than older forms of proof.[100] The members of these juries were drawn from the body of manorial tenants, as were other officers of the manor court, such as the affeerors. Beyond the manor court, villagers, especially the free, were obliged to attend the hundred and shire or county courts, especially during the eyres and assizes.[101] Individual villagers were also obliged to attend at the behest of other authority, such as their lords. Maddicott has suggested that villagers attended county courts in official capacity, often as mainpernors for their lords at times of election. When elections for parliament were held in the county court, mainpernors attended to guarantee that their lords, if elected, would present themselves at parliament. Maddicott suggests that these mainpernors included reeves who, although manorial officers, were also servile.[102]

Peasants as active agents

The effect of systems of law, taxation, and the devastations of warfare, was not solely to oppress the peasantry, although this was undoubtedly achieved to certain measure. Engagement with systems of government and the travails and struggles of political elites also served to educate and to involve the peasantry, or certain sections of the peasantry. Attendance on campaign was, for instance, an opportunity to gain a clearer sense of the political purpose and the nature of government.[103] Similarly, whilst the importance of the labour legislation of the late fourteenth century and its antecedents has been assessed from a number of perspectives, its most enduring effect may have been to alter the 'political attitudes of peasant society'. Legal historians, notably Palmer, have emphasised the ways in which legislation after the Black Death encouraged a greater regard for obligation and promoted a culture of obedience.[104] This education and involvement was then redeployed by the peasantry in matters closer to home but it also encouraged members of the peasantry to seek an active participating membership in the community of the realm. In this final section, an attempt will be made to establish some of the ways in which medieval peasants attempted to effect change in what they perceived as their own political circumstance. This will also encourage us to consider the limits of the political horizons of the peasantry.

We have already seen that, on the manor, in dealings between tenant and lord as well as between tenant and tenant, individual peasants and collectives could take initiative in attempting to ameliorate their condition. In their contact with law and government, peasants were capable of displaying the same initiative. Whilst the peasantry, despite the provisions of the Assize of Arms and the Statute of Winchester, may not have been equipped to do a great deal more than flee physical force, such as the marauding armies of the Scots, in other encounters with 'external politics', peasants were able to play a more self-determined role.

In their obligations to the machinery of government, as minor administrators and as payers of tax, peasants were not slavish. Most obviously, peasants did not always pay what was expected of them. As direct forms of taxation increased in their frequency, so peasants learned the techniques of evasion.[105] The responses to the Inquisitions of the Ninth in 1340 illustrate not just the poverty of communities but their ability to spin a line. Excuses for failure to match the demands of the taxors included insistence that flocks had been decimated by disease and cereals by the weather. Most interestingly of all, communities were not beyond using the levy of previous taxes as an excuse for non-payment, as at Long Stowe (Cambridgeshire), where the villagers explained that their poor return was on account of the greater part of the 'land remaining uncultivated because of the weakness of the tenants who are vexed and destroyed by the frequent taxes and tallages of the king'.[106] Military levies could be similarly avoided, to the extent that campaigns had to be aborted, as happened in 1316. In that year, villagers at Wakefield (Yorkshire) refused, in large number, to respond to the summons for a Scottish campaign.[107] Although villagers paid for their non-attendance with amercements and fines, they achieved their primary aim.

In these responses, peasants were not always behaving according to shared agendas. At Wakefield, Thomas Beghe of Holne, having been elected to the king's army in 1316, and having subsequently withdrawn himself, was forced to pay a fine of 20s 'for his delivery and restoration of status', his dereliction presumably a threat to the community which would have been fined for failing to meet their obligation.[108] Similarly, there is, as has already been discussed in an earlier chapter, indication that villagers attempted to avoid taxation on moveables by converting moveable wealth into immoveable wealth, that is, land. The effect of this may have been to pass the burden of taxation on to neighbours in much the same way as the corrupt local assessors and collectors were also capable of advantaging themselves at the expense of their fellow villagers.[109]

What was true for taxation and other levies was also the case for office-holding and the law. In the first place, jurors and suitors might simply fail to attend court as Goheen's recent analysis of fifteenth-century quarter session juries shows.[110] The jurors empanelled to inquire into wrongdoing did not always respond in the ways that law and government expected of them.[111] The authors of the Statute of Winchester (1285) recognised the significance of this problem, complaining that

> forasmuch as from day to day, robberies, murders, burnings and thefts be more often used than they have been heretofore, and felons cannot be attainted by the oath of jurors which had rather suffer felonies done to strangers to pass without pain, than to indict the offenders of whom great part be people of the same country.

Henceforth, felons were to be dealt with according to the full force of the law and, in order to achieve this,

> cries shall be solemnly made in all counties, hundreds, markets, fairs, and all other places where great resort of people is, so that none shall exempt himself by ignorance.[112]

Willful ignorance could not be so easily combated and jurors recognised obligations to more than just the law and the crown. Both in their desire to avoid penalty for failure to apprehend criminals or detect crimes and in their unwillingness to hand over members of their communities to the justices, village jurors employed their own devices to circumvent the expectations of law and to escape its censure. This is especially obvious when corpses moved at night, villagers choosing to relocate homicide victims to neighbouring jurisdictions in order to 'minimize their inevitable financial obligations for murdrum fines, felons' chattels, deodands and amercements of all kinds'.[113]

Whilst individuals and communities could and did distort their relationship with government and the law in order to accommodate their own needs and designs but principally to avoid further penalty, peasants also chose to engage with the 'state' during this period. The seeking out by the peasantry of relationships with elements of government encourages us to abandon notions of a peasantry passive in the face of the high and late medieval crown and its bureaucracy. Villagers may have sought official and administrative roles in order to secure financial benefit, as we have seen in the case of tax-assessors, but there is good reason to assume that motive for taking office was also political. To attend the county court as a juror or suitor, for instance, was to enter the world of county politics and, by extension, national politics. By the late fourteenth and early fifteenth centuries, villagers attending the county court may have begun to threaten 'real' political engagement since, in 1429, parliamentary legislation was issued to set property and legal status qualifications on those persons eligible to vote for members of parliament. Two decades later, in 1445/6, parliament refused yeomen and those of inferior rank the right to stand as prospective members of parliament.[114]

Deliberate peasant engagement in this respect is perhaps best revealed through the use of law. In their dealings with lords, as we have seen, villagers were prepared to employ courts to contest seigneurial rights.[115] In their personal actions, the peasantry also reveal an acquaintance with the law which was, in part, product of their attendance as jurors but also borne of an acceptance that the remedies, titles and protection that the law offered were worth having. In their variety of legal activities, peasants displayed, *inter alia*, an acquaintance with due process, statute, land law, litigation techniques and the possessory assizes. They were also aware of the range of courts available to them as well as being versed in the tactics of law, including the interchange of extra-curial violence and resort to legal remedy.[116]

Beyond the organs of the state, the peasantry showed a further engagement in their apparent awareness of matters of high politics. The fifteenth-century commonplace book of Robert Reynes, an East Anglian reeve, contains, for instance, the dates and battles of the Wars of the Roses.[117] Isobel Harvey has recently surveyed a number of instances of popular political violence in the late-fourteenth and fifteenth centuries, beginning with the events in Essex in 1400 when peasants lynched the earl of Huntingdon in revenge for his part in the murder of Thomas, duke of Gloucester. She suggests that such acts were informed and that, by the fifteenth century, the changed social and economic circumstance had sharpened the popular political consciousness.[118] Whilst that may be true to a degree, there is also little doubt that thirteenth and fourteenth century villagers also enjoyed a fairly developed sense of high politics. The initiatives of peasant communities were frequently timed to coincide with and take full advantage of moments of political upheaval or uncertainty. Claims by tenants for alleged ancient demesne status not infrequently coincided with periods of unrest, such as 1327, the year of the deposition of Edward II, or of apparent opportunity, as at the succession of Edward I, and may have been attempts to hijack broader political issues. That, for instance, pleas relating to ancient demesne increased in the early years of Edward I's reign may indicate that peasants saw their chance with the succession of a vigorous new king who had attached himself to the early stages of the baronial reform movement.[119]

Peasant awareness of high politics throughout the period went beyond a rudimentary grasp of the major events. The events at Peatling Magna (Leicestershire) in 1265, when peasants attacked a royalist captain and his men because they were against 'the welfare of the community of the realm', were but one indication of the willingness of the peasantry to take sides in the baronial disputes of the thirteenth century.[120] Two hundred years later, the events of Cade's revolt were precipitated by a strong sense of the failings of the duke of Suffolk.[121] While personalities and simple slogans may have dominated a good deal of the sense of high politics amongst the peasantry in this period, there is also evidence to suggest that the peasantry was capable of a rather more nuanced engagement with government and the machinations of the realm. A remarkable feature of the Peasants' Revolt is that the revolt was not just a series of personal vendettas but a mass movement with more generalised aims, principally of a 'political character'.[122] As Harding has shown, the concerns of the rebels in 1381 to return to the communal policing envisaged in the late thirteenth-century Statute of Winchester reflects not only an ongoing debate concerning the administration of justice in the countryside but also echoes debates in the parliament of 1380.[123]

Even if we accept that a combination of obligation and their own volition provided medieval English peasants with a reasonably sophisticated sense of government and politics, did this transform them into active participants or leave them as moderately well-informed victims? Although peasants had no actual voice in politics and government, and were excluded from real authority, they did enjoy access to the lower rungs of administration. As we have seen, they could effect significant changes in the nature of their obligation to the crown and improve their lot as individuals accordingly. It was, however, in their cumulative responses to the demands and policies of the crown that peasants effected signal changes in key aspects of government. The apprehension which the perceived collectivity of the peasantry caused those in power had direct effect on governmental initiatives.

It is clear, for instance, that contemporaries were aware of the potential threat which high levels of taxation contained for society. Time and again, in the thirteenth and fourteenth centuries, counsellors to the king warned of the dangers of provoking those who paid taxes.[124] The poems of the early fourteenth century also speak powerfully of the oppressions which the poor suffered on account of poor harvests and high levels of frequent taxation. In the *Song against the King's Taxes* (*c*.1338–9?), the poet declares that the people would rise if they could find a leader,

> Such tribute cannot be paid forever;
> Lacking, who can give or touch with hands?
> People suffer such ill that they can give no more;
> I don't doubt that, if they had a leader, they would rise.[125]

Lords were also forced to acknowledge the potential threat of their own tenantry in the face of excessive taxation: it was not just concerns over their own economic loss which prompted lords to bribe royal taxers during this period.[126] Similar issues were associated with lawlessness in this period and the perception that it was the responsibility of the crown to maintain the rule of law. Failure to do so, or to meet the expectations of the mass of the population in this regard, could lead to revolt, as the events of 1381 most readily testify.

It was, however, not just in the fear of uprising that a response to the demands of the peasantry was to be found. The establishment of occasional commissions to inquire into a particular distress or wrongdoing indicates that government was alive to the threat. Subsequent to the crisis of 1297, for instance, an inquest into the failings of the system of taxation was established.[127] It has also been suggested that purveyance remained a political issue into the fourteenth century because lords feared that purveyance would cause their tenantry to revolt.[128] Other attempts to appease the peasantry can be found. Developments in the later thirteenth-century manor court may, for example, evidence lordly efforts 'to appease the peasants who took sides and were deeply involved in the civil war'; if this was the case, and it is tendentious, then the ability of medieval peasants to act as a political force capable of precipitating change in the policy of their lords and of encouraging the evolution of institutions of local government, is illustrated in a rather startling fashion.[129] It was also, according to Carpenter, 'a mixture of self-interest and idealism' that prompted the barons in 1259 in the Provisions of Westminster to meet some significant expectations of the peasantry, both as regards the rapacity of royal officials and the excesses of lordship.[130] Similarly, when, in 1327, the emergent Commons in Parliament demanded that the obligations of military service should be conducted according to the Statute of Winchester and not be arbitrary or excessively onerous, they were, it has been suggested, acting as 'the mouthpiece for . . . peasant opinion'.[131] Finally, although the Peasants' Revolt achieved none of the stated aims of the rebels in 1381 in the short term, both crown and landlords baulked at the prospect of aggressive treatment of the peasantry in later years.[132]

In so far, then, as this discussion of peasant involvement in 'politics', in its various forms, has revealed a peasantry prepared to enter, through a variety of means, into a dialogue with, typically, its social superiors, we must also assume a peasantry informed of rights and insistent upon certain obligations. It is clear, as we have seen, that some of that sense of right arose from everyday dealing and the acquaintance of peasants with law, administration and the trappings of government. But that sense, in its perception of moral obligation, of duty, of charity and of equity, also drew upon the church and its teaching.

9

PEASANTS AND RELIGION

As in previous chapters, a study of the religious experience of English peasantry in the late Middle Ages illustrates the potential inter-connectedness of the peasantry with worlds which extended not only beyond localities and regions but also beyond nations. There were clearly differences of access to religion between those living in towns and those living in the countryside but, in essentials, there were no fundamental distinctions of faith or understanding between the major-ity of rural dwellers and urban townspeople. Where differences did exist, as for instance in attendance at the sermons of the greater preachers of the day, they were consequences of the relative immedi-acy of urban life, and, importantly, rural dwellers could still enjoy occa-sional access, as sermons directed at the peasantry clearly reveal.[1] The argument of this chapter is that both through personal enquiry and through the institutions of church, the peasantry was integrated into far-reaching religious and intellectual communities. There were, of course, local peculiarities to that experience and, generally speaking, religious expression in the countryside lacked the sophistication of that in towns but these differences of scale were likely to be less significant than the shared beliefs and assumptions which such universal mem-bership helped generate.

As Christians, medieval English peasants were members of an inter-national community of believers, members, in other words, of Chris-tendom. In that sense, they lived their lives under the general aegis of the Papacy and Papal representatives. In the later Middle Ages, matters of faith and of worship were formulated by the central organs of the church but these formulations were capable of being adapted by the laity, as seems to have happened with the doctrine of purgatory in this period.[2] That faith was not a wholly imposed experience but was, to a degree, negotiable illustrates the vitality of religious life throughout late medieval society. Although developments in access to faith and its practice typically appear first in an urban context in this period, the vibrancy of the lay experience of religion appears to have been as real in the countryside as it was in the towns. As we shall see, villagers found a variety of outlets for the expression of their religiosity and, in the changing of that expression over the period, revealed that they did not lag behind nor were indifferent to developments in the towns. The basic tenets of faith were, in the late Middle Ages, given substance in the Creeds, statements of faith produced by the authority of the church. The Apostles' Creed was, in theory, familiar to all Christians in the Middle Ages, providing the laity with the articles of faith: belief in God, Jesus Christ, the Holy Ghost, the catholic church, communion, confession, salvation, the immaculate conception, the resurrection, the last judgement. As a statement of faith it serves to remind us that, even in the most remote of English farmsteads, there were tenets of belief which its inhabitants shared not only with neighbouring villagers but with villagers as far afield as the Baltic and the Mediterranean.[3] The immersion of the English peasantry in this collectivity of shared beliefs was, of course, the product of centuries, but the maintenance of those beliefs and their developments were significant features of the lives of rural dwellers in the last centuries of the Middle Ages.

Throughout an individual's life, the union with the church was maintained through the sacraments which, organised around vital moments in that life, reaffirmed a relationship with church and God. Through the sacrament of baptism, a sacrament typically administered within hours of birth, the newborn were admitted into membership of the church while, at the point of death, the sacrament of extreme unction prepared the penitent for death and membership of a new congregation in the life everlasting. In between these two 'moments', other sacraments strengthened the relationship between the church and the individual – the marriage rites also employed a key moment in the individual life-cycle to confirm the close role which the church played in the lives of men and women, while confession, and, perhaps most importantly, the eucharist, were reasonably regular reminders of this bond. Confirmation, for the majority, and ordination, for a smaller male minority, again provided further evidence of membership of a community of all believers.

Aside from the sacraments, the liturgical round of the religious year drew, through a regular and structured ordering of the church's calendar, members of the church into religious observance and appropriate forms of spiritual response. Such response included attendance at church on Sundays and the celebration of Christian festivals. The main Christian feasts of Easter and Christmas were supported by a range of religious festivals and feast-days, some of which were peculiar to localities or regions whilst others enjoyed a wider currency. Important in the lives of urban and rural dwellers to differing degrees, the liturgical round resonated powerfully in the agricultural year. Significant feast-days marked transitions from winter to spring (Lent), Rogationtide in early summer, the onset of the harvest towards the end of summer (Lammas – 1 August), the close of the harvest and the arrival of winter (Michaelmas – 29 September), while local feasts punctuated this round providing foci and convenient dates for a range of secular activities, such as the holding of local courts or the annual or bi-annual views of frankpledge. It is difficult to appreciate fully the role which feast-days may have played in the lives of late medieval men and women but annual allowances, recorded in manorial accounts, for labour services lost as a result of feast-days illustrate the considerable intrusion holy days made into the working lives of the peasantry. On the Westminster Abbey manor of Bourton-on-the-Hill (Gloucestershire), the villeins of the abbot of Westminster were permitted at least 39 holy days in addition to extended four-day holidays at Easter and Whitsun. In this sense, at least, the formal demands of religious observance may have brought a degree of latitude and choice into the lives of the peasantry, even if that choice, at least at the beginning of the period, was constrained by economic necessities.[4]

The 'moments' of the sacraments and of feast-days and other religious celebration were the particular expressions of a faith which, at least for some, defined their everyday lives and which informed their understanding of the world they encountered and of the world yet to come. For others, undoubtedly, the personal dictates of faith were not so severe but, for all, some basic instruction in a Christian message may have helped sustain their sense of neighbourliness, of charity, of propriety. Furthermore, there cannot have been a villager or town-dweller in late medieval England who had not made at least a casual acquaintance with the institutions of the church and its representatives. Points of contact between ecclesiastics, such as the parish priest or wandering friar, and the laity offered the potential for lay instruction through the imitation of the virtues of the church's representative, but also raised the possibility that secular society would see in its spiritual guides no more than the palest imitations of the Christian message, if not indeed a total mockery of that message. The diverse religious responses of the laity in the medieval countryside will be considered in more detail below; for the moment, we need to consider the structures which furthered the promotion of religious belief and conditioned expressions of worship in the medieval countryside.

Church Structure

Shared assumptions and beliefs grounded in the Christian message, as with the celebration of the sacraments, feast-days and the liturgical round, were manifestations of membership of a church ultimately regulated and ordered by a Pope many hundreds of miles away from the small parishes and village churches of late medieval England. The villagers of late medieval England came into immediate contact with the church through their parish priest. Other points of contact included local religious houses and the wandering mendicants. Contact with the formal institutions of the church came in a number of ways other than attendance at the parish church. They could attend places of worship other than their own parish church. Chapels within parishes or larger churches, cathedrals and abbey churches might serve as regular or occasional places of worship. The peasantry might also hear sermons delivered either in nearby towns or by friars who had travelled to their village; peasants could also seek charity from neighbouring religious houses. Finally, villagers might, of course, be tenants of ecclesiastics or of religious houses but in such respects the relationship was largely a secular one.

The parish priest was not an isolated figure but rather the final link in a chain of command which extended from the Papal Curia. By the twelfth century, the Papacy's influence in matters of church government and administration was paramount whilst its role in secular matters throughout western Europe was also vast. Underpinning its role as moral arbiter in the high politics of western Europe, the Papacy had real financial and legal influence in the emergent states of Christendom. Papal taxation of the clergy was a significant drain on the income of secular rulers whilst the courts Christian and the canon law offered a partial challenge to the authority of secular rule of law.[5] In matters of ecclesiastical rights and landholding, the Papal Curia was a court of final resort. By the close of the twelfth century, for instance, English churchmen would take even apparently minor disputes over territory to the Pope.[6] Meanwhile the political machinations of the Papacy, which from the mid-thirteenth century would see it increasingly embroiled in Europe's secular politics, ensured that Papal involvement in high politics and the sanctions it chose to apply also affected the religious lives of the laity and their regard for the sanctity and rectitude of the church. The excommunication of King John in 1209 and the interdict placed over the country in the previous year reveal the powers at the disposal of the Papacy; by contrast, the rivalries and the vicissitudes that resulted in schism in the late fourteenth century are evidence of the weakening of Papal authority from the late thirteenth century and its reliance upon association with the emerging monarchical states of western Europe.[7]

All of these assocations between Papacy and locality had implications for dwellers in countryside and town. The financing of crusades was, for instance, supported by the preaching of crusades at the local level and the collection of donations, notably in the form of redemption payments for the revocation of crusading vows. The Papacy, throughout the high Middle Ages, was prepared to encourage such preaching campaigns in rural areas and looked to raise significant financial support from the countryside.[8] If Papal-inspired preaching campaigns served to inform the faithful of the threats within and beyond the borders of Christendom, Papal pronouncement on rights to land or to office might materially affect the condition of those who lived on the land or who fell within the aegis of the office-holder. Most obviously, a Papal interdict or the fall-out from schism severely incapacitated the aspects of personal worship and religious experience. The interdict of 1208 meant that churches in England remained effectively closed to parishioners until 1214, by which time John had conceded his position on ecclesiastical appointments. During the period of the interdict, for instance, it was ordered that 'church doors remain shut save at the chief festival of the church' and that 'neither gospel nor church hours be observed in the accustomed place, nor any other, though the people assemble in the same'.[9] While the sacraments did continue to be administered in muted form, the fact of interdict could not have escaped the attention of parishioners who must, as a consequence, have contemplated their own needs and the role of king and Pope in denying them. Similar observations could be made of later upheavals and challenges to Papal authority. The Great Schism of the later fourteenth and early fifteenth centuries, by dividing both lay and spiritual allegiances, threatened the security and normalcy of worship since, to quote Ullmann, 'in many dioceses public worship was an impossibility, and the populace was left in a confused state of bewilderment and cynicism'.[10]

It was, perhaps, the efforts of the Papal government to effect changes in the religious experience of the laity that best revealed the role that Popes and their representatives could play in everyday lives. The work of church councils, most notably the Fourth Lateran Council of 1215, attempted to regulate the religious lives of the laity. Prefaced by a statement of faith, the legislation of the Fourth Lateran Council sought to establish the appropriate form of worship and the spiritual responsibilities of the Christian laity.[11] Most importantly, by encouraging a regular regard for the sacraments, especially the eucharist but also confession, the Council promoted a religiosity which was given new energy and direction by secular society, a point to which we shall return. Finally, the elements of Papal power outlined here were not universally applicable throughout the whole of the period. We should recognise a weakening of the Papacy's control *vis-à-vis* the rule of the emergent nation-state between *c*.1200 and *c*.1500. In England, attempts by secular government to reduce Papal influence within the country, best evidenced by the statutes of provisors and praemunire (1351, 1353; repeated with additions, 1391, 1393) had implications for, *inter alia*, the ability of the Papacy to tax and to extend the rule of canon law.

How did the rulings of Popes and Councils reach that portion of the flock of believers who lived in the medieval English countryside? In England, as elsewhere, church organisation was based upon dioceses, with each diocese subject to the authority of a bishop. Dioceses were composed of archdeaconries, which in turn were made up of rural deaneries; there was, to a greater or lesser extent dependent upon the particular diocese, some similarity of physical structure between rural deaneries and the divisions of counties, the hundreds or wapentakes: thus, in Lincolnshire, the limits of deaneries corresponded to the organisation of the secular wapentakes in the county. While the bishop headed the diocese, administration and governance at the various levels were in the hands of functionaries including archdeacons and rural deans. This organisational structure also provided a framework for ecclesiastical courts in England, with canon law jurisdiction passing

along the same chains of command from bishops and consistory courts
to the local courts of rural deans. At the lowest level of diocesan organisation was the parish, from which the deaneries were composed, and
of which there were approximately 9000 in the late Middle Ages in
England and Wales.

Parish and priest

At the parish level, the parish priest was responsible for the religious
life of the parish, the moral well-being of his parishioners as well as
the everyday administration of matters pertaining to the church,
including the management of church land, the collection of tithes and
the occasional levying of clerical taxation. The parish might also
provide the smallest unit of canon law jurisdiction, priests occasionally
holding 'rural chapters' in their parish churches.[12]

By the late Middle Ages, the parish priest was as likely to be a vicar
as a rector. Distinctions between rectors and lesser clergy, such as vicars,
centre upon issues of revenue – whilst rectors enjoyed the living of the
parish through a portion of the income generated by the parish, principally through tithes, vicars and chaplains operated as substitutes for
rectors and were paid something more akin to a salary. Where a vicar
rather than a rector was parish priest, the revenue of the parish was
'appropriated' by the individual or institution that owned the right to
appoint the parish priest, the advowson. Whereas before the twelfth
century all parishes had been in the care of a rector, many rectories
were replaced by vicarages in the thirteenth and fourteenth centuries.
This development is to be explained both in terms of the piety of
secular landlords and the financial preoccupations of religious houses.
Where once landowners had affirmed their faith through pious
donation of land to the church, and in particular to religious houses,
strictures of government (which reflected a fear for the flood of land
disappearing into clerical hands and, thereby, beyond the reach of tax
collectors) and economic realities encouraged the donation simply of
the advowson, the right of appointment to a rectory. Once a monastery
came into possession of the advowson of a parish church, it frequently,
counting itself as rector, appointed a vicar or one of its own monks
to fulfil the necessary spiritual functions. The appointee normally
received a salary while the monastery appropriated the balance of
the revenue of the parish. Monasteries frequently claimed pressing
financial needs for such a policy, as, in the first half of the fourteenth

century, did the abbot and convent of Cockersand, whose monastery
was situated by the shore of Morecambe Bay. Some new source of
revenue was necessary, it was explained, to build up the walls of the
monastery, 'beaten and shaken twice in the day and night by the waves
and heady tides of the said sea' or else the monastery would soon be
brought to 'pitiable ruin'. Although, in the late fourteenth and fifteenth
centuries, there was, in some few parishes, a reversal of the process,
with institutions 'reappropriating' churches so that vicars once again
found themselves in full possession of the parochial revenue, the moti-
vation for such a reversal was also often fiscal rather than charitable
or pastoral. Failing parishes, where the flock had been decimated by
a combination of recurrent epidemic disease and out-migration, were
no longer capable of providing the wants of religious houses: as a
consequence, the holders of the advowson, in such instances, aped the
behaviour of secular landlords and replaced the uncertainty of fluctuating parochial income with the reduced risk of a farm or pension paid
by the incumbent. Thus, in Yorkshire in 1455 the rectorial tithes of the
village of Thorpe-by-Newark, appropriated many years earlier by the
prior and convent of Haverholme, were restored to the vicar there in
return for an annual sum.[13]

The 'reappropriation' of churches in the fifteenth century was but
one response to the larger problem of depopulation in the late fourteenth and fifteenth centuries. In parts of the country, some of the
parish churches, once the religious focus for dense and bustling centres
of rural populations, became redundant in the wake of the demographic shifts of the later Middle Ages. This frequently led to the amal-
gamation of parishes, as occurred at Dunsthorpe, Lincolnshire, in the
early to mid-fifteenth century where, 'on account of the lack of parishioners, the fewness of peasants, their low wages, the bareness of lands,
the lack of cultivation, pestilences, and epidemics', there were insufficient funds to support a chaplain, let alone a rector. The parishioners
petitioned the bishop of Lincoln that they should be permitted to amal-
gamate with the neighbouring parish of Hameringham. Amalgama-
tion was not a solution for all parish churches in the late Middle Ages:
some simply persisted as pale imitations of themselves, poor, their
parishioners lacking in most of their spiritual needs. By contrast, of
course, as certain parishes failed, others prospered, particularly in the
newer centres of rural industry, such as the cloth-making villages of
southern Suffolk.[14] At nearby Bottisham, in the late fourteenth century,
a medium-sized Cambridgeshire village could accommodate a rector,

four chaplains and two members of the household of the bishop of
Ely, a feature which has been explained in terms of the economic
advantages of the community.[15] Finally, it is also the case that even
where churches were not appropriated or fell into poverty, the rector
may still have been absent and a lesser cleric placed there in his stead.
In the later Middle Ages, some, particularly the non-inheriting offspring of the landed, obtained Papal dispensation to hold more than
a single benefice. This pluralism was not unusual in the late Middle
Ages although Bogo de Clare, a son of the earl of Gloucester and Here-
ford who, at his death in 1291 held, amongst other offices, 24 parishes
and the income they generated (more than £2000), was atypical in his
assiduity.[16]

Whether parishioners found themselves under the aegis of a rector
or of a vicar or lesser cleric, such as a parish chaplain, may have been
a matter of some significance. Where a rector enjoyed the living of the
parish, the parishioners, if the rector was actually present, benefited
from the spiritual leadership of a man who may, perhaps, have had a
university education; the parishioners would also, in theory, have been
advantaged in financial terms since the community would recover a
proportion of the tithe paid to the rector in the form of alms to the
local poor. By contrast, lesser clergy were likely to be lacking in formal
education. Furthermore, as we have seen, where a cleric other than a
rector was in charge of a parish, the tithe paid by parishioners was
appropriated to the individual or the institution in possession of the
advowson; as a consequence, the proportion of that tithe traditionally
allocated to local charitable provision became unavailable. The dual
effects of appropriation and pluralism were frequently therefore to
reduce both the quality of spiritual guidance available to parishioners
and the extent of charity formally administered within the parish.[17] At
the same time, it has been argued, these processes, by encouraging
within parishioners a sense of their own potential to manage directly
the provisions and practice of their faith, did not have a wholly
deleterious effect upon communities or upon collective religious
experience in the late Middle Ages.[18]

Parishioners

Throughout the later Middle Ages, parishioners, in both rural and
urban parishes, were expected to fulfil certain obligations to the

church. Some of these obligations were matters of personal faith and observance, such as regular confession or attendance at mass, while others, the maintenance of the fabric of the church, for instance, were more collective in their nature. In terms of this study, these manifestations of observance and of duty evidence not only the obligations which parishioners owed but also, to a certain extent, the piety of villagers. That the willingness of parishioners to contribute directly to the celebration of their faith shifted considerably over this period can be characterised, in part, as the product of changing economic conditions: by the early fifteenth century piety was comfortably affordable in ways that it was not a century earlier. Alongside the economic forces that may have influenced degrees of piety, there were other, less tangible, forces which prompted changes in observance, as attitudes, for instance towards the clergy, shifted.

The responsibilities of the parishioners towards their parish, whilst undergoing significant developments between 1200 and 1500, can be grouped into three broad categories of attendance and observance, payment, and maintenance of the fabric of the church. Religious dictates such as these served to draw the faithful into closer association with the community of the church while regular observance effected a confirmation of membership of that community. Hidden within these categories is the rise of the layman as an officer and administrator of the church: by 1500 the laity had involved themselves in the day to day running of their parish churches in ways that could not have been envisaged three centuries previously. Further, the expectations which the church placed upon its parishioners were also important in fostering within the laity a heightened sense of their own spirituality: the obligations of the church were transformed, in their performance, into pious expression. This is one of the more significant features of lay religious behaviour in this period. Most importantly, perhaps, the congregation themselves imbued religious celebration with particular meaning, as in the cultic status accorded the sacrament of the eucharist; by introducing a degree of self-regulation and control into their religiosity, the laity admitted themselves into a fuller membership of the church. In English villages, between the thirteenth and fifteenth centuries, the extension and maturation of that relationship is to be seen in various forms of pious expression, forms which tended to undergo significant shifts of scale and complexity as the economic security of individuals and communities altered. The main elements of that expression, aside from payments to the church and maintenance of the fabric of the church, were divided between individual and collective acts of piety. A combination of burgeoning literacy, improved standards of living, and institutional developments, means that we are better informed about fifteenth-century piety than we are pious behaviour in the thirteenth century. Although the religious experience of English villagers undoubtedly underwent important developments between 1200 and 1500, common elements, such as the parish guild, the veneration of the host, and charitable bequests in wills, are evident across the three centuries. These we shall return to but it is perhaps best to begin with the institutionalised forms of Christian worship.

Attendance and observance

Most obviously, as an individual, the villager displayed his or her faith through public attendance at the parish church and through the celebration of the sacraments and the liturgy. In this display, the orthodox Christian was doing no more than meeting the expectations of the church. The Fourth Lateran Council of 1215 had made explicit the church's expectations of its flock in terms of observance. The 'pastoral revolution' which that Council initiated determined secular religious experience throughout the closing centuries of the Middle Ages and touched the lives of the English peasantry in significant ways, as it did lives throughout the towns and countryside of Christendom. In particular, the Lateran Council had called for the regular (annual) celebration of communion and for frequent confession.

Requirements of communion and confession brought the orthodox into reasonably regular contact with their church. The prescribed celebration of the significant moments in the religious calendar also brought the Christian within the orbit of an imposed religiosity. That there was an element of prescription and imposition about the observance of faith in the late Middle Ages does not mean that the orthodox were religious automatons who did no more than the mechanical fulfilment of their obligations, a point to which we will need to return. However, in their religiosity, country-dwellers in England, as throughout Christendom, reflected the assimilation of the church's instruction. For example, the marital behaviour of the peasantry, as has already been discussed in an earlier chapter, can and should be discussed in the context of the absorption of Christian teaching and the adoption of norms of behaviour. A close association of nuptiality and fertility, described for the countryside by Smith and others, reveals or looks to reveal observance of the teachings of the church, especially through the church's promotion of the sacrament of marriage. This observance finds its expression in the censure of extra-marital sex and of the bearing of children beyond marriage as well as the evident disregard for the rights of the illegitimate. In 1271 at Park (Hertfordshire), a St Albans manor, it was successfully argued in an inheritance case that one of two brothers, William and Simon atte Leye, was rightful heir 'because he was the first born and because his father had plighted his troth (*affideverat*) with his mother before he was born'.[19]

This observance extended beyond a basic regard for the sacraments. The records of church courts as well as reference in other sources to their use, show the preparedness of villagers to judge each other according to shared cultural norms and a sense of appropriate morality. While ecclesiastical court records abound with accusations of adultery and incest, manor court rolls contain further indication of the willingness of villagers to testify to the moral failings of their peers. On the manor of Wakefield at Alverthorp, jurors in the manor court reported that 'Walter of the Hill retained in adultery Alice, the wife of Roger of the Wodehous' for which it seems Walter was fined in the church courts to his lord's loss.[20] Pleas of defamation also rehearse a code which drew on Christian morality, with individuals suing against accusations of usury, adultery, theft, and so on. To quote one such example, at Hipperholme, again on the manor of Wakefield, the collapse of an agreement between two parties in 1297 led to accusations of usury and the charging of excessive interest.[21] That this morality gained something from Christian teaching seems reasonably clear. Moralising literature, such as the early fourteenth-century poem, *Handlyng Synne*, or later works, notably but not exclusively by writers such as Langland and Gower, is the written expression of a preaching tradition that would, by the thirteenth century, have found its most eloquent voice in the sermons of the mendicant orders. While villagers might have encountered sermons on, for example, the seven deadly sins in visits to market towns or, perhaps, from the preachings of wandering friars, the parish priest was also a principal imparter of this morality. Instruction manuals to priests and collections of sermons provided them with the ammunition with which to assault the limitations of their congregations.[22] Whilst the priest might help to establish the parameters of Christian behaviour for his lay congregation, it was also a function of that congregation to regulate the behaviour of their priest. Episcopal visitations to parishes were reliant upon the preparedness of parishioners to attest to the appropriateness of their clerics' behaviour, attestation which was necessarily conditioned by instilled assumptions regarding ideals of the priestly condition.[23]

Payment

A further important function of the lay Christian, in the countryside as in the town, was to pay. Mason has described the 'ideal parishioner' as 'a dutifully programmed automaton with a limitless purse'.[24] The church claimed, as an annual payment, a tenth part of produce, the tithe, to support its ministry and almost all things fell within the titheable purview. Livestock and grain were the most obvious sources of tithe but income in the form of wages and rent were also subject.[25] Tithes could be commuted to money payments but the rector could exploit an economic situation according to circumstance. On the estates of the prior and convent of Durham, the monks, who owned the advowson, expected to receive tithe in grain in years of poor harvest (when the resale prices were high) but were content with the money in good harvest/low-price years.[26]

In addition to tithe, villagers also made payments in money and in kind, typically at significant moments in the life-cycle and in return for some spiritual function of the priest. Payments at funerals, such as obits, and payments for the churching or purification of women after childbirth were typical of such payments, as were gifts made to the priest on feast-days.[27] We have already had cause to mention occasional payments encouraged by the church, such as sums paid as redemptions of crusading vows.[28] Most infamous was the mortuary payment, a single payment, often of livestock, on the death of the parishioner. Swanson quotes examples from Lincolnshire which reveal how significant these payments could be in rural areas. In one example, in 1400–1, a family, three of whose members had died, lost a horse and two cows in a single year.[29] Finally, here, some account needs to be taken of church court fines. Payment in the form of fines to the parish priest or his senior, the rural dean or the commisary general, were common. Manor court rolls record further financial penalties exacted from unfree tenants who had allowed themselves to be dragged through the church courts for some or other moral indiscretion and had, as a consequence, squandered the rightful property of the lord. At Gidding (Hertfordshire), an individual was set in the stocks not for his repeated adultery but for the alienation of the lord's property as fines to the church.[30]

Organisation and maintenance of the fabric of the church

A further and particular aspect of payment was that directed at the maintenance of the fabric of the church. As we shall discuss below, the impact of rural wealth on church architecture was an important aspect of lay piety in the late Middle Ages but, as importantly, there was already an universal obligation to maintain the fabric and furniture of churches, an obligation which transcended economic sub-groups within the parish. During the high Middle Ages, a distinction of obligations had been agreed between the clergy and their parishioners, with the priest responsible for the maintenance of the chancel while the parish maintained the nave. As well as the fabric of the church, the laity were also obliged to furnish the church with objects necessary for worship, including books, chalices, cloths and vestments, lights and candles. According to Duffy, 'by the mid fourteenth century even obscure village churches were very fully equipped, largely as a result of such lay gifts'.[31] While a significant proportion of this giving was prompted by individual acts of piety, especially at point of death, there was also an important corporate component. In the fifteenth century, it was common, for instance, for fines levied by the community for breaches of village by-laws to be divided between the lord and the parish church.[32] This corporate or communal component responded to an explicit requirement of the church. Conciliar and diocesan orders set out the obligations of parishioners.[33] The effect of such expectations, when made of the parish in this way, was both to encourage a closer association of parishioners with their church and, in the administration of that association, to prompt the development of lay offices responsible to the parish.

The parish priest, the rector or vicar of the parish, was not alone in fulfilling his duties; he was typically supported by other clergy, most especially parochial assistants, so that it is estimated that there were between three and five clerics per parish in the late Middle Ages, with some considerable fluctuation over the period.[34] For instance, holy-water clerks, minor clerics, aided the priest in his duties, received a wage from the parish for doing so, and were recruited from within the parish. That villagers saw financial benefit and some advancement in such offices is suggested by squabbles over the right to hold the office.

At Hinderclay (Suffolk), in 1305, two villagers defamed the holy-water clerk, claiming that he was married and therefore should not hold clerical office. It is also clear that the defamed clerk, who subsequently lost his position, had previously ousted his accusers' son.[35] As well as these minor clerics, there were, increasingly, laymen involved in the running of the church and of matters associated with spirituality, notably the administration of charity.

From the mid-fourteenth century onwards, it is the emergence of the churchwarden that dominates this story of lay involvement. It fell to churchwardens to oversee the collection of and to serve as trustees for funds which could be spent on the maintenance of the church, new building projects and the appropriate distribution of alms gathered by the community. The collective enterprise of the village, co-ordinated by the efforts of churchwardens, sits at the heart of some of the more impressive church-building schemes in late medieval England.[36] This involvement in structure eventually trespassed into matters of a more spiritual nature. Even by the close of the thirteenth century, for example, some Lincolnshire villagers, in opposition to their priest, were claiming the right to appoint parochial assistants.[37] It was however in the middle ground between the administration of charity and charity as an act of faith that the convergence of lay office with pious expression is best evidenced. Bequests left by parishioners for the good of the poor or for the parish were administered by wardens who might, for instance, raise funds from bequeathed moveables or gather rents from land. Churchwardens could also actively raise funds, by organising events such as ales, plays and other entertainments.[38] They might also oversee regular collections, such as payments into the 'common box' of the parish. Finally, in the distribution of these collections, the churchwardens had a vital role in ensuring that the expectations of the community were met and that those who deserved charitable support received it.[39] By the close of the Middle Ages, therefore, a process of appropriation and the concomitant diminution of charitable donation capable of being redirected from tithe payments meant that, in many parishes, churchwardens had usurped the charitable and distributive function of the parish priest. Developments in offices such as that of churchwarden reflected a greater polarisation and a heightened confidence in rural society and helped generate a preoccupation with office and office-holding that found its strongest expression in the early modern period. Increasingly these officers became the embodiment of local responsibility and, unsurprisingly, there was a tendency for institutions of charitable provision to focus upon them. In that sense, parish officers took on the guise of provisioners of communal charity in the fifteenth century and, as a consequence, were the natural administrators of more formal charitable relief under the Tudors.[40]

The Parish and Beyond

The formal obligations of observance may have provided the principal outlets for religious expression in this period but they did not circumscribe it. The religious behaviour of the laity took on an increasingly individualistic hue as the period progressed, and institutionalised religious observance became but one part of the villager's pious expression. Villagers began to take charge of their religiosity in ways that saw them advance newer institutions than did the church, notably the parish guild, but also devote themselves to personal religious 'endeavours', such as individual acts of charity, and an evident regard for the soul and the after-life. There were also, littered throughout the lives of most men and women in the Middle Ages, occasional 'moments' which, at least in their outward expression, suggest piety and engagement with faith: pilgrimages, for instance, but also attendance at feasts, processions, and other celebrations of Christianity, as well as the possession of and absorption of religious works.

As to a deeper understanding of the components of faith, it is reasonable to assume that, as in the towns, some villagers pondered their beliefs. However, although we can gain some sense of lay religious practice from, for example, pious donations evidenced by wills, or individual and collective acts of observance, particularly a regard for the sacraments and for sanctity, there is little which permits us a sense of the extent and depth of religious comprehension in this period. Beyond the normalities of the faith, in the fifteenth century inquisition records cast some light on the beliefs of the unorthodox and heretical; the assertions of heretics and the assumptions of their inquisitors may also help to illustrate commonly held beliefs. The main thrust of charges levelled at heretics within the diocese of Norwich in the early fifteenth century pertained to the sacraments, veneration of saints, morality, and the role of the clergy. Questionnaires devised by the church in order to examine possible heretics include, amongst a range of topics, questions on the nature of the eucharist and the divine grace of the priesthood. It is uncertain whether questionnaires such as these were appropriate responses to the acute religious knowledge of the laity or were hopelessly remote, intellectual documents that baffled uninformed respondents and made heretics of them in the process. It has been suggested, however, that amongst the laity of late medieval England were those who comprehended more than the bare minimum of Christian theology, were alive to contemporary theological debates conducted in the universities, and were prepared to question their own faith accordingly. In attempting to gain insights into the religious beliefs of peasants in the later Middle Ages, it is those who attracted the attention of the church through their challenges to orthodox belief that offer the best guides. Furthermore, heretics and those who fell into doctrinal error were not in any way purely urban phenomena: a discussion of the religious experience of the peasantry in the later Middle Ages needs to take account of the unorthodox and the heretical, a point to which we shall return.[41]

Essentially, the laity, in town or countryside, did not enjoy a theological membership of the community of the church; in the later Middle Ages no more was expected of the laity than that they should absorb the teachings of the church and fulfil their Christian duties with a benign acceptance. To delve into matters of theology was to question the authority of the church and, ultimately, to risk life and limb. Changes in degrees of pious expression and of the church's readiness to accept such changes may have meant that the Christian laity were able to engage more directly with their faith by the close of the Middle Ages than they had been two centuries previously but, throughout our period, the primary role of the lay Christian was to do more than it was to think.

In the countryside, as in the towns, acting as a Christian meant, above all, being charitable. Throughout Christendom, at least from the twelfth century, there had been a growing emphasis on the virtue of charity – *caritas*. New religious orders, particularly the begging or mendicant orders such as the Franciscans and the Augustinians, had placed charitable giving and an imitation of the poverty of Christ at the centre of their faith. The laity followed their lead. Expressions of charitable giving, made explicit in donations recorded in numerous peasant wills surviving from the fourteenth and fifteenth centuries and in the articles of association of rural parish guilds, illustrate the extent to which this movement took root in the hamlets and villages of the late medieval English countryside. Individual acts of charity, though undoubtedly a product of the church's instruction, were given a distinctive focus by the laity in the high and late Middle Ages. Although more wills *per capita* survive from urban or semi-urban centres, the changing attitude of testators in the countryside accords with that to be found in the towns. It is a standard of the literature that attitudes to charity hardened during the late Middle Ages, especially in the decades after the Black Death, when concerns over the undeserving poor are reflected in donations and bequests to specific categories of 'the poor'. This move is evident in wills from villagers, in much the same ways as can be found in wills with an urban provenance. The villein and copyholder testators on the fifteenth-century estates of St Albans Abbey appear chary of indiscriminate bequests. Most wills apportion property amongst named legatees with a final request that the executors distribute the residue 'for the greatest good of my [the testator's] soul according to how they see fit'.[42] Earlier wills are not always so directed. A rare example of a villein will from the early fourteenth century includes a bequest of 37s. of alms to be 'given to the poor on the day of his burial and on the 7th day'.[43] In charitable giving and its modification, individual villagers revealed themselves to be responsive both to the expectations of their faith and the societal norms which conditioned it. The same is also true of acts of charity that were more obviously collective.

Parish guilds offered a collective opportunity to fulfil the charitable duties of the Christian. It has been estimated that by the close of the Middle Ages almost all villages had at least one guild. In their collectivity, guilds reflected the organisation and work of the parish and it was frequently the case that those who operated the local guilds were also officers of the parish. It is also clear that village guilds tended to be composed of the local parishioners with very few outsiders. One example of the localness of rural guilds is provided by the guild of St Peter in Bardwell (Suffolk): almost all of its members in the early sixteenth century were parishioners, the exceptions being three women from the neighbouring village of Barningham who may have been local women who had married out, while almost all adult parishioners were guild members.[44] For many guild members, it seems likely that, in their guild membership, they looked for the security in life and in death which such membership afforded them. Guilds provided charitable support for their members and for the local poor. For members, they assisted financially, helping to fund ventures and to provide at moments of need. The guild of Corpus Christi at

Stretham (Cambridgeshire) maintained a common chest from which members could borrow money whilst other guilds hired out livestock which had been left to the guild by testators to the benefit of poorer peasants.[45] Guilds, as parishes, also organised ales and other events for the benefit of the local poor, including their own members. Some of this charitable provision was dispersed fairly widely, including the financing of general poor relief.[46]

The function of individual or collective piety exemplified by wills and the activity of guilds did not stop with acts of charity. Within the more institutionalised forms of worship, that is, within the parish church, there is evidence that the peasantry, as other social groups, came to take a more energetic involvement in the formal provisions of their faith. The usurpation of formal religious expression, such as the sacrament of the eucharist, has been described in a number of con-texts for western society in the late Middle Ages.[47] Whilst, as we have already seen, the church promoted a growing lay involvement with the sacrament, it is clear that, by the later Middle Ages, this engagement had spilled over into personal preoccupations with the eucharist, including a greater demand for private masses and a heightened desire to attend and receive communion. Parishioners in the English coun-tryside were not left behind in these developments. The developing ritual of the eucharist and its promotion, within England, by church councils, was embraced by worshippers in the late fourteenth- and fifteenth-century countryside. That the elevation of the host during the mass, a moment imbued with powerful meaning for the lay con-gregation, was of real import for rural dwellers also can be seen in the expenditure on the church furnishings necessary to support the ritual. Churchwardens' accounts and wills reveal sums spent on sacring-bells, rung to mark the elevation of the host, and candles and lamps to illu-minate the ritual of the mass.[48] As well as an enthusiastic attendance at the mass, individuals also paid for private masses, as at Hinderclay (Suffolk), where, in 1296, Adam the chaplain sued two villagers for his dues in saying incantations (*pro canobio*) and masses. At Walsham le Willows (Suffolk), in 1338, William Cook attempted to recover a brass bowl worth 4s. from a chaplain, Henry de Wells which, William claimed, he had lent to Henry in order for Henry to be able to celebrate mass for the soul of William's mother, Hilary.[49]

Aside from the mass, the faithful in the countryside also found other opportunities to adapt their faith to their own needs or to empha-sise certain elements of its expression. In the fifteenth century, for example, an early sabbatarian movement found local support in the willingness to postpone secular business on Sundays. Other outlets for piety included the taking of personal vows, the veneration of local saints, and, of course, pilgrimage, such as that undertaken by the five pilgrims from Burgh le Marsh (Lincolnshire) who travelled to Compostella in the middle years of the fourteenth century and who, during the return journey and finding themselves in great peril from a storm at sea, vowed to erect an altar to the saint.[50] All such expressions could be made on an individual basis but there could also be an important collective element to such undertakings. To the extent that their function was spiritual, guilds, for instance, might also maintain chapels and their own clergy or simply an altar or light in praise of their saint. It has been suggested that parish guilds were more in evidence in the villages of the late fourteenth and fifteenth centuries than they were in earlier centuries. The explanation for this rise has been located in the changing economic and demographic circumstances of the late Middle Ages: increased mobility in the post-plague English countryside, it has been suggested, meant that there was greater need for surrogate families and kin groups, alternative families able to provide the sense of mutual surety and protection which family groups might once have offered. This explanation makes certain assumptions about the nature and degree of familial solidarity in the decades before the plague. As we have seen, in certain areas of the country, notably eastern England, the density of kin relations appears to have been fairly weak long before the mid-fourteenth century and the posited rise of parish guilds.[51] It seems as likely that a vital motive force for the growth in parish guilds was a burgeoning secular religiosity possibly allied to an increasing self-awareness amongst the laity as their role as parish administrators developed. Whereas in the towns guilds were often closely associated with crafts, it has been suggested that guilds in the countryside were 'rarely vocational'. Dorothy Owen has represented their rise in the rural parishes of late medieval Lincolnshire as 'spontaneous', reflecting spiritual desires and changing fashions of worship.[52]

Faith could also be proclaimed, both individually and collectively, in prayer for the dead and an abiding regard for remembrance and its display. The growing secular preoccupation with the doctrine of purgatory, described by a number of historians for this period,[53] found expression in the medieval village, most clearly by the mid-fifteenth century. Wills reveal this preoccupation in instructions for prayers for the dead. Where they survive, wills from earlier periods also show this preoccupation with the soul. In his will, which included bequests totalling £13 12s. 4d., the villein William Lene lavished in the region of £4 10s. (33 per cent of bequests, which also amounted to 17 per cent of his total moveable wealth at the time of his death) on his own funeral and commemorative prayers.[54] This preoccupation was displayed in other ways. While some individuals might only invest in prayers for the dead and obits, services on the anniversary of the death, others also chose to express their piety through payments towards the collective endowment of chantry chapels and, by the close of our period, limited investment in funeral art. The churches of rural parishes reflect the relative wealth of communities and their members: in particular, the great fifteenth-century churches of East Anglia and the Cotswolds are testimony to the extraordinary incomes which trade in wool and cloth generated in those regions at the close of the Middle Ages. Bainbridge's investigation of the role of individual testators in furnishing the parish church of All Saints, Elm (Cambridgeshire), reveals a plethora of chapels and altars dedicated to a variety of saints.[55] By the mid- and late-fifteenth century, there were some very wealthy individuals who had risen in the previous generation or two from peasant stock and who now found themselves sufficiently advantaged to celebrate their wealth and their piety in additions to the architecture and furnishings of parish churches. The perpendicular of the fifteenth-century wool churches, their sumptuous new chapels, panellings, brasses and transi-tombs reveal, but only in part since there are also mixed messages about wealth, power and dynasty here, the piety of the *nouveau riche* of the later Middle Ages. For most individuals in the countryside, the expression of piety through endowment was conducted less extravagantly. The wills of peasants on the estates of St Albans in the fifteenth century contain numerous examples of small bequests for the maintenance of lamps, to support funds for the high altar or for the bells of the parish church.[56]

Although a scale of investment in church architecture and interiors similar to that found in the wealthiest wool- and cloth-rich parts of the country is largely lacking in other, poorer, areas, parish churches in most parts of the country underwent extensive rebuilding and furnishing in the last century and a half of the Middle Ages, a process supported by individual endowment by villagers.[57] In their collective piety, villagers revealed the same preoccupations. Guilds helped provide for the funerals of their members, as well as for obits and masses for the dead. Whilst neither the endowment of chantries, chapels established for the saying of prayers for the soul of, typically, the beneficiary, nor investment in funeral art, such as *memento mori* and lavish tombs, were within the financial reach of individual peasants, it is evident that collectively, through parish and guild, some permanent expression revealing attitudes to death and the life hereafter could be established.

Faith and excessive piety could also serve as a stick with which to beat the unfaithful. Such opportunities were relatively few in later medieval England, particularly after the expulsion of the Jews at the close of the thirteenth century. That said, pockets of the perceived godless could still be found and suitably chastised, as revealed by local antagonism towards heretical sects and religious deviants, especially in the fifteenth century. By the early fifteenth century, convocation had agreed modes of enquiry with regard to heretical sects; it was incumbent upon communities to report on those who gathered in conventicles or failed to celebrate the sacraments. In this way, the church used the local community to report on religious 'deviance' and thereby transformed acts of scrutiny and vigilance into standards of orthodoxy.[58] Furthermore, the potential, once present even for the peasantry, to transform piety into crusading zeal and 'take the cross' had all but disappeared by the fourteenth century. Earlier, as thirteenth-century lists of those who took crusading vows indicate, even poor villagers committed themselves to crusade and, to judge by a Lincolnshire example, some appear to have attempted to meet their obligations.[59] The potential for militarised piety in the late Middle Ages came in the form of warfare closer to home, between countries whose identity as nations was developing fairly rapidly. The Hundred Years' War, which ground to a halt in the second half of the fifteenth century, was a conflict fought increasingly between 'nations' rather than feudal amalgams, and each nation claimed God as its own. It is certainly stretching a point to claim that peasant involvement in such campaigns was, first and foremost, an expression of piety, but it also seems inappropriate to claim that there was no spiritual sense of 'right' attached to such involvement. Undoubtedly, also, the rhetoric of the intranational disputes and civil wars in which, as we have also seen, the peasantry was prepared to take sides, included, as a significant element, claims of moral and spiritual justification. The fourteenth-century wall-paintings that decorate the north aisle of South Newington church (Oxfordshire) deliberately juxtapose Thomas of Lancaster, beheaded in the reign of Edward II, with images of the murdered Thomas à Becket. If the parishioners at South Newington were responsible for this work, then they had chosen to depict a 'political saint', whose head had been 'cut off for the peace of England' and 'at whose tomb health is given to the sick, that the truth may now be clear to all'. In the same measure, William Lene's bequest in 1329 'for the expenses of one going to [the shrine of] St Thomas of Lancaster' offers us a rather opaque marrying of faith and politics.[60] In an extremely limited sense, however, support for nation or faction, either through direct action or in some less direct way, such as the payment of taxes, villagers may have been encouraged to imbue their act with a religious overtone.[61]

Beyond everyday religiosity, villagers, especially male villagers, could also extend their access to faith through education and clerical office. Priests employed local men in minor offices, such as holy-water clerks, and also offered rudimentary education to the sons of villagers. There is only limited evidence for serfs and villeins becoming clerics but it has been suggested that opportunities for the unfree to enter the priesthood may have increased in the late fourteenth and fifteenth century as villeins employed their new wealth in social and spiritual advancement.[62] Also in this context, it is important to recognise that the shared assumptions of faith, outlined above, meant that particularly able individuals within the village were not divorced from the beliefs of those who were their social superiors and, where the strictures of institutions permitted, they were able to be assimilated, as Robert Grosseteste, bishop of Lincoln, 1235–53, but a man of humble peasant stock, into the hierarchy of the church whose mind-set they already shared.[63]

Whilst delving into faith was in part encouraged by the church, a dialogue with belief also led some rural dwellers into unorthodoxy and heresy, a development especially evident in England from the late fourteenth century. Alternative and distorted views of the life hereafter and of the tenets of faith were the product of a number of sources. In the first place, the echoes from a pre-Christian past, a persistent 'alternative' to Christianity, are heard in the association of wells and springs with healing miracles, as at Linslade (Buckinghamshire) where, by the close of the thirteenth century, a spring in a field had become a focus for veneration, much to the concern of the bishop.[64] But distortion also, and more evidently, emerged directly through the church's teachings, sermons and the dissemination of theological and pastoral works. In its most ordinary expression, faith was employed to explain the

threatening and the unknown.[65] Some late fourteenth-century Yorkshire 'ghost-stories' include sufficient detail to indicate that they had a
local provenance whilst they also suggest ways in which the preaching
of the church was set to meet the more basic fears of the laity. One
tale records how, after his burial, a villager from Kilburn (Yorkshire),
Robert de Boltebi, continued to rise from his grave by night and to
disturb the villagers. Some youths seized the wayward corpse and held
him fast until a priest could be fetched. The priest heard his confession, after which the corpse was allowed to rest in peace whilst the
priest abjured the youths who had apprehended the ghost that they
should disclose no detail of the dead man's confession.[66] The last point,
stressing the force and the sanctity of the sacrament of confession, was
no doubt the purpose of the story. The transmission of instruction in
the form of *exempla*, as in the example just cited, whilst it informed the
laity, in accessible form, of matters spiritual, was also capable both of
misdirecting and of encouraging further investigation and consequent
misconstruction.

A feature of changing society during this period was the expansion
of literacy and the extension of access to texts. Robert Reynes of
Acle (Norfolk), a substantial East Anglian villager of the late fifteenth
century, compiled a commonplace book in which he recorded his daily
activities as well as snippets of morality and current affairs. The largest
portion of the book was given over to religious matters and reveals
something of his religious preoccupations. He was a churchwarden
and a guild officer, and both roles are reflected in his record of purchases and of material relevant to the life of the guild saint. Moralising literature on death and on the sacraments is also represented, as
are the principal elements of the liturgy. As Duffy remarks, although
Reynes gathered charms and zodiacal material in his commonplace
book, most of his material was entirely orthodox and revealed 'little
evidence of . . . deep religious introspection and interiority'. Nor was
there an apparent interest in matters of doctrine.[67]

If the religion of men such as Reynes was, for the most part, safely
contained within the parameters of orthodoxy, the potential for villagers' religiosity to overstep the mark increased during this period.
The work of the Fourth Lateran Council had, as we have seen, encouraged a closer engagement of the laity with their faith and this almost
inevitably encouraged questioning and error. Whilst most spiritual
energy amongst the laity of high and late medieval England seems
to have been directed at the celebration of faith within the bounds

established by the church, there were undoubtedly those who delved deeper and queried some of the fundamental tenets of doctrine. This is most evident in the fifteenth century when the Wycliffite heresy of the late fourteenth century had lost its early momentum but had spawned pockets of dissent and unorthodoxy in town and countryside. The association of the university-based theology of John Wycliffe with the unorthodox and heretical Lollard movements of the fifteenth century raises difficult questions regarding the transmission of ideas from the schools of Oxford to the everyday locations of provincial and rural England. However, there is some indication that debate over doctrine, and of more than the most basic kind, had found its way into the English countryside by at least the early fifteenth century. Especially, it seems, in areas of rural industry, stocked with an artisanal, mobile and reasonably well-paid labour force, heresy survived in fairly robust clusters. Here, in small groups, texts, including the Bible in the vernacular, were read and discussed, sermons pondered and questions of faith mulled over. Aston quotes an example from the early sixteenth century of a Lollard, William Sweeting, who read to heretical groups in the fields and hedgerows, whilst they were 'keeping beasts'.[68] Unorthodox sermons on theology by renegade priests were also a source of heresy. In the early years of the fifteenth century, the vicar of Manuden (Essex), Thomas Bagley, had preached to his congregation of villagers on the subject of transubstantiation, denying both that the host was transformed into the body of Christ and that priests could, by force of words, effect such a transformation. Towards the close of the century, the rector of Letcomb Basset (Berkshire) made similar observation, claiming that the eucharist was 'pure brede and nowgth els'.[69] From such sources Wycliffite views on, *inter alia*, the eucharist and transubstantiation found their way into rural religiosity. Hudson cites an example of a villager from Upton (Berkshire) in the early sixteenth century who appears to have employed Wycliffite imagery in discussing the eucharist.[70] Whilst such views may not have found a fertile seed-bed in the religious sensibilities of the majority of rural dwellers in later medieval England, they did take hold amongst some and are testimony to the receptiveness and the vitality of late medieval rural religion. It was also, as we have seen, in their rejection by the orthodox that such ideas reveal the same receptiveness and vitality.

Similar points could be made about expressions of anti-clericalism in this period. For the greater part, criticism of the church reflected lay concerns over effective 'management' more than it did something of a more fundamental order. In this, expressions of anger or disillusionment reflected 'the developing relationship between clergy and people'.[71] In Lincolnshire, for instance, in the late thirteenth century, disputes over tithe and other payments centred on the inappropriate demands which priests seemed to be making of their parishioners whilst later, early fifteenth-century, disturbances may have reflected the influence of Lollardy. Brief outbreaks of anti-clericalism in the mid-fourteenth century may, as Owen has suggested, reveal parishioners' censure of 'unscrupulous' priests in the aftermath of plague.[72]

Without doubt the church and faith did not mean the same thing to all rural dwellers in this period. For some perhaps, the church served its principal role as a convenient centre of community, as a market and a place of business. It is certainly difficult to separate out modes of behaviour and to classify them as pious or impious. There was no room for expressions of unbelief in medieval England and doubts of such a fundamental kind are mostly hidden from us. Instead, for the greater part, as this chapter has been intended to show, we have to content ourselves with the outward expression of faith. In that expression we also see a reception of ideas and an engagement with faith which speaks of a countryside integrated within an international church. But, as we have seen in other contexts, this integration was not able to impose a uniformity of experience. It is, inevitably, the case that close proximity of Christian moral teaching did not have uniform consequences for the behaviour of all individuals. On occasion, the message could be lost or substituted. At Romsley (Worcestershire) in 1271, Hawis and two of her three daughters were attacked in their home by the husband of the third daughter because they had tried to exclude the husband and the daughter from the house, to which they had just returned from a charitable ale (*cervisia*).[73] The ale, rather than the lesson of *caritas*, was more evidently absorbed on this occasion.

Certainly, also, expressions of piety were conditioned by economic, social and legal circumstances. The pious donors of the thirteenth century, who financed the establishment of lamps in parish churches, did so through the rental of free land. Less scope existed for villeins to act in this way or to attach such obligations to their holdings. Similarly, lords were chary of their unfree tenants' recourse to church courts and attempted to restrict activity there.[74] Heresy responded similarly to circumstance: its home in the countryside was, typically, not amongst 'traditional' peasant stock but amongst an emergent rural labouring and artisanal sector.[75] Finally, where there was polarisation of landholding, as, for instance in fourteenth-century Cornwall or more generally in the fifteenth-century countryside, the wealthiest peasant landholders were able to invest substantial sums in pious expression.

10

CONCLUSION

In their membership of a broad array of institutions – manor, market, state and church – peasants in medieval England enjoyed a superficially 'common' experience and in the expression of that membership emerged bonds and indications of membership and non-membership which could be employed to the advantage and further security of 'community'.

But what community do we have in mind? The message of much of this study of the English peasantry in the Middle Ages has been the diversity of experience: the label of 'peasant' is as all-encompassing and as general as that of 'Christian' or 'layman' but it hides, as is well known, multiplicities of experience. We gain our clearest sense of this, hardly surprisingly, when we encounter peasants for whom we have unusually detailed information. The early fourteenth-century villein testator, William Lene, whom we have encountered in more than one context, is a case in point. From his probate and from the record of his death in the manor court rolls, we learn that William was owed substantial sums of money; we also know that he held large amounts of chattels and a good deal of land. From earlier court rolls, we also see that he was actively engaged in the land market, frequently buying holdings during the previous decade of heightened dearth and falling land prices. From his will we gain some sense of the size of his family, which was large by contemporary standards, and included an illegitimate son. We are offered some indication of his intentions and priorities: his bequests to his family, to the church, to the poor. In his request that someone attend the shrine of St Thomas of Lancaster, we are also presented with some sense of his piety and politics.[1] But this, clearly, does not mean we know him: his actions, viewed from our present, are devoid of motive. How we should we read him? As the pious giver, careful to reward family and friends, the church and the poor, an extender of credit during times of shortage; as the supporter of a martyred saint? Or, alternatively, as the aggressive acquisitor, who preyed on his neighbours' disadvantage, was unfaithful to his wife, and publically supported Thomas of Lancaster because that was where advantage may have lain by 1329, when he died?

One hundred and fifty years later, Robert Reynes of Acle, in the late fifteenth century, the villein compiler of a commonplace book, and therefore also something of a rarity in our sources, offers, similarly, little real insight into his own sense of community and of his place within it.[2] We know that he was a reeve, a bondsman, a guild officer. We might reasonably suspect he was other things as well: a father, husband, brother. He may have also, as some of his references suggest, conceived of other memberships – of political communities, of the community of the realm, of those who upheld the law, of those who were not criminals, not heretics, not foreign, not women, not beggars. Reynes viewed society from the perspective of a wealthy villager whose own expectations of society and of his place in it had been moulded by a plethora of influences. The exploration of the variety and force of these influences has been a central endeavour of this book. Robert Reynes was, of course, the product of unseen forces but this is not the place to attempt a psycho-history of the late medieval peasant. We can, however, itemise some of the more obvious factors that may have played upon his life: the ties that bound him to his family, the society of his fellow villagers, the expectations and obligations owed to his lord. Beyond manor and village, Reynes may have gathered his life-experiences in market towns and county courts, he may have joined pilgrimages or military levies. He may, as his commonplace book suggests, have gained other facets of his world-view from reading or from listening to priests and sermonisers. In turn, these influences informed his choices and his actions. Reynes may have been conditioned to respond in ways that, as McIntosh has shown, many of his contemporaries were.[3] He may have moralised and condemned the deviant; he may also have shown compassion and regard for those less fortunate than himself; he may have been aggressive in his marketing or complacent and content with his lot; perhaps a doting family man or a brute. We do not know and we can only risk inference from observation of action. But in an awareness of the complexity of influences that informed action, we are at least encouraged to show some regard for the potential variety of responses possible.

If we look beyond villagers like Reynes and Lene, the wealthier, more substantial members of their communities, our view is murkier still and our observations even less certain. The smallholders and the landless can be accommodated into more general arguments as regards social, economic and demographic change in this period but we know relatively little of them. Glimpses come typically through the unfamiliar and the unusual – random acts of violence, encounters in courts for breach of service, heresy trials which cast light on book-owning rural artisans – but they are capable of offering insights into the preoccupations of lowlier rustics. Similar observations could be made for peasant women; again, we are best informed about wealthy village women, as Bennett's 'biography' of Cecilia Penifader of Brigstock illustrates.[4] We know much less about the women who crop up now and again in our records, as regraters, raisers of the hue and cry, or fined for having children out of wedlock. Finally, the individuals who wandered from village to village, the *extranei* who were housed illegally during gleaning, are, for the most part, only names to us.

Despite these uncertainties and lacunae, we can, however, gain sufficient from our records to be confident that the lives of these individuals were integrated into complex, long-standing and broad social, cultural, political, economic and demographic systems and, what is more, their own actions within these systems mattered.

NOTES

Note: For ease of reference, full publication details of a work are cited afresh under each chapter.

CHAPTER 1 INTRODUCTION

1. J. A. Raftis, *Tenure and Mobility. Studies in the Social History of the Medieval English Village* (Toronto, 1964); E. B. Dewindt, *Land and People in Holywell-cum-Needingworth. Structures of Tenure and Patterns of Social Organization in an East Midlands Village, 1252–1457* (Toronto, 1971); E. Britton, *The Community of the Vill* (Toronto, 1977); S. Olson, *A Chronicle of all that Happens. Voices from the Village Court in Medieval England* (Toronto, 1996).

2. M. M. Postan, *Essays on Medieval Agriculture and General Problems of the Medieval Economy* (Cambridge, 1973).

3. Z. Razi, *Life, Marriage and Death in a Medieval Parish. Economy, Society and Demography in Halesowen (1270–1400)* (Cambridge, 1980); R. M. Smith, 'Marriage processes in the English past: some continuities', in L. Bonfield, R. Smith and K. Wrightson (eds), *The World we have Gained. Histories of Population and Social Structure* (Oxford, 1986).

4. C. Dyer, *Standards of Living in the Later Middle Ages. Social Change in England, c.1200–1520* (Cambridge, 1989).

5. For further discussion, see pp. 53–4 (Chapter 4). M. M. Postan, 'The charters of the villeins', in *idem, Essays on Medieval Agriculture*; D. Thorner, B. Kerblay and R. E. F. Smith (eds), *A.V. Chayanov on the Theory of Peasant Economy* (Madison, WI, 1986); P. R. Hyams, 'The origins of a peasant land market in England', *Economic History Review*, 23 (1970); P. D. A. Harvey (ed.), *The Peasant Land Market in Medieval England* (Oxford, 1984); R. M. Smith, 'Some thoughts on "hereditary" and "proprietary" rights in land under customary law in thirteenth and early fourteenth century England', *Law and History Review*, 1 (1983).

6. E. King, *Peterborough Abbey, 1086–1310. A Study in the Land Market* (Cambridge, 1973), ch. 6; note especially the two essays by R. M. Smith in *idem* (ed.), *Land, Kinship and Life-Cycle* (Cambridge, 1984).

7. R. H. Britnell, *The Commercialisation of English Society, 1100–1500* (Cambridge, 1993); J. Masschaele, *Peasants, Merchants and Markets. Inland Trade in Medieval England, 1150–1350* (Basingstoke, 1997).

8. F. W. Maitland, 'The history of a Cambridgeshire manor', *English Historical Review*, 9 (1894), repr. in H. M. Cam (ed.), *Selected Historical Essays of F. W. Maitland* (Cambridge, 1957).

9. F. G. Davenport, *The Economic Development of a Norfolk Manor, 1086–1565* (Cambridge, 1906); A. Clark, 'Serfdom on an Essex manor, 1308–1378', *English Historical Review*, 20 (1905).

10. P. Vinogradoff, *Villainage in England* (Oxford, 1892); *Select Pleas in Manorial and other Seignorial Courts*, ed. F. W. Maitland (Selden Society, vol. 2, 1889); P. R. Hyams, *Kings, Lords and Peasants in Medieval England. The Common Law of Villeinage in the Twelfth and Thirteenth Centuries* (Oxford, 1980).

11. See, for example, A. E. Levett, *The Black Death on the Estates of the See of Winchester* (Oxford, 1916); R. H. Hilton, *The Economic Development of some Leicestershire Estates in the Fourteenth and Fifteenth Centuries* (Oxford, 1947); E. Miller, *The Abbey and Bishopric of Ely. The Social History of an Ecclesiastical Estate from the Tenth to the Early Fourteenth Century* (Cambridge, 1951); F. R. H. DuBoulay, *The Lordship of Canterbury. An Essay on Medieval Society* (London, 1966); J. A. Raftis, *The Estates of Ramsey Abbey. A Study in Economic Growth and Organization* (Toronto, 1957); King, *Peterborough Abbey*; G. A. Holmes, *The Estates of the Higher Nobility in Fourteenth-Century England* (Cambridge, 1957); B. F. Harvey, *Westminster Abbey and its Estates in the Middle Ages* (Oxford, 1977); C. Dyer, *Lords and Peasants in a Changing Society. The Estates of the Bishopric of Worcester, 680–1540* (Cambridge, 1980).

12. E. A. Kosminsky, *Studies in the Agrarian History of England in the Thirteenth Century* (Oxford, 1956); J. R. Maddicott, *The English Peasantry and the Demands of the Crown, 1294–1341*, Past and Present Supplement 1 (1975), repr. in T. H. Aston (ed.), *Landlords, Peasants and Politics in Medieval England* (Cambridge, 1987) (from which subsequent references are taken); R. H. Hilton, *The Decline of Serfdom in Medieval England* (Cambridge, 1966); J. Hatcher, 'English serfdom and villeinage: towards a reassessment', *Past and Present*, 90 (1981), repr. in Aston (ed.), *Landlords, Peasants and Politics* (from which subsequent references are taken); J. Whittle, 'Individualism and the family–land bond: a reassessment of land transfer patterns among the English peasantry, c.1270–1580', *Past and Present*, 160 (1998).

13. For a fairly comprehensive but now slightly dated list of many relevant published sources, see E. L. C. Mullins, *Texts and Calendars. An Analytical Guide to Serial Publications* (Royal Historical Society, 2 vols, 1978, 1983).

14. R. H. Tawney, *The Agrarian Problem in the Sixteenth Century* (London, 1912); W. Hudson, 'The prior of Norwich's manor of Hindolveston: its early organisation and rights of the customary tenants to alienate their strips of land', *Norfolk Archaeology*, 20 (1921).

15. G. C. Homans, *English Villagers of the Thirteenth Century* (Harvard, 1941).

16. For discussion of community in the Middle Ages, see S. Reynolds, *Kingdoms and Communities in Western Europe, 900–1300* (2nd edn, Oxford, 1997); R. M. Smith, '"Modernization" and the corporate village community', in A. H. R. Baker and D. Gregory (eds), *Explorations in Historical Geography* (Cambridge, 1984); C. Wickham, *Community and Clientele in Twelfth Century Tuscany. The Origins of the Rural Commune in the Plain of Lucca* (Oxford, 1998). The theoretical and more generally discursive literature is large, beginning with F. Tönnies, *Community and Association (Gemeinschaft und Gesellschaft)* (1887); see, for example, C. Calhoun, 'History, anthropology and the study of communities', *Social History*, 3 (1978); *idem*, 'Com-

munity: towards a variable conceptualization for comparative research', *Social History*, 5 (1980).

17. M. Rubin, 'Small groups: identity and solidarity in the late Middle Ages', in J. Kermode (ed.), *Enterprise and Individuals in Fifteenth Century England* (Stroud, 1991), 134.

18. S. H. Rigby, *English Society in the Later Middle Ages. Class, Status and Gender* (Basingstoke, 1995).

19. D. Thorner, 'Peasant economy as a category in economic history', in T. Shanin (ed.), *Peasants and Peasant Societies* (Harmondsworth, 1971); also discussions, J. Whittle, *The Development of Agrarian Capitalism. Land and Labour in Norfolk, 1440–1580* (Oxford, 2000), 11–16; Rigby, *English Society in the Later Middle Ages*, 25.

20. M. M. Postan, *The Medieval Economy and Society. An Economic History of Britain in the Middle Ages* (Harmondsworth, 1972), ch. 3.

21. T. H. Aston and C. H. E. Philpin (eds), *The Brenner Debate. Agrarian Class Structure and Economic Development in Pre-Industrial Europe* (Cambridge, 1985).

Part I   Land

CHAPTER 2   LAND: TENURE, LANDHOLDING AND RENT

1. Technically speaking, this land formed part of the lord's demesne.

2. F. W. Maitland, *Domesday Book and Beyond. Three Essays in the Early History of England* (Cambridge, 1897), 43–6.

3. For a recent revisionist argument, see R. Faith, *The English Peasantry and the Growth of Lordship* (Leicester, 1997), ch. 10; see also P. R. Hyams, *Kings, Lords and Peasants in Medieval England. The Common Law of Villeinage in the Twelfth and Thirteenth Centuries* (Oxford, 1980).

4. Hyams, *Kings, Lords and Peasants*, 240.

5. On definitions of 'freedom', see R. H. Hilton, 'Freedom and villeinage in England', *Past and Present*, 31 (1965), reprinted in R. H. Hilton (ed.), *Peasants, Knights and Heretics. Studies in Medieval English Social History* (Cambridge, 1976) (from which subsequent references are taken).

6. See Hyams, *Kings, Lords and Peasants*; this also from R. H. Hilton, *The Decline of Serfdom in Medieval England* (Cambridge, 1966), 14–19; Faith, *English Peasantry and the Growth of Lordship*, 251.

7. C. Howell, *Land, Family and Inheritance in Transition. Kibworth Harcourt, 1280–1700* (Cambridge, 1983), 53; *Halmota Prioratus Dunelmensis. Containing Extracts from the Halmote Court or Manor Rolls of the Prior and Convent of Durham*, ed. J. Booth (Surtees Society, vol. 82, 1886), 33; see also discussion in P. D. A. Harvey, 'Conclusion', in *idem* (ed.), *The Peasant Land Market in Medieval England* (Oxford, 1984), 334–5.

8. *English Historical Documents. Vol. 5, 1485–1558*, ed. C. H. Williams (Oxford, 1971), 273.

9. We should not ignore the possibility that, as serfdom drifted into oblivion, there were some landlords who made exaggerated claims of it, in which case Arundel might look even more like a medieval landlord than did medieval landlords themselves.

10. Henry de Bracton, *De legibus et consuetudinibus Angliae*, f.207, quoted in A. W. B. Simpson, *An Introduction to the History of the Land Law* (1961), 72–3.

11. Villeins did however have access to the king's court in other matters and we would be wholly wrong to view them as unfamiliar with the workings of the common law: see pp. 81–2.

12. Other payments could also have been used as evidence, see pp. 50–1.

13. *Curia Regis Rolls* (hereafter *CRR*), 1233–1237, 108.

14. Hyams, *Kings, Lords and Peasants*, 194–7; for further discussion of tenants' obligations, see pp. 26–33.

15. R. H. Hilton, 'Peasant movements in medieval England', *Economic History Review*, 2nd ser., 2 (1949), repr. in E. M. Carus-Wilson (ed.), *Essays in Economic History. Vol. 2* (London, 1962), 79–80 (from which subsequent references are taken); Z. Razi, 'The struggles between the abbots of Halesowen and their tenants in the thirteenth and fourteenth centuries', in T. H. Aston, P. R. Coss, C. Dyer and J. Thirsk (eds), *Social Relations and their Ideas. Essays in Honour of R. H. Hilton* (Cambridge, 1983), 154–6; see also pp. 30–1.

16. J. Hatcher, 'English serfdom and villeinage: towards a reassessment', *Past and Present*, 160 (1998).

17. M. J. McIntosh, *Autonomy and Community. The Royal Manor of Havering, 1200–1500* (Cambridge, 1986), 42–9; for discussion of ancient demesne and villein sokemen, see also R. S. Hoyt, *The Royal Demesne in English Constitutional History, 1066–1272* (Ithaca, NY, 1950), 192–207; B. P. Wolffe, *The Royal Demesne in English History. The Crown Estate in the Governance of the Realm from the Conquest to 1509* (London, 1971), 17–26. See also pp. 163–4.

18. E. Miller (ed.), *The Agrarian History of England and Wales. Vol. 3, 1348–1500* (Cambridge, 1991), ch. 7, *passim*.

19. Howell, *Kibworth Harcourt*, 52–3.

20. Harvey, 'Conclusion', 328; also Hilton, *Decline of Serfdom*, 48.

21. J. Hatcher, *Rural Economy and Society in the Duchy of Cornwall, 1300–1500* (Cambridge, 1970), 52–3.

22. C. Dyer, 'The English medieval village community and its decline', *Journal of British Studies*, 33 (1994), 411.

23. Westminster Abbey Muniments 25423; Bodleian Library, Suffolk Rolls 21.

24. E. Miller, *The Abbey and Bishopric of Ely. The Social History of an Ecclesiastical Estate from the Tenth to the Early Fourteenth Century* (Cambridge, 1951), 104.

25. B. F. Harvey, *Westminster Abbey and its Estates in the Middle Ages* (Oxford, 1977), 251–4.

26. C. Dyer, *Lords and Peasants in a Changing Society. The Estates of the Bishopric of Worcester, 680–1540* (Cambridge, 1980), 120; R. A. Lomas, 'Developments in land tenure on the prior of Durham's estate in the later Middle Ages', *Northern History*, 13 (1977), 27–43.

27. C. Dyer, 'Tenant farming and tenant farmers: E. The West Midlands', in Miller (ed.), *Agrarian History of England and Wales. Vol. 3*, 640.

28. T. Lomas, 'South-east Durham: late fourteenth and fifteenth centuries', in Harvey (ed.), *Peasant Land Market*, 311–13.

29. P. R. Schofield, 'Tenurial developments and the availability of customary land in a later medieval community', *Economic History Review*, 49 (1996), 257.

30. E. King, 'Tenant farming and tenant farmers: D. The East Midlands', in Miller (ed.), *Agrarian History of England and Wales. Vol. 3*, 629.

31. Dyer, 'West Midlands', 639.

32. For Hakeford Hall, see B. M. S. Campbell, 'Population pressure, inheritance and the land market in a fourteenth-century peasant community', in R. M. Smith (ed.), *Land, Kinship and Life-Cycle* (Cambridge, 1984), 120–7.

33. L. Slota, 'Law, land transfer and lordship on the estates of St Albans Abbey in the thirteenth and fourteenth centuries', *Law and History Review*, 6 (1988), 132.

34. See pp. 60–1, for example.

35. E. A. Kosminsky, *Studies in the Agrarian History of England in the Thirteenth Century* (Oxford, 1956), 205–6, 228; Hilton, *Decline of Serfdom*, 19.

36. For a general discussion of developments in free tenure, see Simpson, *History of Land Law*, ch. 3. On *Quia Emptores*, see also p. 60.

37. Westminster Abbey Muniments 25568.

38. A. E. Levett, *The Black Death on the Estates of the See of Winchester* (Oxford, 1916), 22–5. The remaining two tenants holding what appear to have been fractions of virgates held, respectively, a messuage and eight acres and a two-acre holding (without a messuage), suggesting that a quarter-virgate had begun to disintegrate: *ibid.*, 24; for further discussion of the fragmentation of such holdings, see pp. 55–6, 66, 68.

39. Levett, *Black Death*, 23–4.

40. Kosminsky, *Studies in the Agrarian History of England*, 216, 223; E. Miller and J. Hatcher, *Medieval England. Rural Society and Economic Change, 1086–1348* (Harlow, 1978), 143–4; C. Dyer, *Standards of Living in the Later Middle Ages. Social Change in England, c.1200–1520* (Cambridge, 1989), 120.

41. Levett, *Black Death*, 23–4.

42. Hatcher, *Duchy of Cornwall*, 225–52; A. J. Winchester, *Landscape and Society in Medieval Cumbria* (Edinburgh, 1987), 62–4. But, for clear indications of open-field agriculture in Cornwall, see *The Cornish Lands of the Arundells of Lanherne. Fourteenth to Sixteenth Centuries*, ed. H. S. A. Fox and O. J. Padel (Devon and Cornwall Record Society, n.s., 41, 2000), ch. 5.

43. R. M. Smith, 'Families and their land in an area of partible inheritance: Redgrave, Suffolk, 1260–1320', in *idem* (ed.), *Land, Kinship and Life-Cycle*, 139–44.

44. *The Sibton Abbey Estates. Select Documents, 1325–1509*, ed. A. H. Denney (Suffolk Records Society, vol. 2, 1960), 72–4.

45. A. R. H. Baker, 'Some fields and farms in medieval Kent', *Archaeologia Cantiana*, 80 (1965), 158.

46. *Feudal Documents from the Abbey of Bury St Edmunds*, ed. D. C. Douglas (British Academy Records of the Social and Economic History of England and Wales, vol. 8, 1932), 40–1; *The Kalendar of Abbot Samson of Bury St Edmunds and Related Documents*, ed. R. H. C. Davis (Camden, 3rd ser., vol. 84, 1954), 47; *A Suffolk Hundred in the Year 1283. The Assessment of the Hundred of Blackbourne for a Tax of One Thirtieth, and a Return Showing the Land Tenure there*, ed. E. Powell (Cambridge, 1910), 22.
47. See pp. 61–2, 63–9.
48. I. M. W. Harvey, 'Bernwood in the Middle Ages', in J. Broad and R. Hoyle (eds), *Bernwood. The Life and Afterlife of a Forest* (Preston, 1997), 16.
49. M. Stinson, 'Assarting and poverty in early fourteenth-century western Yorkshire', *Landscape History*, 5 (1983).
50. See pp. 55, 72–5, 85–6.
51. Hatcher, 'English serfdom and villeinage', 255–6.
52. See also pp. 15, 50–1.
53. Levett, *Black Death*, 23–5.
54. P. D. A. Harvey, *A Medieval Oxfordshire Village. Cuxham, 1240–1400* (Oxford, 1965), 119.
55. Hatcher, *Duchy of Cornwall*, 64–8.
56. R. M. Smith, 'Some thoughts on "hereditary" and "proprietary" rights in land under customary law in thirteenth and early fourteenth century England', *Law and History Review*, 1 (1983), 116–17; see also pp. 66–7.
57. Hatcher, *Duchy of Cornwall*, 59.
58. Hilton, 'Freedom and villeinage'.
59. *Ibid.*, 182; also Hatcher, 'English serfdom and villeinage', 256–7, makes similar points about rents and unassessed exactions; A. L. Poole, *Obligations of Society in the Twelfth and Thirteenth Centuries* (Oxford, 1946), 20–1.
60. Harvey, *Westminster Abbey and its Estates*, 113–14.
61. M. C. Hill, *The Demesne and the Waste. A Study of Medieval Enclosure on the Manor of High Ercall, 1086–1399* (Transactions of the Shropshire Archaeological Society, vol. 62, 1984), 23–4.
62. F. G. Davenport, *The Economic Development of a Norfolk Manor, 1086–1565* (Cambridge, 1906), 70; E. King, *Peterborough Abbey, 1086–1310. A Study in the Land Market* (Cambridge, 1973), ch. 6.
63. Miller, *Abbey and Bishopric of Ely*, 109.
64. For example, Miller, *Abbey and Bishopric of Ely*, 107; Smith, ' "Hereditary" and "proprietary" rights', 118.
65. R. H. Hilton, 'Gloucester Abbey leases of the late thirteenth century', *University of Birmingham Historical Journal*, 4 (1953), reprinted *idem, The English Peasantry in the Later Middle Ages* (Oxford, 1975), 150–2.
66. Hatcher, *Duchy of Cornwall*, 86–92.
67. Miller, *Abbey and Bishopric of Ely*, 111; Harvey, *Westminster Abbey and its Estates*.

CHAPTER 3   DETERMINANTS OF PEASANT LANDHOLDING

1. *English Historical Documents. Vol. 2, 1042–1189*, ed. D. C. Douglas and G. W. Greenaway (Oxford, 2nd edn, 1981), 875–6.

2. S. Harvey, 'Domesday England', in H. E. Hallam (ed.), *The Agrarian History of England and Wales. Vol. 2, 1042–1350* (Cambridge, 1988), 77–8.
3. See pp. 163–4.
4. See pp, 21, 38.
5. See pp. 31–2.
6. P. D. A. Harvey, 'The English inflation of 1180–1220', *Past and Present*, 61 (1973), repr. in Hilton (ed.), *Peasants, Knights and Heretics* (from which subsequent references are taken); M. Mate, 'High prices in early fourteenth-century England: causes and consequences', *Economic History Review*, 2nd ser., 28 (1975); N. J. Mayhew, 'Numismatic evidence and falling prices in the fourteenth century', *Economic History Review*, 2nd ser., 27 (1974).
7. M. M. Postan and J. Hatcher, 'Population and class relations in feudal society', *Past and Present*, 78 (1978), repr. in T. H. Aston and C. H. E. Philpin (eds), *The Brenner Debate. Agrarian Class Structure and Economic Development in Pre-Industrial Europe* (Cambridge, 1985). For a fuller discussion of demographic change, see pp. 91–2.
8. J. Hatcher, 'English serfdom and villeinage: towards a reassessment', *Past and Present*, 90, repr. in T. H. Aston (ed.), *Landlords, Peasants and Politics in Medieval England* (Cambridge, 1987), from which subsequent references are taken: 'The emphasis which was increasingly placed upon extraordinary charges relating to marriages, deaths and successions of vassals and their families was to a large extent an inevitable consequence of the inflexibility of ordinary sources of revenue in the face of the rising value of land and the falling value of money' (p. 257).
9. Hatcher, 'English serfdom and villeinage', 262 and references there, n.36. See also p. 42.
10. C. Dyer, *Lords and Peasants in a Changing Society. The Estates of the Bishopric of Worcester, 680–1540* (Cambridge, 1980), ch. 13; B. F. Harvey, *Westminster Abbey and its Estates in the Middle Ages* (Oxford, 1977), 270; P. R. Schofield, 'Tenurial developments and the availability of customary land in a later medieval community', *Economic History Review*, 49 (1996), 258–60; T. Lomas, 'South-east Durham: late fourteenth and fifteenth centuries', in P. D. A. Harvey (ed.), *The Peasant Land Market in Medieval England* (Oxford, 1984), 261.
11. J. Birrell, 'Peasant craftsmen in the medieval forest', *Agricultural History Review*, 17 (1969), 96.
12. *Feudal Documents from the Abbey of Bury St Edmunds*, ed. D. C. Douglas (British Academy Records of the Social and Economic History of England and Wales, vol. 8, 1932), cxxxii, n. 4; see also, N. Neilson, *Customary Rents* (Oxford, 1910), ch. 1.
13. It has recently been suggested that such difference may have been more apparent than real, R. Faith, *The English Peasantry and the Growth of Lordship* (Leicester, 1997), 121–5.
14. See, for instance, G. C. Homans, *English Villagers of the Thirteenth Century* (Harvard, 1941), 116–20; *idem*, 'Partible inheritance of villagers' holdings', *Economic History Review*, 8 (1937), 48–56; *idem*, 'The Frisians in East Anglia', *Economic History Review*, 2nd ser., 10 (1957–8), 189–206. For a contrary interpretation, see R. J. Faith, 'Peasant families and inheritance

customs in medieval England', *Agricultural History Review*, 14 (1966); also *idem*, *English Peasantry and the Growth of Lordship*, 135–7.

15. See, for instance, Homans, *English Villagers*.

16. *Select Cases in Manorial Courts, 1250–1550. Property and Family Law*, ed. L. R. Poos and L. Bonfield (Selden Society, 1998), 10, 19–20.

17. *Court Rolls of the Manor of Wakefield. Vol. 2, 1297 to 1309*, ed. W. P. Baildon (Yorkshire Archaeological Society, vol. 36, 1906), 208.

18. *The Court Rolls of Walsham le Willows, 1303–1350*, ed. R. Lock (Suffolk Records Society, vol. 41, 1998), 154–5; see, for further examples, J. A. Raftis, *Tenure and Mobility. Studies in the Social History of the Medieval English Village* (Toronto, 1964), 88.

19. Essex Record Office D/DU 267/29, court of 17 March 1338.

20. Z. Razi, 'Family, land and the village community in later medieval England', *Past and Present*, 93 (1981), repr. in Aston (ed.), *Landlords, Peasants and Politics* (from which this and subsequent references are taken), 383.

21. See pp. 159–65.

22. M. K. McIntosh, *Controlling Misbehavior in England, 1370–1600* (Cambridge, 1998); M. Spufford, 'Puritanism and social control', in A. Fletcher and J. Stevenson (eds), *Order and Disorder in Early Modern England* (Cambridge, 1985).

23. See, for example, pp. 71–2, 167–9.

24. *Court Rolls of the Manor of Wakefield. Vol. 3, 1313 to 1316, and 1286*, ed. J. Lister (Yorkshire Archaeological Society, vol. 57, 1917), 155; *Court Rolls of Walsham le Willows*, ed. Lock, 128.

25. *The Peasants' Revolt of 1381*, ed. R. B. Dobson (2nd edn, London, 1983), 165.

26. R. H. Hilton, *Bond Men Made Free. Medieval Peasant Movements and the English Rising of 1381* (London, 1973), 232.

27. See pp. 68–9, 111.

28. Harvey, 'English inflation', 63.

29. Harvey, *Westminster Abbey and its Estates*, 130–1; Harvey, 'English inflation', 60; E. Miller, 'England in the twelfth and thirteenth centuries: an economic contrast?', *Economic History Review*, 2nd ser., 24 (1971), 8–9.

30. See pp. 26–8.

31. J. M. W. Bean, 'Landlords', in E. Miller (ed.), *The Agrarian History of England and Wales. Vol. 3, 1348–1500* (Cambridge, 1991), 575–6.

32. J. Hatcher, *Rural Economy and Society in the Duchy of Cornwall, 1300–1500* (Cambridge, 1970), 85–6. In other cases some of the smaller lay lords leased their demesnes much earlier: J. A. Tuck, 'Tenant farming and tenant farmers: A. The Northern Borders', in Miller (ed.), *Agrarian History of England and Wales*, vol. 3, 587. For useful summaries see, for example, J. L. Bolton, *The Medieval English Economy, 1150–1500* (London, 1980), 220; T. A. R. Evans and R. J. Faith, 'College estates and university finances, 1350–1500', in J. L. Catto and T. A. R. Evans (eds), *The History of the University of Oxford. Vol. 2, Late Medieval Oxford* (Oxford, 1992), 671 (and for further references see *ibid.*, n.120).

33. For this and similar examples, see P. D. A. Harvey, 'Tenant farming and tenant farmers: G. The Home Counties', in Miller (ed.), *Agrarian History of England and Wales, Vol. 3*, 667.

34. M. M. Postan, 'The chronology of labour services', *Transactions of the Royal Historical Society*, 4th ser., 20 (1937), repr. in *idem, Essays on Medieval Agriculture*, 91 (from which this and subsequent references are taken).

35. M. Mate, 'Tenant farming and tenant farmers: H. Kent and Sussex', in Miller (ed.), *Agrarian History of England and Wales, Vol. 3*, 683.

36. See, for example, C. Dyer, 'Tenant farming and tenant farmers: E. The West Midlands', in Miller (ed.), *Agrarian History of England and Wales, Vol. 3*, 639.

37. F. R. H. DuBoulay, 'Who were farming the English demesnes at the end of the Middle Ages?', *Economic History Review*, 2nd ser., 17 (1964–5); B. F. Harvey, 'The leasing of the abbot of Westminster's demesnes in the later Middle Ages', *Economic History Review*, 2nd ser., 22 (1969) for later lessees; on peasant lessees in the eleventh and twelfth centuries, R. Lennard, *Rural England, 1086–1135. A Study of Social and Agrarian Conditions* (Oxford, 1959), 153–5; Harvey, 'English inflation', 62.

38. Bean, 'Landlords', 575–6; on the agenda of minor landlords more generally, see R. H. Britnell, 'Minor landlords in England and medieval agrarian capitalism', *Past and Present*, 89 (1980), repr. in Aston (ed.), *Landlords, Peasants and Politics*. For the further and separate distinction that direct management could not be imposed on manors held by the king, see Harvey, 'English inflation', 65–7.

39. See also p. 66.

40. Britnell, 'Minor landlords'.

41. We should note, however, that the percentages given include tithe corn from appropriated churches as well as grain from the rectory farms: Harvey, *Westminster Abbey and its Estates*, 140–8.

42. See for example pp. 164–5; note also that a contrary argument, based on productivity, can also be offered here. If, as Stone has shown, customary labour was less effective than hired labour, then those demesnes which were orientated towards the market may, in fact, have relied less on labour services in order to maximise yields. On the productivity of customary labour, see D. Stone, 'The productivity of hired and customary labour: evidence from Wisbech Barton in the fourteenth century', *Economic History Review*, l (1997).

43. See p. 15.

44. On implied manumission, see P. R. Hyams, *Kings, Lords and Peasants in Medieval England. The Common Law of Villeinage in the Twelfth and Thirteenth Centuries* (Oxford, 1980), 45; for actual manumission see, for example, A. L. Poole, *Obligations of Society in the Twelfth and Thirteenth Centuries* (Oxford, 1946), 30–4.

45. P. D. A. Harvey, 'Initiative and authority in settlement change', in M. Aston, D. Austin and C. Dyer (eds), *Rural Settlements of Medieval England* (Oxford, 1989).

Chapter 4   The Transfer of Peasant Land

1. See pp. 101–2, 140, 143–6.

2. A. Macfarlane, *The Origins of English Individualism* (Oxford, 1978).

3. *Carte Nativorum. A Peterborough Cartulary of the Fourteenth Century*, eds

C. N. L. Brooke and M. M. Postan (Northamptonshire Record Society, vol. 20, 1960), xxxiv. The introduction to this edition is reprinted as M. M. Postan, 'The charters of the villeins', in *idem, Essays on Medieval Agriculture* (from which subsequent references are taken). See also, D. Thorner, B. Kerblay and R. E. F. Smith (eds), *A.V. Chayanov on the Theory of Peasant Economy* (Madison, WI, 1986); the Chayanovian model as applied to the study of the English peasant land market is discussed in detail by R. M. Smith, 'Some issues concerning families and their property in rural England, 1250–1800', in *idem* (ed.), *Land, Kinship and Life-Cycle* (Cambridge, 1984), 6–21.

4. P. R. Hyams, 'The origins of a peasant land market in England', *Economic History Review*, 23 (1970), 19–20.

5. Z. Razi, 'Family, land and the village community in later medieval England', *Past and Present*, 93 (1981), 373–5; Razi's views are modified in *idem*, 'The myth of the immutable English family', *Past and Present*, 140 (1993), 22–33.

6. R. R. Davies, *Lordship and Society in the March of Wales, 1284–1400* (Oxford, 1978), 430.

7. R. J. Faith, 'Berkshire: fourteenth and fifteenth centuries', in P. D. A. Harvey (ed.), *The Peasant Land Market in Medieval England* (Oxford, 1984), 128; A. Jones, 'Bedfordshire: fifteenth century', *ibid.*, 203. The situation was mirrored elsewhere: see, for example, J. Z. Titow, 'Lost rents, vacant holdings and the contraction of peasant cultivation after the Black Death', *Agricultural History Review*, 42 (1994); see also R. J. Faith, 'Peasant families and inheritance customs in medieval England', *Agricultural History Review*, 14 (1966), 86–92.

8. B. F. Harvey, *Westminster Abbey and its Estates in the Middle Ages* (Oxford, 1977), ch. xi; P. R. Schofield, '*Extranei* and the market for customary land on a Westminster Abbey manor in the fifteenth century', *Agricultural History Review*, 49 (2001), 5 (table 1).

9. C. Dyer, *Lords and Peasants in a Changing Society. The Estates of the Bishopric of Worcester, 680–1540* (Cambridge, 1980), 301–5.

10. For example, Davies, *Lordship and Society*, 431. See Razi, 'Immutable English family', 28–31.

11. R. H. Hilton, *The Economic Development of some Leicestershire Estates in the Fourteenth and Fifteenth Centuries* (Oxford, 1947), 100–5; also P. D. A. Harvey, 'Conclusion', in *idem* (ed.), *The Peasant Land Market in Medieval England* (Oxford, 1984), 340–4, 349–53.

12. E. Miller, 'Tenant farming and tenant farmers: B. Yorkshire and Lancashire', in *idem* (ed.), *Agrarian History of England and Wales, Vol. 3, 1348–1500* (Cambridge, 1991), 601.

13. Hyams, 'Origins of a peasant land market'.

14. E. Miller and J. Hatcher, *Medieval England. Rural Society and Economic Change, 1086–1348* (Harlow, 1978), 145; R. M. Smith, 'Some thoughts on "hereditary" and "proprietary" rights in land under customary law in thirteenth and fourteenth century England', *Law and History Review*, 1 (1983), 107–10.

15. See p. 39, for example.

16. R. M. Smith, 'Human resources', in G. Astill and A. Grant (eds), *The Countryside of Medieval England* (Oxford, 1988), 196–202.
17. See pp. 25–6.
18. D. Moss, 'The economic development of a Middlesex village', *Agricultural History Review*, 28 (1980), 108–9.
19. P. R. Schofield, 'Access to credit in the early fourteenth-century English countryside', in *idem* and N. J. Mayhew (eds), *Credit and Debt in Medieval England c.1180–c.1350* (Oxbow, 2002).
20. E. M. Carus-Wilson, 'Evidences of industrial growth on some fifteenth-century manors', *Economic History Review*, 2nd ser., 12 (1959).
21. See pp. 150–1; also E. B. Fryde, *Peasants and Landlords in Later Medieval England* (Stroud, 1996), 87–104; P. R. Schofield, 'Dearth, debt and the local land market in a late thirteenth-century village community', *Agricultural History Review*, 45 (1997), 11–12.
22. See pp. 118, 171–5, 192, 194.
23. Schofield, 'Dearth, debt and the local land market', 15–17.
24. *Thomas Wright's Political Songs of England from the Reign of John to that of Edward II*, ed. P. R. Coss (Cambridge, 1996), 186, 196.
25. On the boost given to a market in free land, see J. M. W. Bean, *The Decline of English Feudalism, 1215–1540* (Manchester, 1968), ch. 2.
26. See pp. 65–9. Issues of subinfeudation did not apply to unfree land which was, *de iure*, the free holding of the lord; consequently transfer of unfree land was always effected by substitution of the outgoing tenant by the incoming tenant. In this, at least, a market in unfree land in the thirteenth century was less encumbered than was a market in free land, see J. H. Baker, *An Introduction to English Legal History* (London, 3rd edn, 1990), 298.
27. See also pp. 184–5.
28. Z. Razi and R. M. Smith, 'The origins of the English manorial court rolls as a written record: a puzzle', in Razi and Smith (eds), *Medieval Society and the Manor Court* (Oxford, 1996), 45–6.
29. See p. 55.
30. Faith, 'Peasant families and inheritance customs'.
31. See, for instance, the graphs of land sales in B. M. S. Campbell, 'Population pressure, inheritance and the land market in a fourteenth-century peasant community', in R. M. Smith (ed.), *Land, Kinship and Life-Cycle*, 108–9; also pp. 66–7.
32. D. N. McCloskey, 'The open fields of England: rent, risk, and the rate of interest, 1300–1815', in D. W. Galenson (ed.), *Markets in History. Economic Studies of the Past* (Cambridge, 1989).
33. For example, B. F. Harvey, 'The population trend in England between 1300 and 1348', *Transactions of the Royal Historical Society*, 5th ser., 16 (1966), 40–1.
34. R. J. Faith, 'Berkshire: fourteenth and fifteenth centuries', in P. D. A. Harvey (ed.), *The Peasant Land Market in Medieval England* (Oxford, 1984), 124.
35. Davies, *Lordship and Society*, 442.
36. For example, C. Dyer, 'Tenant farming and tenant farmers: E. The West

Midlands', in E. Miller (ed.), *The Agrarian History of England and Wales*, vol. 3, 636. They are also evident in an attempt to ensure that primogeniture, rather than partibility, was the common practice for inheritance, for which see pp. 68–9.

37. Harvey, *Westminster Abbey and its Estates*, 299–307.
38. R. M. Smith's study of Redgrave found that, although the overall acreage of land suggested that most land in this Suffolk manor was transferred at point of death, the vast majority of actual land transfers were *inter-vivos* and generated by far the greater part of manorial revenue *c*.1300: 'Some thoughts on "hereditary" and "proprietary" rights in land', 116–17. Compare also Harvey, *Westminster Abbey and its Estates*, 286–7 with *ibid.*, 206–7. For further examples from eastern England, see E. Miller, *The Abbey and Bishopric of Ely. The Social History of an Ecclesiastical Estate from the Tenth to the Early Fourteenth Century* (Cambridge, 1951), 138–9, 151–2.
39. R. M. Smith, 'Families and their land in an area of partible inheritance: Redgrave, Suffolk, 1260–1320', in *idem* (ed.) *Land, Kinship and Life-Cycle* (Cambridge, 1984), 142–3, 156–8; *idem*, 'Some thoughts on "hereditary" and "proprietary" rights in land', 116–17; also J. Williamson, 'Norfolk: thirteenth century', in P. D. A. Harvey (ed.), *The Peasant Land Market in Medieval England* (Oxford, 1984), 57–8.
40. Smith, 'Families and their land', 165–71.
41. Harvey, *Westminster Abbey and its Estates*, 300.
42. *Ibid.*, 205ff., 300ff.
43. For examples, see Harvey, 'Population trend', 40; F. R. H. DuBoulay, *The Lordship of Canterbury. An Essay on Medieval Society* (London, 1966), 214–18; H. C. Darby, *The Medieval Fenland* (Cambridge, 1940), 42–55.
44. See pp. 25–6; for an example, see M. C. Hill, *The Demesne and the Waste. A Study of the Medieval Enclosure of the Manor of High Ercall, 1086–1399* (Transactions of the Shropshire Archaeological Society, vol. 62, 1984), 23–4.
45. See pp. 131–4 for the chronology of market foundation.
46. Williamson, 'Norfolk: thirteenth century', 57–8; Dyer, *Lords and Peasants in a Changing Society*, 106–7; Harvey, *Westminster Abbey and its Estates*, 299–300; Harvey, 'Conclusion', 348. See also pp. 107–13.
47. See pp. 101–2.
48. For references, see above, nn.5 and 6; also C. Howell, *Land, Family and Inheritance in Transition. Kibworth Harcourt, 1280–1700* (Cambridge, 1983), 240–1, 249. Further references can also be found in Razi, 'Immutable English family', 33, n.114.
49. See also pp. 53, 55.
50. For a recent contribution which returns to the issues of lordship as a challenge to the family–land bond, see J. Whittle, 'Individualism and the family–land bond: a reassessment of land transfer patterns among the English peasantry, *c*.1270–1580', *Past and Present*, 160 (1998).
51. We should acknowledge that recovery of land by widows is also symptomatic of an active land market, a view contrary to that of, say, G. C. Homans. Homans had also noted that widows often returned to court to

claim land alienated by their husbands prior to their deaths, their claim based on their inability to gainsay their husbands who had sold away their dower rights in land. He interpreted this as an indication that rights of alienation were, on certain manors in central England, limited to the lifetime of the grantor or of the grantee: Homans, *English Villagers of the Thirteenth Century* (Harvard, 1941), 195–7. Although this feature is therefore also seen by Homans as consistent with restrictions on alienation, it is in fact important to recognise that such widows were employing devices borrowed from common law, their response evidence both of the active market in land which had created their predicament and the sophistication of local legal fora which had developed in part to service this market.

52. In this context see Williamson, 'Norfolk: thirteenth century', 56–7, who argues that although partibility should have led to significant division of holdings it did not because the peasant family sought to preserve the integrity of the group: hence divisions reform under the headship of one sibling. See also, B. Dodwell, 'Holdings and inheritance in medieval East Anglia', *Economic History Review*, 2nd ser., 20 (1967); see also Smith, 'Families and their land', 137.

53. J. S. Beckerman, 'Procedural innovation and institutional change in medieval English manorial courts', *Law and History Review*, 10 (1992), 223.

54. See also pp. 106–7 for the role of the community in encouraging widow remarriage.

55. For the classic statement on this issue, see R. H. Tawney, *The Agrarian Problem in the Sixteenth Century* (London, 1912), ch. 2.

56. See pp. 101–2.

57. As might be imagined, historians have taken extraordinarily removed positions here. For the view from one position, see J. A. Raftis, *Peasant Economic Development within the English Manorial System* (Stroud, 1997), 129–31.

58. Smith, 'Families and their land', 159–65; Schofield, 'Dearth, debt and the local land market', 9–15; *idem*, 'Peasants and the manor court', 18–20. For intra-communal tensions, see pp. 166–9.

59. See pp. 145–6.

60. Schofield, 'Dearth, debt and the local land market', and pp. 180–1.

61. P. R. Hyams, *Kings, Lords and Peasants in Medieval England. The Common Law of Villeinage in the Twelfth and Thirteenth Centuries* (Oxford, 1980), ch. 5.

62. See pp. 53–4.

63. J. Ravensdale, 'Population changes and the transfer of customary land on a Cambridgeshire manor in the fourteenth century' in Smith (ed.), *Land, Kinship and Life-Cycle* (Cambridge, 1984).

64. Campbell, 'Population pressure, inheritance and the land market', 112–13; Z. Razi, *Life, Marriage and Death in a Medieval Parish* (Cambridge, 1980), 37, 88; Schofield, 'Dearth, debt and the local land market', 1–2.

65. See also pp. 140, 143–4.

Part II Family

1. R. M. Smith, 'Some issues concerning families and their property in rural England, 1250–1800', in R. M. Smith (ed.), *Land, Kinship and Life-Cycle* (Cambridge, 1984), 22ff.

CHAPTER 5 FAMILY, HOUSEHOLD AND KIN

1. A. McFarlane, *The Origins of English Individualism* (Oxford, 1978), 147.
2. P. R. Schofield, 'The family and the village community: England, 1100–1500', in S. H. Rigby (ed.), *The Blackwell Companion to Later Medieval Britain* (forthcoming, Oxford, 2002), for a recent overview of these issues.
3. For an early review of the issues and the need for careful use of terms, see P. Laslett, 'Introduction: the history of the family', in P. Laslett and R. Wall (eds), *Household and Family in Past Time. Comparative Studies in the Size and Structure of the Domestic Group over the Last Three Centuries in England, France, Serbia, Japan and Colonial North America* (Cambridge, 1972), 34–40.
4. G. C. Homans, *English Villagers of the Thirteenth Century* (Harvard, 1941).
5. Homans, *English Villagers*, 119–20; the work of Homans has been criticised, not least because his sample of wealthier villagers in 'champion' England is representative only of a particular type of peasant: R. M. Smith, 'Some issues concerning families and their property in rural England, 1250–1800', in *idem* (ed.), *Land, Kinship and Life-Cycle* (Cambridge, 1984), 16.
6. See pp. 154–6, for example.
7. For a recent edition of some county returns, C. Fenwick, *The Poll Taxes of 1377, 1379, and 1381. Pt.1: Bedfordshire–Leicestershire* (Oxford, 1998). Sections of the 1379 and 1380 poll-taxes are quoted in, *inter alia*, J. P. J. Goldberg, *Women in England, c.1275–1525* (Manchester, 1995), 181–2 (1379). Sir C. Oman, *The Great Revolt of 1381* (Oxford, 1906), app. 3 (1380). The 1377 poll-tax also contains 'a handful . . . of nominative listings': J. P. J. Goldberg, *Women, Work and Life-Cycle* (Oxford, 1992), 305; for a brief example, *idem*, *Women in England*, 130–1.
8. J. C. Russell, *British Medieval Population* (Albuquerque, 1948), 26–9; cf. J. Krause, 'The medieval household: large or small?', *Economic History Review*, 2nd ser., 9 (1956–7).
9. H. E. Hallam, 'Some thirteenth-century censuses', *Economic History Review*, 2nd ser., 10 (1958); R. M. Smith, 'Hypothèses sur la nuptialité en Angleterre aux xiiie–xive siècles', *Annales: Économies, Sociétés, Civilisations* (1983), 120.
10. On the Spalding Priory manors, in the thirteenth century, a few households (less than 4%) also contained only one person: H. E. Hallam, 'Some thirteenth-century censuses', 352–3.
11. Z. Razi, *Life, Marriage and Death in a Medieval Parish. Economy, Society and Demography in Halesowen (1270–1400)* (Cambridge, 1980), 93.

12. C. Howell, *Land, Family and Inheritance in Transition. Kibworth Harcourt, 1280–1700* (Cambridge, 1983), 232–5.

13. Razi, *Life, Marriage and Death*, 83–6, 140–4.

14. The concept of the complex familial group as a standard of the later Middle Ages giving way to the nucleated family in the early modern period has now been supplanted by the thesis that it was the predominance of nuclear families that defined the familial system of the peasantry in the late Middle Ages as well as in the early modern period. See, for example, R. M. Smith, 'Some reflections on the evidence for the origins of the "European marriage pattern" in England', in C. Harris (ed.), *The Sociology of the Family. New Directions for Britain* (Keele, 1979). For earlier views, see, for example, L. Stone, *The Family, Sex and Marriage in England, 1500–1800* (London, 1977) and the brief discussion of the same by J. M. Bennett, *Women in the Medieval English Countryside. Gender and Household in Brigstock before the Plague* (Oxford, 1987), 48–9.

15. E. Miller and J. Hatcher, *Medieval England. Rural Society and Economic Change, 1086–1348* (Harlow, 1978), 140; Hallam, 'Some thirteenth-century censuses', 352.

16. Homans, *English Villagers*, 144–5; also Z. Razi, 'Family, land and the village community in later medieval England', *Past and Present*, 93 (1981), repr. in T. H. Aston (ed.), *Landlords, Peasants and Politics in Medieval England* (Cambridge, 1987), 364.

17. C. Dyer, *Standards of Living in the Late Middle Ages. Social Change in England, 1200–1520* (Cambridge, 1989), 168, quoting an example from Enstone (Oxon.).

18. P. R. Schofield, 'Tenurial developments and the availability of customary land in a later medieval community', *Economic History Review*, 49 (1996), 261; L. R. Poos, *A Rural Society after the Black Death. Essex, 1350–1525* (Cambridge, 1991), 199.

19. G. Beresford, 'Three deserted medieval settlements on Dartmoor: a report on the late E. Marie Minter's excavations', *Medieval Archaeology*, 23 (1979), 133 (houses 7 and 4), 139.

20. Z. Razi, 'The myth of the immutable English family', *Past and Present*, 140 (1993), 30; see also, for examples, R. H. Hilton, *The Economic Development of some Leicestershire Estates in the Fourteenth and Fifteenth Centuries* (Oxford, 1947), 94–105; T. Lomas, 'South-east Durham: late fourteenth and fifteenth centuries', in P. D. A. Harvey (ed.), *The Peasant Land Market in Medieval England* (Oxford, 1984), 316; J. N. Hare, 'The demesne lessees of fifteenth-century Wiltshire', *Agricultural History Review*, 29 (1981), 10–12.

21. Dyer, *Standards of Living*, 162–3, 167.

22. See Chapter 5, *passim*.

23. Hallam, 'Some thirteenth-century censuses', 352.

24. Razi, 'Immutable English family', 6.

25. *Ibid.*, 9.

26. Hence, before the plague, a high proportion (83%) of both *post mortem* and *inter-vivos* transfers were intra-familial: *ibid.*, 17.

27. *Ibid.*, 11; also, see pp. 88, 119–27.
28. *Ibid.*, 16ff; 19–22.
29. *Ibid.*, *passim*.
30. *Ibid.*, 25.

CHAPTER 6　PEASANT MARRIAGE AND HOUSEHOLD FORMATION

1. E. A. Wrigley and R. S. Schofield, *The Population History of England and Wales, 1541–1871. A Reconstruction* (Cambridge, 1981); research associated with this project has informed the work of a number of medievalists who have sought to employ the sixteenth-century demographic landscape as a 'starting point' for their own investigations. See, for example, L. R. Poos, *A Rural Society after the Black Death* (Cambridge, 1991), 127–9.
2. For example, E. Miller and J. Hatcher, *Medieval England. Rural Society and Economic Change, 1086–1348* (Harlow, 1978), vii–x.
3. C. Dyer, *Standards of Living in the Later Middle Ages. Social Change in England, c.1200–1520* (Cambridge, 1989), 262–3, 264.
4. I. Kershaw, 'The Great Famine and agrarian crisis in England, 1315–1322', *Past and Present*, 59 (1973), repr. in R. H. Hilton (ed.), *Peasants, Knights and Heretics. Studies in Medieval English Social History* (Cambridge, 1976); Z. Razi, *Life, Marriage and Death in a Medieval Parish* (Cambridge, 1980), 39–40; B. M. S. Campbell, 'Population pressure, inheritance and the land market in a fourteenth-century peasant community', in R. M. Smith (ed.), *Land, Kinship and Life-Cycle* (Cambridge, 1984), 99, 113; A. J. Pollard, *North-Eastern England during the Wars of the Roses. Lay Society, War and Politics, 1450–1500* (Oxford, 1990), 46–8; *idem*, 'The north-eastern economy and the agrarian crisis of 1438–40', *Northern History*, 25 (1989); J. P. J. Goldberg, 'Mortality and economic change in the diocese of York, 1390–1514', *Northern History*, 43 (1900); Dyer, *Standards of Living*, 267–8; cf. J. Walter and R. Schofield, 'Famine, disease and crisis mortality in early modern society', in J. Walter and R. Schofield (eds), *Famine, Disease and the Social Order in Early Modern Society* (Cambridge, 1989), 28ff.
5. Razi, *Life, Marriage and Death*, ch. 3; R. Lock, 'The Black Death in Walsham le Willows', *Proceedings of the Suffolk Institute of Archaeology and History*, 37 (1992); Campbell, 'Inheritance and the land market', 96–7.
6. There is some suggestion that, in the fifteenth century at least, life in the countryside was healthy relative to life in the towns. This assumption is based largely upon the belief that, by the fifteenth century, communicable diseases, especially plague, were mostly resident in towns and areas of dense population. However, historical evidence for plague outbreaks becomes less robust in the fifteenth century, and if, as has been recently suggested, plague established itself as enzootic in the rodent population in the late fourteenth and fifteenth centuries, plague remained a threat wherever rodents and humans came into contact. R. S. Gottfried, *Epidemic Disease in Fifteenth Century England. The Medical Response and the Demographic Consequences* (Leicester, 1978); J. L. Bolton: 'The world upside

down: plague as an agent of economic and social change', in M. Ormrod and P. Lindley (eds), *The Black Death in England* (Stamford, 1996), 25; Poos, *A Rural Society*, 112, n. 4.

7. C. Howell, *Land, Family and Inheritance in Transition. Kibworth Harcourt, 1280–1700* (Cambridge, 1983), 225–6; B. F. Harvey, *Living and Dying in England, 1100–1540. The Monastic Experience* (Oxford, 1993), 127–9; J. Hatcher, 'Mortality in the fifteenth century: some new evidence', *Economic History Review*, 2nd ser., 39 (1986), 31–6.

8. Separate studies have produced broadly comparable results, although early studies by Postan and Titow, and Hallam, are more pessimistic than is the later research of Razi, Poos and Hallam. M. M. Postan and J. Z. Titow, 'Heriots and prices on Winchester manors', *Economic History Review*, 2nd ser., 11 (1959), 392–417, repr. in *Postan, Essays on Medieval Agriculture and General Problems of the Medieval Economy* (Cambridge, 1973); H. E. Hallam, 'Age at first marriage and age at death in the Lincolnshire Fenland, 1252–1478', *Population Studies*, 39 (1985), 64–5; Razi, *Life, Marriage and Death*, 34–45; Poos, *A Rural Society*, 118. See also the general observations of R. M. Smith, 'Demographic developments in rural England, 1300–48: a survey', in B. M. S. Campbell (ed.), *Before the Black Death. Studies in the 'Crisis' of the Early Fourteenth Century* (Manchester, 1991), 58.

9. For example, P. Franklin, 'Malaria in medieval Gloucestershire: an essay in epidemiology', *Transactions of the Bristol and Gloucestershire Archaeological Society*, 101 (1983), 111–22.

10. Hatcher, 'Mortality in the fifteenth century', 27–9; Harvey, *Living and Dying in England*, 129; G. Rosser, *Medieval Westminster, 1200–1540* (Oxford, 1989), 177–80.

11. Smith, 'Demographic developments', 59–60; Poos, *A Rural Society*, 118–20.

12. Wrigley and Schofield, *The Population History of England and Wales*, 249–52.

13. Miller and Hatcher, *Medieval England. Rural Society and Economic Change*, viii; cf. Smith, 'Demographic developments', 60.

14. Poos, *A Rural Society*, 121–7; cf. M. Bailey, 'Demographic decline in late medieval England: some thoughts on recent research', *Economic History Review*, 49 (1996).

15. W. C. Jordan, *The Great Famine. Northern Europe in the Early Fourteenth Century* (Princeton, NJ, 1996), 123 and nn. 107–8.

16. Literary evidence offers some 'anecdotal' insights, the most obvious of which is contained in Chaucer's Wife of Bath's prologue, where it is, perhaps, suggested that the Wife was first married at the age of twelve: *The Riverside Chaucer*, ed. L. D. Benson (3rd edn, Oxford, 1987), p.105, l.4.

17. See p. 121.

18. C. Dyer, 'Changes in diet in the late Middle Ages: the case of harvest workers', *Agricultural History Review*, 36 (1988), repr. in *idem, Everyday Life in Medieval England* (London, 1994); *idem*, 'English diet in the late middle Ages', in T. H. Aston, P. R. Coss, C. Dyer and J. Thirsk (eds), *Social Relations and their Ideas: Essays in Honour of R. H. Hilton* (Cambridge, 1983); *idem, Standards of Living*, 157–60.

19. On rural miners, see, for example, I. Blanchard, 'The miner and the agri-
    cultural community in medieval England', *Agricultural History Review*, 20
    (1972); *idem*, 'Stannator Fabulosus', *Agricultural History Review*, 22 (1974).
20. Broadly, here, we mean those endogenous factors which Thomas Malthus
    termed 'preventive checks' and which stand in contrast to the 'positive
    checks' of the exogenous, such as disease or weather. Smith, 'Demo-
    graphic developments', 26–30.
21. B. A. Hanawalt, *The Ties that Bound. Peasant Families in Medieval England*
    (Oxford, 1986), ch. 12, espec. 202, 204.
22. J. Hajnal, 'European marriage patterns in perspective', in D. V. Glass and
    D. E. V. Eversley (eds), *Population in History: Essays in Historical Demogra-
    phy* (London, 1965); *idem*, 'Two kinds of household formation systems',
    Population and Development Review, 8 (1982).
23. G. C. Homans, *English Villagers of the Thirteenth Century* (Harvard, 1941),
    133–76; see also the comments of Razi, *Life, Marriage and Death*, 50; Smith,
    'Demographic developments', 64–5.
24. Hallam, 'Age at first marriage and age at death in the Lincolnshire
    fenland, 1252–1478', 59; see also the comments of Smith, 'Demographic
    developments', 72–3; Poos, *A Rural Society*, 144–5.
25. See pp. 119–27.
26. Discussion of medieval marriage and its formulation by the church is
    extensive. Amongst the most important contributions are C. Donahue,
    'The policy of Alexander the Third's consent theory of marriage', in S.
    Kuttner (ed.), *Proceedings of Medieval Canon Law. Monumenta Iuris Canon-
    ici, c:5* (Vatican City, 1976), 251–81; *idem*, 'The canon law on the forma-
    tion of marriage and social practice in the later Middle Ages', *Journal of
    Family History*, 8 (1983), 144–58, espec. 144–5; M. M. Sheehan, 'Marriage
    and family in English conciliar and synodal legislation', in M. M. Sheehan,
    Marriage, Family and Law in Medieval Europe. Collected Studies (Toronto,
    1996) (from which subsequent references are taken); *idem*, 'Marriage
    theory and practice in the conciliar legislation and diocesan statutes
    of medieval England', *Mediaeval Studies*, 40 (1978), repr. in Sheehan,
    Marriage, Family and Law. For a general discussion, see J. A. Brundage,
    Medieval Canon Law (Harlow, 1995), 72–5. See also pp. 196–7 for discus-
    sion of peasant understanding of canon law of marriage.
27. M. M. Sheehan, 'Choice of marriage partner in the Middle Ages: devel-
    opment and mode of application of a theory of marriage', *Studies in
    Medieval and Renaissance History*, new ser., 1 (1978), repr. in Sheehan, *Mar-
    riage, Family and Law*, 91–2 (from which this and subsequent references
    are taken).
28. *Court Roll of Chalgrave Manor, 1278–1313*, ed. M. K. Dale (Bedfordshire
    Historical Record Society, vol. 28, 1948), 40.
29. For example, Poos has explored defamation and other pleas in ecclesias-
    tical courts, in *A Rural Society*; also *idem*, 'Sex, lies, and the church courts
    of pre-Reformation England', *Journal of Interdisciplinary History*, 25 (1995);
    on issues of familial love and hatred as revealed in other sources, notably
    coroners' records, see Hanawalt, *Ties that Bound*.
30. Poos, *A Rural Society*, 138; see also, Hanawalt, *Ties that Bound*, 199–
    200.

31. E. Clark, 'The decision to marry in thirteenth- and early fourteenth-century Norfolk', *Mediaeval Studies*, 49 (1987).
32. Razi, *Life, Marriage and Death*, 51–2; R. M. Smith, 'Families and their land in an area of partible inheritance: Redgrave, Sulfolk, 1260–1320', in *idem* (ed.) *Land, Kinship and Life-Cycle* (Cambridge, 1984), 174–5; Poos, *A Rural Society*, 141.
33. A. E. Levett, *Studies in Manorial History* (Oxford, 1938), 230–1.
34. F. M. Page, 'The customary poor law of three Cambridgeshire manors', *Cambridge Historical Journal*, 3 (1929), 129; see also, Clark, 'Decision to marry', 507.
35. J. M. Bennett, 'Conviviality and charity in medieval and early modern England', *Past and Present*, 134 (1992), 31–3.
36. Clark, 'Decision to marry', 500–1, where the work of selecting future married couples is the community's; see also this volume, pp. 116–17.
37. *Select Cases in Manorial Courts, 1250–1550. Property and Family Law*, ed. L. R. Poos and L. Bonfield (Selden Society, 1998), lxxxviii, 14–16.
38. Sheehan, 'Choice of marriage partner', 99–100, writes, 'This was the first general and organized system for negative control of the choice of marriage partner by powers other than the couple'; also *idem*, 'The formation and stability of marriage in fourteenth-century England: evidence of an Ely register', *Mediaeval Studies*, 33 (1971), repr. in Sheehan, *Marriage, Family and Law*, 45 (from which this and subsequent references are taken).
39. For instance, Sheehan, 'Choice of marriage partner', 111–17; R. Faith, 'Seigneurial control of women's marriage', *Past and Present*, 99 (1983), 135–7; Homans, *English Villagers*, 173. On, for example, the memory of marriage rites in cases of legitimacy/illegitimacy, see R. M. Smith, 'Marriage processes in the English past: some continuities', in L. Bonfield, R. Smith and K. Wrightson (eds), *The World we have Gained. Histories of Population and Social Structure* (Oxford, 1986), 57–64.
40. F. Pedersen, 'Did the medieval laity know the canon law rules on marriage? Some evidence from fourteenth-century York cause papers', *Mediaeval Studies*, 56 (1994), 123–4.
41. See also pp. 70–2.
42. See p. 168.
43. *Select Cases in Manorial Courts*, ed. Poos and Bonfield, 18–19.
44. *Court Rolls of the Manor of Wakefield. Vol. 1, 1274 to 1297*, ed. W. P. Baildon (Yorkshire Archaeological Society, vol. 29, 1900), 118–19.
45. *Select Cases in Manorial Courts*, ed. Poos and Bonfield, 38–40.
46. *Select Cases in Manorial Courts*, ed. Poos and Bonfield, cviii–cix; also, J. S. Beckerman, 'Procedural innovation and institutional change in medieval English manorial courts', *Law and History Review*, 10 (1992), 216–17.
47. *Select Cases in Manorial Courts*, ed. Poos and Bonfield, 2–3. The fact that villagers brought such questions to the manor court is testimony to a sophisticated sense of legal argument, see also Chapter 8.
48. Beckerman, 'Procedural innovation', 218–19, 224–6. *Select Cases in Manorial Courts*, ed. Poos and Bonfield, 33–43, for fifteenth-century examples.
49. Clark, 'Decision to marry in Norfolk', 500–1.
50. P. Franklin, 'Peasant widows' "liberation" and remarriage before the Black Death', *Economic History Review*, 2nd ser., 39 (1986), 195.

51. M. M. Postan, 'The charters of the villeins', in *idem*, *Essays on Medieval Agriculture*, 115–16.

52. C. Dyer, 'Changes in the size of peasant holding in some West Midlands villages, 1400–1540', in Smith (ed.), *Land, Kinship and Life-Cycle*, 289; R. M. Smith, 'The manorial court and the elderly tenant in late medieval England', in M. Pelling and R. M. Smith (eds), *Life, Death and the Elderly. Historical Perspectives* (Routledge, 1991), 45–8.

53. Essex Record Office, D/DU 267/29, courts of 18 Oct. 1331, 12 Feb. 1332.

54. See pp. 15, 36, 50.

55. J. M. Bennett, 'Medieval peasant marriage: an examination of marriage fines in *Liber Gersumarum*', in J. A. Raftis (ed.), *Pathways to Medieval Peasants* (Toronto, 1981), 200–2.

56. See p. 38, for example.

57. E. Searle, 'Seigneurial control of women's marriage: the antecedents and function of merchet in England', *Past and Present*, 82 (1979), 19ff., espec. 21–2; also Bennett, 'Medieval peasant marriage', 200.

58. Searle, 'Seigneurial control of women's marriage', 19ff.

59. On personal status, Faith, 'Seigneurial control of women's marriage', 146; on exogamy, P. A. Brand and P. R. Hyams, 'Seigneurial control of women's marriage', *Past and Present*, 99 (1983), 130–1.

60. See pp. 97, 105. See also, on customary tenants' access to free land, B. F. Harvey, *Westminster Abbey and its Estates in the Middle Ages* (Oxford, 1977), 296, where she describes family custom and the manorial rule as being 'at odds with each other'.

61. See pp. 66–7.

62. See pp. 68–9, 122.

63. See pp. 122, 123.

64. H. S. A. Fox, 'Exploitation of the landless by lords and tenants in early medieval England', in Z. Razi and R. M. Smith (eds), *Medieval Society and the Manor Court* (Oxford, 1996).

65. On this last point, see Postan, 'Charters of the villeins', 116.

66. On post-plague incidence of merchet payments, C. Dyer, 'The social and economic background to the rural revolt of 1381', in R. H. Hilton and T. H. Aston (eds), *The English Rising of 1381* (Cambridge, 1984), 23; Poos, *A Rural Society*, 246; on the fifteenth century, Faith, 'Seigneurial control of women's marriage', 147.

67. Z. Razi, 'The myth of the immutable English family', *Past and Present*, 140 (1993), 38–42.

68. On the range of these exactions, see pp. 171–5.

69. N. Ritchie (née Kenyon), 'Labour conditions in Essex in the reign of Richard II', *Economic History Review*, 4 (1934), repr. in E. M. Carus-Wilson (ed.), *Essays in Economic History* (London, 1962), vol. 2; see also L. R. Poos, 'The social context of the Statute of Labourers enforcement', *Law and History Review*, 1 (1983).

70. Bailey, 'Demographic decline'; Poos, *A Rural Society*, part V; J. P. J. Goldberg, *Women, Work and Life-Cycle* (Oxford, 1992), ch. 8; see also, S. A. C. Penn, 'Female wage earners in late fourteenth-century England', *Agricultural History Review*, 35 (1987).

71. *Proceedings before the Justices of the Peace in the Fourteenth and Fifteenth Centuries. Edward III to Richard II*, ed. B. H. Putnam and T. F. T. Plucknett (Ames Foundation, London, 1938), 358.

72. On *cui in vita sua*, see *Select Cases in Manorial Courts*, ed. Poos and Bonfield, 103; for the development of forms of tenure advantageous to women, R. M. Smith, 'Women's property rights under customary law: some developments in the thirteenth and fourteenth centuries', *Transactions of the Royal Historical Society*, 5th ser., 36 (1986); *idem*, 'Coping with uncertainty: women's tenure of customary land in England, *c*.1370–1430', in J. Kermode (ed.), *Enterprise and Individuals in Fifteenth Century England* (Stroud, 1991), 134.

73. For which, see, for example, M. M. Sheehan, *The Will in England. From the Conversion of the Anglo-Saxons to the End of the Thirteenth Century* (Toronto, 1963); see also, *idem*, 'Report of a thesis on the will', *Mediaeval Studies*, 23 (1961), 368–71, repr. in Sheehan, *Marriage, Family and Law*, 5–6.

74. See J-L. Flandrin, *Families in Former Times. Kinship, Household and Sexuality* (Cambridge, 1979), 24, where he calculates that where, in each generation, a model population had produced one boy and one girl from each marriage, a marriageable youth would be prevented from marrying 2731 cousins of his own generation as well, of course, as numerous relatives of previous and later generations.

75. For a brief discussion of rules of consanguinuity and their implementation, see M. M. Sheehan, 'The European family and canon law', *Continuity and Change*, 6 (1991), repr. in Sheehan, *Marriage, Family and Law*, 253–6 (from which this reference is taken); for English conciliar rulings on prohibited degrees of marriage, see, for example, Sheehan, 'Marriage and family in English conciliar and synodal legislation', 81–6.

76. C. E. Woodruff, 'Some early visitation rolls preserved at Canterbury', *Archaeologica Cantiana*, 32 (1917), 150; A. Gransden, 'Some late thirteenth-century records of an ecclesiastical court in the archdeaconry of Sudbury', *Bulletin of the Institute of Historical Research*, 32 (1959), 64–9.

77. M. M. Sheehan, 'Theory and practice: marriage of the unfree and the poor in medieval society', *Mediaeval Studies*, 50 (1988), repr. in Sheehan, *Marriage, Family and Law*, 242–6 (from which this and subsequent references are taken). See also pp. 197–8.

78. Flandrin, *Families in Former Times*, 98–102.

79. Sheehan, 'The formation and stability of marriage', 45; *idem*, 'Marriage of the unfree and the poor', 211–46, espec. 244–5.

80. Smith, 'Marriage processes', 43.

81. B. A. Hanawalt, 'Childrearing among the lower classes of late medieval England', *Journal of Interdisciplinary History*, 8 (1977), 9–20; M. M. McLaughlin, 'Survivors and surrogates: children and parents from the ninth to the thirteenth centuries', in L. deMause (ed.), *The History of Childhood. The Untold Story of Child Abuse* (London, 1974), 120–1; for a psycho-historical approach and a response to the same, see B. A. Kellum, 'Infanticide in England in the later Middle Ages', *History of Childhood Quarterly*, 1 (1974); R. H. Helmholz, 'Infanticide in the Province of Canterbury during the fifteenth century', *History of Childhood Quarterly*, 2 (1975).

82. *Court Roll of Chalgrave*, ed. Dale, 10–11; see also the earlier statement of custom in respect of mortuary and heriot payments, *ibid.*, 9.
83. As discussed above, p. 102 and more fully on pp. 204–4, 205–7.
84. E. Clark, 'Charitable bequests, deathbed land sales, and the manor court in later medieval England', in Razi and Smith (eds), *Medieval Society and the Manor Court*.
85. Sheehan, 'European family and canon law', 252; L. Bonfield and L. R. Poos, 'The development of the deathbed transfer in medieval English manor courts', *Cambridge Law Journal*, 47 (1988), repr. in Razi and Smith (eds), *Medieval Society and the Manor Court*.
86. For example, F. M. Page, *The Estates of Crowland Abbey. A Study in Manorial Organisation* (Cambridge, 1934), 110, although Page was very aware of the potential for the non-inheriting to be provided with small plots of land from within the family holding: *ibid.*, 111; also 'Customary poor law', 128–9.
87. Smith, 'Demographic developments', 65; *idem*, 'Some issues concerning families and their property in rural England, 1250–1800', in *idem* (ed.) *Land, Kinship and Life-Cycle*; 46–50.
88. See pp. 53–4.
89. Poos, *A Rural Society*, 142.
90. See pp. 101–2; also Page, *Estates of Crowland Abbey*, 111.
91. *Court Rolls of the Manor of Hales, 1272–1307. Part 1*, ed. J. Amphlett and S. G. Hamilton (Worcestershire Historical Society, 1910), 166–7.
92. C. Dyer, *Standards of Living in the Later Middle Ages. Social Change in England, c.1200–1520* (Cambridge, 1989), 152–4.
93. Searle, 'Seigneurial control of women's marriage', 23.
94. P. P. A. Biller, 'Birth-control in the west in the thirteenth and early fourteenth centuries', *Past and Present*, 94 (1982), 25.
95. Razi, *Life, Marriage and Death*, 66–9.
96. Fox, 'Exploitation of the landless'.
97. Razi, 'Immutable English family', 11.
98. See, for instance, p. 67.
99. M. Stinson, 'Assarting and poverty in early fourteenth-century western Yorkshire', *Landscape History*, 5 (1983).
100. H. S. A. Fox, 'Servants, cottagers and tied cottages during the later Middle Ages: towards a regional dimension', *Rural History*, 6 (1995), 128–31. We might also speculate that family members also remained on the family farms and may well have remained in the same households.
101. Bailey, 'Demographic decline'; see also pp. 93–4.

Part III   Worlds Beyond: Market, Crown and Church

CHAPTER 7   PEASANTS AND THE MARKET

1. R. H. Britnell, *The Commercialisation of English Society, 1100–1500* (Cambridge, 1993), 1: 'English experience between 1000 and 1500

was not that of transition from "natural economy" to "market economy". Throughout the period there was a market sector which affected the lives of almost everybody.'

2. R. H. Britnell, 'The proliferation of markets in England, 1200–1349', *Economic History Review*, 2nd ser., 34 (1981). See also the summary in E. Miller and J. Hatcher, *Medieval England. Towns, Commerce and Crafts, 1086–1348* (Harlow, 1995), 159–60.

3. Miller and Hatcher, *Medieval England. Towns, Commerce and Crafts*, 160.

4. But see for a recent lower estimate, B. M. S. Campbell, *English Seigniorial Agriculture, 1250–1450* (Cambridge, 2000), ch. 8.

5. For example, Britnell, *Commercialisation*, 103–5. See also, M. Bailey, *A Marginal Economy? East Anglian Breckland in the Later Middle Ages* (Cambridge, 1989), 8–11.

6. E. Miller, *The Abbey and Bishopric of Ely* (Cambridge, 1951), for example.

7. E. Miller and J. Hatcher, *Medieval England. Rural Society and Economic Change, 1086–1348* (Harlow, 1978), 149; J. Z. Titow, *English Rural Society, 1200–1350* (London, 1969), 79–80; see also R. M. Smith, 'A periodic market and its impact upon a manorial community: Botesdale, Suffolk, and the manor of Redgrave, 1280–1300', in Z. Razi and R. M. Smith (eds), *Medieval Society and the Manor Court* (Oxford, 1996), 468, using Dyer's estimates of smallholder consumption requirements.

8. E. A. Kosminsky, *Studies in the Agrarian History of England in the Thirteenth Century* (Oxford, 1956), ch. iv; discussed by Miller and Hatcher, *Medieval England. Rural Society and Economic Change*, 143–4. The figures have also recently been discussed by J. Masschaele, *Peasants, Merchants and Markets. Inland Trade in Medieval England, 1150–1350* (Basingstoke, 1997), 50–1. See also pp. 22–6.

9. D. Farmer, 'Marketing the produce of the countryside, 1200–1500', in E. Miller (ed.), *Agrarian History of England and Wales, Vol. 3, 1348–1500* (Cambridge, 1991), 337–9

10. Britnell, *Commercialisation*, 166–7.

11. In terms of market integration, see Farmer, 'Marketing the produce of the countryside', 329–30, and the discussion of his data in Smith, 'A periodic market', 453–60.

12. For example, Smith, 'A periodic market', 453–61, especially 453, quoting Britnell, 'The proliferation of markets', 215, and Farmer, 'Marketing the produce of the countryside'.

13. Miller and Hatcher, *Medieval England. Rural Society and Economic Change*, 129; Miller, *Abbey and Bishopric of Ely*, 131–2; P. D. A. Harvey, 'Introduction', in *idem* (ed.), *The Peasant Land Market in Medieval England* (Oxford, 1984), 28.

14. Bailey, *A Marginal Economy?*, 143–58.

15. G. Astill and A. Grant, 'The medieval countryside: efficiency, progress and change', in Astill and Grant, *Countryside of Medieval England* (Oxford, 1988), 218; see also Miller, *Abbey and Bishopric of Ely*, 135; A. Appleby, *Famine in Tudor and Stuart England* (Liverpool, 1978), chs 3, 6; J. Walter and R. Schofield, 'Famine, disease and crisis mortality in early modern

society', in *idem* (eds), *Famine, Disease and the Social Order in Early Modern Society* (Cambridge, 1989), 21–5.

16. See pp. 62, 67, 74–5.

17. M. M. Postan, 'Medieval society in its prime: England', in *idem* (ed.), *The Cambridge Economic History of Europe. Vol. 1, The Agrarian Life of the Middle Ages* (2nd edn, Cambridge, 1966), 620.

18. See pp. 65–6.

19. C. Dyer, 'Were peasants self-sufficient? English villagers and the market, 900–1350', in E. Mornet (ed.), *Campagnes médiévales: l'homme et son espace. Études offertes à Robert Fossier* (Publications de la Sorbonne, 1995), 653–4.

20. See the recent discussion in S. H. Rigby, *English Society in the Later Middle Ages. Class, Status and Gender* (Basingstoke, 1995), 61–6.

21. See p. 66. See also the comments of R. M. Smith, 'Some issues concerning families and their property in rural England, 1250–1800', in *idem* (ed.), *Land, Kinship and Life-Cycle* (Cambridge, 1984), 65; also note R. H. Hilton, 'Introduction', in *idem* (ed.), *The Transition from Feudalism to Capitalism* (London, 1976), 15: 'the survival in 14th-century England of large estates characterised by big demesnes using labour services from dependent tenures was exceptional'.

22. C. Dyer, *Standards of Living in the Later Middle Ages* (Cambridge, 1989), 110–17.

23. J. Radley, 'Holly as a winter feed', *Agricultural History Review*, 9 (1961), 89–92.

24. A. J. Winchester, *Landscape and Society in Medieval Cumbria* (Edinburgh, 1987), 111.

25. R. Hodges, *Primitive and Peasant Markets* (Oxford, 1988), ch. 5.

26. There is a large theoretical literature, for inroads into which see references in Smith, 'A periodic market', 460–1.

27. But see also pp. 148–55.

28. See the contentious comment of Z. Razi, 'Family, land and the village community in later medieval England', *Past and Present*, 93 (1981), 368: 'the village economy in the late Middle Ages remained largely a subsistence economy'.

29. *Court Roll of Chalgrave Manor, 1278–1313* ed. M. K. Dale, (Bedfordshire Historical Record Society, vol. 28, 1948), 32.

30. *Manorial Records of Cuxham, c.1200–1349*, ed. P. D. A. Harvey (Oxfordshire Record Society, vol. 50, 1976), 627–9.

31. See also p. 143.

32. See also pp. 202–4.

33. R. M. Smith, 'Transactional analysis and the measurement of institutional determinants of fertility: a comparison of communities in present-day Bangladesh and pre-industrial England', in J. C. Caldwell, A. G. Hill and V. J. Hull (eds), *Micro-Approaches to Demographic Research* (London and New York, 1988), 226–39.

34. See pp. 99–102.

35. J. A. Raftis, *Peasant Economic Development within the English Manorial System* (Stroud, 1997), 12–13; Masschaele, *Peasants, Merchants and Markets*, 45–6;

P. R. Schofield, 'Dearth, debt and the local land market in a late thirteenth-century village community', *Agricultural History Review*, 45 (1997), 11, 17. For further discussion of taxation, see pp. 171–5.

36. See pp. 42, 75–6, 167–9.

37. R. M. Smith, 'Kin and neighbours in a thirteenth-century Suffolk community', *Journal of Family History*, 4 (1979), 246–9; P. R. Schofield, 'The late medieval view of frankpledge and the tithing system: an Essex case study', in Z. Razi and R. M. Smith, (eds), *Medieval Society and the Manor Court* (Oxford, 1996), 422–6. See also M. Pimsler, 'Solidarity in the medieval village? The evidence of personal pledges at Elton, Huntingdonshire', *Journal of British Studies*, 17 (1977); D. Postles, 'Personal pledging: medieval "reciprocity" or "symbolic capital"?' *Journal of Interdisciplinary History*, 26 (1996).

38. See p. 73.

39. For the late thirteenth and early fourteenth centuries, R. M. Smith, 'Families and their land in an area of partible inheritance: Redgrave, Suffolk, 1260–1320', in *idem* (ed.), *Land, Kinship and Life-Cycle* (Cambridge, 1984), 160–3; Schofield, 'Dearth, debt and the local land market', 10; for the fifteenth century, see, for example, Schofield, '*Extraneii* and the market for customary land on a Westminster Abbey manor in the fifteenth century', *Agricultural History Review*, 49 (2001), 5–6.

40. J. P. J. Goldberg, *Women, Work and Life-Cyle* (Oxford 1992), 161, 165–7.

41. R. M. Karras, *Common Women. Prostitution and Sexuality in Medieval England* (Oxford, 1996), 24–5.

42. Vulnerability includes exploitation of poorer peasants by the wealthier, not just in terms of their appropriation of property but in a refusal to pay for services rendered.

43. Masschaele, *Peasants, Merchants and Markets*, 39–40, 45–6, 51–4. For the Walsham example, *The Court Rolls of the Manor of Walsham le Willows, 1303–1350*, ed. R. Lock, (Suffolk Records Society, vol. 41, 1998), 230.

44. *Court Rolls of Walsham le Willows*, ed. Lock, 131.

45. *Court Roll of the Manor of Downham, 1310–1327*, ed. M. Clare Coleman (Cambridgeshire Records Society, vol. 11, 1996), 65; *Court Rolls of the Manor of Wakefield. Vol. 4*, ed. J. Lister (Yorkshire Archaeological Society, vol. 78, 1930), 99.

46. E. Clark, 'Debt litigation in a late medieval English vill', in J. Raftis (ed.), *Pathways to Medieval Peasants* (Toronto, 1981), 275, n. 43. For other examples, see *ibid.*, 274, n. 40 (sheep), 275, n. 44 (cow), n. 47 (butter).

47. L. R. Poos, *A Rural Society after the Black Death. Essex, 1350–1525* (Cambridge, 1991), 22–5.

48. Smith, 'A periodic market', 468.

49. M. Bailey, 'Rural society', in R. Horrox (ed.) *Fifteenth Century Attitudes* (Cambridge, 1994), 164–6.

50. J. M. Bennett, *Women in the Medieval English Countryside. Gender and Household in Brigstock before the Plague* (Oxford, 1987), 120–1; also *idem*, *Ale, Beer and Brewsters in England* (Oxford, 1997); also note the suggestion of Smith that poorer villagers brewed ale: Smith, 'Some issues concerning families

and their property', 27–30; cf. Z. Razi, *Life, Marriage and Death in a Medieval Parish* (Cambridge, 1980), 76–7.

51. P. D. A. Harvey, *A Medieval Oxfordshire Village. Cuxham, 1240–1400* (Oxford, 1965), 71–2; see also *Manorial Records of Cuxham*, ed. Harvey, 153.

52. See, for example, S. Pearson, *The Medieval Houses of Kent. An Historical Analysis* (London, 1994), 33, 146–7, and *passim*. I am grateful to Professor Christopher Dyer for drawing my attention to this reference.

53. Westminster Abbey Muniments 25469–25497.

54. Z. Razi and R. M. Smith, 'The origins of the English manorial court rolls as a written record: a puzzle', in Razi and Smith (eds), *Medieval Society and the Manor Court* (Oxford, 1996), 57–67; also P. R. Schofield, 'Peasants and the manor court: gossip and litigation in a Suffolk village at the close of the thirteenth century', *Past and Present*, 159 (1998), 15, n.47.

55. See Chapter 4.

56. J. Whittle, *The Development of Agrarian Capitalism. Land and Labour in Norfolk, 1440–1580* (Oxford, 2000), 110–19.

57. *Ibid.*, 112–14.

58. *Ibid.*, 116–17, 171.

59. M. M. Postan, 'Credit in medieval trade', *Economic History Review*, 1st ser., 1 (1928), repr. in *idem*, *Essays on Medieval Trade and Finance* (Cambridge, 1973), 11–12.

60. *Court Roll of the Manor of Downham*, ed. Coleman, 105–6.

61. Schofield, 'Peasants and the manor court', 2–5 and *passim*; also p. 166.

62. Schofield, 'Dearth, debt and the local land market'.

63. Razi, *Life, Marriage and Death*, 37.

64. J. Ravensdale, 'Population changes and the transfer of customary land on a Cambridgeshire manor in the fourteenth century', in R. M. Smith (ed.) *Land, Kinship and Life-Cycle*, 216: 'One wonders how many surrenders *ad opus* are foreclosures on mortgages in such a desperate market for holdings [in the early fourteenth century]'.

65. Whittle, *Agrarian Capitalism*, 116–18.

66. Ravensdale, 'Population changes and the transfer of customary land', 215, on widows and credit in the medieval village; more generally, and for a later period, B. A. Holderness, 'Widows in pre-industrial society: an essay upon their economic functions', in Smith (ed.) *Land, Kinship and Life-Cycle*, 435–42.

67. Recent investigations of rural markets include Smith, 'A periodic market'; R. H. Hilton, 'Small town society in England before the Black Death', *Past and Present*, 109 (1984); C. Dyer, 'The consumer and the market in the later Middle Ages', *Economic History Review*, 2nd ser., 43 (1990), reprinted in *idem*, *Everyday Life in Medieval England* (London, 1994); M. Kowaleski, *Local Markets and Regional Trade in Medieval Exeter* (Cambridge, 1995) (from which subsequent references are taken). For further discussion of the establishment of local markets and their geography, see the works listed by Smith, 'A periodic market', 461, n.19.

68. See p. 132.

69. For earlier views regarding marketing and rent, see p. 135; R. H. Hilton,

'Low-level urbanization: the seigneurial borough of Thornbury in the Middle Ages', in Razi and Smith (eds), *Medieval Society and the Manor Court*, 482.

70. Smith, 'A periodic market', 472–3.

71. I. M. W. Harvey, 'Bernwood in the Middle Ages', in J. Broad and R. Hoyle (eds), *Bernwood. The Life and Afterlife of a Forest* (Preston, 1997), 14.

72. *Court Rolls of Walsham le Willows*, ed. Lock, 199–200.

73. Dyer, 'Consumer and the market', 274; Poos, *A Rural Society*, 162–4.

74. C. Dyer, 'The hidden trade of the Middle Ages: evidence from the West Midlands', *Journal of Historical Geography*, 18 (1992), repr. in *idem, Everyday Life in Medieval England*, 299.

75. Britnell, *Commercialisation*, 88ff.

76. E. W. Moore, *The Fairs of Medieval England. An Introductory Study* (Toronto, 1985); see also, for an example, *Select Pleas in Manorial and other Seignorial Courts*, ed. F. W. Maitland (Selden Society, vol. 2, 1888), 152.

77. Miller and Hatcher, *Medieval England. Towns, Commerce and Crafts*, ch. 4; also, M. M. Postan, 'The trade of medieval Europe: the north', in M. M. Postan and E. E. Rich (eds), *The Cambridge Economic History of Europe, Vol. 2* (Cambridge, 1952), repr. in Postan, *Essays on Medieval Trade and Finance* (from which this and subsequent references are taken), 105–6.

78. Masschaele, *Peasants, Merchants, and Markets*, 47–52; also N. J. Mayhew, 'Modelling medieval monetisation', in R. H. Britnell and B. M. S. Campbell (eds), *A Commercialising Economy* (Manchester, 1995), 58–9.

79. M. Bailey, 'The rabbit and the medieval East Anglian economy', *Agricultural History Review*, 36 (1988), 10–15; also *idem, A Marginal Economy?*, 115–58.

80. A. Watkins, 'Cattle grazing in the forest of Arden in the later Middle Ages', *Agricultural History Review*, 37 (1989), 17–20.

81. B. M. S. Campbell, J. A. Galloway, D. Keene and M. Murphy, *A Medieval Capital and its Grain Supply. Agrarian Production and Distribution in the London Region, c.1300* (London, 1993), 88.

82. Masschaele, *Peasants, Merchants and Markets*, 53.

83. Postan, 'The trade of medieval Europe: the north', 140, on monastic and other landlords buying up wool in the countryside, the *collecta*; also E. B. Fryde, *Peasants and Landlords in Later Medieval England, c.1380–c.1525* (Stroud, 1996), 87; E. E. Power, *The Wool Trade in Medieval English History* (Oxford, 1941), 44–6.

84. Postan, 'The trade of medieval Europe: the north', 141; *Rotuli Parliamentorum (1278–1503)* (6 vols, Record Commission, London, 1783), vol. 5, 334–5.

85. On the mid-fifteenth century depression, see J. Hatcher, 'The great slump of the mid-fifteenth century', in R. Britnell and J. Hatcher (eds), *Progress and Problems in Medieval England. Essays in Honour of Edward Miller* (Cambridge, 1996); on the competition between larger wool producers and the peasantry in this period, and the low price of wool, see Power, *Wool Trade in Medieval English History*, 38–40; Fryde, *Peasants and Landlords*, 94, 100–4.

86. See pp. 48, 55; Britnell writes, 'Investment in land permitted richer villagers to live more comfortably than in the past and created opportunities for commercial farming among families who could not previously have enjoyed them': R. H. Britnell, *Growth and Decline in Colchester, 1300–1525* (Cambridge, 1986), 259; also, on the move towards pastoral husbandry and, in particular, sheep farming, *ibid.*, 255.

87. J. N. Hare, 'The demesne lessees of fifteenth-century Wiltshire', *Agricultural History Review*, 29 (1981), 10–13; also Fryde, *Peasants and Landlords*, 111–12.

88. Hare, 'Demesne lessees', 15.

89. J. L. Bolton, *The Medieval English Economy, 1150–1500* (London, 1980), 267–73; Poos, *A Rural Society*, ch. 3; Winchester, *Landscape and Society*, 116–20.

90. Sue Degnan, 'Research in 1985. Excavations. Buckinghamshire. Westbury, Shenley Brook End, Milton Keynes. The pottery', *Medieval Village Research Group. Thirty-Third Annual Report* (1985), 16.

91. Britnell, *Commercialisation*, 112–13; M. L. Ryder, 'Livestock remains from four medieval sites in Yorkshire', *Agricultural History Review*, 9 (1961), 106.

92. A. Burl, *Prehistoric Avebury* (Yale, 1979), 39.

93. Farmer, 'Marketing the produce of the countryside', 348, for this and other examples.

94. *Court Rolls of the Manor of Walsham le Willows*, ed. Locke, 92; for which, see also, P. R. Schofield, 'Access to credit in the early fourteenth-century countryside', in P. R. Schofield and N. J. Mayhew (eds), *Credit and Debt in Medieval England, c.1180–c.1350* (Oxbow, 2002).

95. For the use of legal protections for debt in the context of local courts, see R. L. Henry, *Contracts in the Local Courts of Medieval England* (London, 1926). Also, note Yoram Ben-Porath, 'The F-connection: families, friends and firms and the organization of exchange', *Population and Development Review*, 6 (1980).

96. *Court Rolls of the Manor of Wakefield, Vol. 4*, ed. Lister, 202–3.

97. *Court Roll of Chalgrave*, ed. Dale, 49.

98. Poos, *A Rural Society*, 197–200; P. R. Schofield, 'Tenurial developments and the availability of customary land in a later medieval community', *Economic History Review*, 49 (1996), 260–4.

99. Goldberg, *Women, Work and Life-Cycle*, 161.

100. E. Rutledge, 'Immigration and population growth in early fourteenth-century Norwich: evidence from the tithing roll', *Urban History Yearbook 1988*, 15–30 (Norwich); R. H. Hilton, 'Lords, burgesses and hucksters', *Past and Present*, 97 (1982), 10 (Halesowen). For comments on Halesowen, see also Goldberg, *Women, Work and Life-Cycle*, 283, 288. Also, R. M. Smith, 'Demographic developments in rural England, 1300–48: a survey', in B. M. S. Campbell (ed.), *Before the Black Death. Studies in the 'Crisis' of the Early Fourteenth Century* (Manchester, 1991), 75–6.

101. Poos, *Rural Society*, ch. 9; Goldberg, *Women, Work and Life-Cycle*, ch. 6, espec. table 6.1 and 290ff.; see also the qualifying comments of M. Bailey, 'Demographic decline in late medieval England: some thoughts on recent research', *Economic History Review*, 49 (1996), 11–12.

102. See pp. 67–8, 72, 75–6.
103. Masschaele, *Peasants, Merchants and Markets*; Raftis, *Peasant Economic Development*.

CHAPTER 8   PEASANTS AND POLITICS

1. See, for example, R. H. Hilton, 'Peasant movements in England before 1381', *Economic History Review*, 2nd ser., 2 (1949), repr. in E. M. Carus-Wilson (ed.), *Essays in Economic History*. *Vol. 2* (from which subsequent references are taken); R. H. Hilton, *Bond Men Made Free. Medieval Peasant Movements and the English Rising of 1381* (London, 1973).
2. For example, Z. Razi, 'The struggles between the abbots of Halesowen and their tenants in the thirteenth and fourteenth centuries', in T. H. Aston, P. R. Coss, C. Dyer and J. Thirsk (eds), *Social Relations and their Ideas. Essays in Honour of R. H. Hilton* (Cambridge, 1983); P. Franklin, 'Politics in manorial court rolls: the tactics, social composition and aims of a pre-1381 peasant movement', in Z. Razi and R. Smith (eds), *Medieval Society and the Manor Court* (Oxford, 1996), 166, 176–7.
3. Hilton, 'Peasant movements', 77–8, 86; *idem, English Peasantry in the Later Middle Ages* (Oxford, 1975), 51–5; also, *idem*, 'Reasons for inequality amongst medieval peasants', *Journal of Peasant Studies*, 5 (1978). See also the comments of R. M. Smith, '"Modernization" and the corporate medieval village community', in A. H. R. Baker and D. Gregory (eds), *Explorations in Historical Geography* (Cambridge, 1984), 143.
4. J. A. Raftis, *Peasant Economic Development within the English Manorial System* (Stroud, 1997).
5. See Chapter 7, espec. pp. 149–56.
6. For the work of the 'Toronto' historians, see, for example, E. B. Dewindt, *Land and People in Holywell-cum-Needingworth* (Toronto, 1971); E. Britton, *The Community of the Vill* (Toronto, 1997); Raftis, *Peasant Economic Development*. For an important statement on integration from this 'school', see A. R. Dewindt, 'Defining the peasant community in medieval England', *Journal of British Studies*, 26 (1987). See also S. H. Rigby's comments on stratification, *English Society in the Later Middle Ages. Class, Status and Gender* (Basingstoke, 1995), 47–9.
7. P. R. Hyams, 'The origins of a peasant land market in England', *Economic History Review*, 23 (1970).
8. J. R. Maddicott, 'Magna Carta and the local community, 1215–1259', *Past and Present*, 102 (1984); *idem*, 'The county community and the making of public opinion in fourteenth-century England', *Transactions of the Royal Historical Society*, 5th ser., 28 (1978); D. A. Carpenter, 'English peasants in politics, 1258–1267', *Past and Present*, 136 (1992).
9. J. R. Maddicott, 'The English peasantry and the demands of the crown, 1294–1341', *Past and Present, Supplement 1* (1975), repr. in T. H. Aston (ed.), *Landlords, Peasants and Politics in Medieval England* (Cambridge, 1987), (from which subsequent references are taken). See also, for earlier work,

A Lincolnshire Assize Roll for 1298 (PRO Assize Roll No. 505), ed. W. S. Thomson (Lincolnshire Record Society, vol. 36, 1944).

10. Not all historians have been inclined to couch lord–tenant relations in terms of conflict; instead, negotiation and perceived mutual advantages have dominated some analyses. See, for one example, Raftis, *Peasant Economic Development*.

11. E. B. Fryde and N. Fryde, 'Peasant rebellion and peasant discontents', in E. Miller (ed.), *The Agrarian History of England and Wales. Vol. 3, 1348–1500* (Cambridge, 1991), 765.

12. J. Hatcher, 'English serfdom and villeinage: towards a reassessment', *Past and Present*, 90 (1981), 262, citing Z. Razi, *Life, Marriage and Death in a Medieval Parish* (Cambridge, 1980), 29–30.

13. Fryde and Fryde, 'Peasant rebellion and peasant discontents', 766, citing F. R. H. DuBoulay, *The Lordship of Canterbury. An Essay on Medieval Society* (London, 1966), 189.

14. Hilton, 'Peasant movements', 90; cf. Hatcher, 'English serfdom and villeinage', 270.

15. Hilton, 'Peasant movements', 82; Franklin, 'Politics in manorial court rolls', 166, 176–7.

16. Franklin, 'Politics in manorial court rolls', 179; Hilton, 'Peasant movements', 82–3. Also, R. J. Faith, 'The "Great Rumour" of 1377 and peasant ideology', in R. H. Hilton and T. H. Aston (eds), *The English Rising of 1381* (Cambridge, 1984), 66–8, who writes of the creation of 'local traditions of resistance' (68).

17. N. J. Hone, *The Manor and Medieval Records* (London, 1906), 153.

18. See, for example, cases of violence and abuse of the lord's men at Wakefield, *Court Rolls of the Manor of Wakefield. Vol. 1*, ed. W. P. Baildon (Yorkshire Archaeological Society, vol. 29, 1900), 161, 163 (resistance to bailiff in both cases); *Court Rolls of the Manor of Wakefield. Vol. 3*, ed. J. Lister (Yorkshire Archaeological Society, vol. 57, 1917), 161 (earl's men); *Court Rolls of the Manor of Wakefield. Vol. 4*, ed. J. Lister (Yorkshire Archaeological Society, vol. 78, 1930), 43 (contempt shown to under-bailiff). Also, *Manorial Records of Cuxham, c.1200–1349*, ed. P. D. A. Harvey, (Oxfordshire Record Society, vol. 50, 1976), 618 (throwing a stone at the lord's granger).

19. For examples, see pp. 70–2.

20. See Chapters 2, 3 and 4.

21. P. R. Schofield, 'Peasants and the manor court: gossip and litigation in a Suffolk village at the close of the thirteenth century', *Past and Present*, 159 (1998), 22.

22. *Chronica Monasterii de Melsa*, ed. E. A. Bond (Rolls series, 3 vols, 1866–68), vol. 3, 126–7.

23. L. R. Poos, *A Rural Society after the Black Death. Essex, 1350–1525* (Cambridge, 1991), 246.

24. See pp. 29–30; also E. King, *Peterborough Abbey, 1086–1310. A Study in the Land Market* (Cambridge, 1973), 99–100.

25. *The Cartulary of the Abbey of Eynsham*, ed. H. E. Salter (Oxford Historical Society, 2 vols, 1907, 1908), vol. 51, 19–20; also see p. 46.

26. J. F. Nichols, 'An early fourteenth century petition from the tenants of

Bocking to their manorial lord', *Economic History Review*, 2 (1929–30), 300–7; also, N. Denholm-Young, *Seigneurial Administration in England* (London, 1937), 154.

27. For one such example, see Hilton, 'Peasant movements', 80; also, this volume, p. 15. Cf. Hatcher, 'English serfdom and villeinage', 270 and n. 61.

28. *The Pinchbeck Register*, ed. Lord F. Hervey (2 vols, Brighton, 1925), vol. 1, 323. The case is given in full, *ibid.*, 321–4; see also C. Dyer, 'The rising of 1381 in Suffolk', *Proceedings of the Suffolk Institute of Archaeology and History*, 36 (1988), repr. in *idem*, *Everyday Life in Medieval England* (London, 1994), 225–7 (from which this and subsequent references are taken).

29. On ancient demesne, see pp. 16–17; M. J. McIntosh, *Autonomy and Community. The Royal Manor of Havering 1200–1500* (Cambridge, 1986), 37–9; Hilton, 'Peasant movements', 80–1; Faith, 'Great Rumour', 43–73; C. Dyer, 'Memories of freedom: attitudes towards serfdom in England, 1200–1350', in M. Bush (ed.), *Serfdom and Slavery. Studies in Legal Bondage* (Harlow, 1996), 277–95; see also p. 183.

30. E. A. Kosminsky, *Studies in the Agrarian History of England in the Thirteenth Century* (Oxford, 1956), 344; see also Hilton, 'Peasant movements', 81.

31. Kosminsky, *Studies in the Agrarian History of England*, 343; R. H. Hilton, 'A thirteenth century poem on disputed villein services', *English Historical Review*, 56 (1941).

32. For example, J. Canning, *A History of Medieval Political Thought, 1300–1450* (London, 1996), 163–4.

33. Razi, 'Struggles between the abbots of Halesowen and their tenants'; for an example of seigneurial violence directed towards tenants, see *ibid.*, 162–3.

34. Dyer, 'The rising of 1381 in Suffolk', 227–8.

35. See, for instance, Hervey, *Pinchbeck Register*, 106, 107 for a Thomas de Mildenhal listed amongst those who, amongst other enormities, 'came to the gates of the Abbey and feloniously burned them'. For further examples, see Hilton, 'Peasant movements', 83.

36. Razi, 'Struggles between the abbots of Halesowen and their tenants', 164–6.

37. On the events at St Albans and interpretations of their meaning, Faith, 'Great Rumour', 66, 68; S. Justice, *Writing and Rebellion. England in 1381* (California, 1996), 168–9.

38. C. Dyer, 'The social and economic background to the rural revolt of 1381', in Hilton and Aston (eds), *The English Rising of 1381*, 11–14.

39. Dyer, 'Social and economic background'; Hilton, *Bond Men Made Free*, ch. 7.

40. Dyer, 'Memories of freedom', 288–91.

41. Raftis, *Peasant Economic Development*, ch. 7.

42. See pp. 73–6, 139–46.

43. For example, Razi, *Life, Marriage and Death*, 77, 78, n. 148; Schofield, 'Peasants and the manor court', 22–5.

44. L. Bonfield, 'The nature of customary law in the manor courts of

medieval England', *Comparative Studies in Society and History*, 31 (1989); Schofield, 'Peasants and the manor court'.

45. W. O. Ault, *Open-Field Farming in Medieval England* (London, 1972).

46. For example, *Walter of Henley and other Treatises in Estate Management and Accounting*, ed. D. Oschinksy (Oxford, 1971), 278–9.

47. A moot point. See Bonfield, 'Customary law'; *idem*, 'What did Edwardian villagers mean by "customary law"?', in Z. Razi and R. M. Smith (eds), *Medieval Society and the Manor Court* (Oxford, 1996); J. Beckerman, 'Toward a theory of medieval manorial adjudication: the nature of communal judgements in a system of customary law', *Law and History Review*, 13 (1995). On manor court jurors, see, for example, S. Olson, 'Jurors of the village court: local leadership before and after the plague in Ellington, Huntingdonshire', *Journal of British Studies*, 30 (1991).

48. W. A. Morris, *The Frankpledge System* (New York, 1910); D. A. Crowley, 'The later history of frankpledge', *Bulletin of the Institute of Historical Research*, 48 (1975), 1–2.

49. See pp. 197, 200–1, 214.

50. J. S. Beckerman, 'Procedural innovation and institutional change in medieval English manorial courts', *Law and History Review*, 10 (1992), 212–14; also pp. 178–9.

51. Crowley, 'Later history of frankpledge', 10. On hue and cry, Dewindt, *Land and People in Holywell-cum-Needingworth*, 271; also S. Olson, *A Chronicle of All that Happens. Voices from the Village Court in Medieval England* (Toronto, 1996), 97–9.

52. M. K. McIntosh, *Controlling Misbehavior in England, 1370–1600* (Cambridge, 1998), 18, 31–2, 34–42; *idem*, 'Finding language for misconduct: jurors in fifteenth-century local courts', in B. A. Hanawalt and D. Wallace (eds), *Bodies and Disciplines. Intersections of Literature and History in Fifteenth-Century England* (Minnesota, 1996); see also pp. 200–1.

53. For the suggestion that there were late thirteenth and early fourteenth century antecedents to early modern 'puritanism', M. Spufford, 'Puritanism and social control', in A. Fletcher and J. Stevenson (eds), *Order and Disorder in Early Modern England* (Cambridge, 1985), 48–57.

54. Britton, *The Community of the Vill*, 38–43; B. A. Hanawalt, *The Ties that Bound* (Oxford, 1986), ch. 12; also pp. 102–4, 116–17.

55. See pp. 42–3, 71.

56. Justice, *Writing and Rebellion*, 184–5; also Hilton, 'Peasant movements', 84–5, on early peasant unrest and the tendency for juries to conceal offences.

57. Hatcher, 'English serfdom and villeinage', 256, n.22, citing *Select Pleas in Manorial and other Seigneurial Courts*, ed. F. W. Maitland (Selden Society, vol. 2, 1888), 95.

58. Nichols, 'An early fourteenth century petition'; also Franklin, 'Politics in manorial court rolls', 179ff.

59. For example, McIntosh, *Controlling Misbehavior in England*, passim; Spufford, 'Puritanism and social control', 50–3.

60. For instance, E. R. Wolf, *Peasants* (London, 1966), 12–17.

61. G. W. S. Barrow, *Robert Bruce* (London, 1965), 196–8 and *passim*; J. V.

Scammell, 'Robert I and the north of England', *English Historical Review*, 78 (1958); A. J. Winchester, *Landscape and Society in Medieval Cumbria* (Edinburgh, 1987), 135.

62. *Johannis de Trokelowe et Henrici de Blaneforde Chronica et Annales,* ed. H. T. Riley (Rolls series, 1866), 91.

63. J. E. Morris, *The Welsh Wars of Edward I* (Oxford, 1901), 112, 120; R. R. Davies, *The Revolt of Owain Glyn Dwr* (Oxford, 1995), 234–5.

64. E. Searle and R. Burghart, 'The defence of England and the Peasants' Revolt', *Viator*, 3 (1972).

65. *Chronicle of Adam Murimuth,* ed. E. M. Thompson (Rolls series, 1889), 33.

66. A. J. Pollard, *North-Eastern England during the Wars of the Roses. Lay Society War and Politics, 1450–1500* (Oxford, 1990), 45.

67. *Chronica Monasterii de Melsa,* ed. Bond, vol. 2, 6–7.

68. For a useful summary of significant developments and references to more detailed work, see A. L. Brown, *The Governance of Late Medieval England, 1272–1461* (London, 1989), ch. 4; on fifteenth-century lay subsidies, see also C. Dyer, 'Taxation and communities in late medieval England', in R. Britnell and J. Hatcher (eds), *Progress and Problems in Medieval England* (Cambridge, 1996).

69. Hilton, *Bond Men Made Free*, 146–7; also Maddicott, *The English Peasantry and the Demands of the Crown*, 286.

70. W. M. Ormrod, 'The crown and the English economy, 1290–1348', in B. M. S. Campbell (ed.), *Before the Black Death* (Manchester, 1991), 153; Maddicott, 'The English peasantry and the demands of the crown', 290.

71. Maddicott, 'The English peasantry and the demands of the crown', 291.

72. M. Bailey, 'Introduction', in *Hertfordshire Lay Subsidy Rolls, 1307 and 1334*, ed. J. Brooker and S. Flood (Hertfordshire Record Society, vol. 14, 1998), xiv–xv.

73. Maddicott, 'The English peasantry and the demands of the crown', 335; cf. Dyer, 'Taxation and communities', 173, but also 189–90.

74. Maddicott, 'The English peasantry and the demands of the crown', 301–6.

75. *Ibid.*, 304–5.

76. *Halmota Prioratus Dunelmensis. Containing Extracts from the Halmote Court or Manor Rolls of the Prior and Convent of Durham*, ed. J. Booth (Surtees Society, vol. 82, 1886), 3.

77. T. H. Lloyd, *The Movement of Wool Prices in Medieval England* (Cambridge, 1973), 18–20.

78. *The Peasants' Revolt of 1381*, ed. R. B. Dobson (2nd edn, London, 1983), 136, citing *Chronicon Henrici Knighton*.

79. *The Peasants' Revolt*, ed. Dobson, 54–9; Hilton, *Bond Men Made Free*, 162; W. M. Ormrod, 'The politics of pestilence: government in England after the Black Death,' in *idem* and P. Lindley (eds), *The Black Death in England* (Stamford, 1996), 159–67.

80. See, for example, Dobson, *The Peasants' Revolt*, 161, 164–5, citing *Anonimalle Chronicle*.

81. P. Spufford, *Origins of the English Parliament* (London, 1972), 208.

82. Brown, *Governance*, 85–99, especially, 93–4; Maddicott, 'The English peasantry and the demands of the crown', 318–29.

83. H. J. Hewitt, *The Organization of War under Edward III* (Manchester, 1966), 47–8; Maddicott, 'The English peasantry and the demands of the crown', 328–9.

84. J. F. Willard, *Parliamentary Taxes on Personal Property, 1290–1334*, (Cambridge, MA, 1934).

85. S. Reynolds, *Kingdoms and Communities in Western Europe, 900–1300* (2nd edn, Oxford, 1997), on law as a force for state-building.

86. For instance, A. Musson and W. M. Ormrod, *The Evolution of English Justice. Law, Politics and Society in the Fourteenth Century* (Basingstoke, 1999), 93–6.

87. *Ibid.*, 91.

88. P. R. Hyams, 'What did Edwardian villagers understand by law?', in Razi and Smith, *Medieval Society and the Manor Court*, 88.

89. *Statutes of the Realm (1101–1713)*, ed. A. Luders *et al.* (11 vols, Record Commission, London, 1810–28) vol. 1, 96.

90. For felonies, see, for example, Musson and Ormrod, *Evolution of English Justice*, 17.

91. For useful summaries of jurisdictions in this context, see Hyams, 'Edwardian villagers', 89–90; Brown, *Governance*, 106–12.

92. Maddicott, 'County community and the making of public opinion', 29–30.

93. For a recent discussion of the eyre and the commissions, see Musson and Ormrod, *Evolution of English Justice*, 43–50; also Brown, *Governance*, 116–17.

94. See, for example, *South Lancashire in the Reign of Edward II as Illustrated by the Pleas at Wigan Recorded in Coram Rege Roll no. 254*, ed. G. H. Tupling (Chetham Society, 3rd ser., vol. 1, 1949), xxxix–xliii.

95. For the Assize of Clarendon, see W. Stubbs, *Select Charters and other Illustrations of English Constitutional History from the Earliest Times to the Reign of Edward the First* (Oxford, various editions), 8th edition (1895), 143–6.

96. Schofield, 'Peasants and the manor court', 4.

97. *A Lincolnshire Assize Roll for 1298 (PRO Assize Roll no. 505)*, ed. W. S. Thomson (Lincolnshire Record Society, vol. 36, 1994), 74, case 323.

98. *Lincolnshire Assize Roll*, ed., Thomson, lxxxviii–ix; also H. M. Cam, *The Hundred and the Hundred Rolls. An Outline of Local Government in Medieval England* (London, 1930), 78–9.

99. R. F. Hunnisett, *The Medieval Coroner* (Cambridge, 1961).

100. Beckerman, 'Procedural innovation and institutional change'.

101. W. A. Morris, *The Early English County Court. An Historical Treatise with Illustrative Documents* (Cambridge, 1926), 103–4.

102. Maddicott, 'County community and the making of public opinion', 32–3.

103. Maddicott, 'The English peasantry and the demands of the crown', 329; see also M. R. Powicke, 'The English commons in Scotland in 1322 and the deposition of Edward II', *Speculum*, 35 (1960).

104. R. C. Palmer, *English Law in the Age of the Black Death, 1348–1381. A Transformation of Governance and Law* (Chapel Hill, 1993); Musson and Ormrod, *The Evolution of English Justice*, 96.

105. For instance, Brown, *Governance*, 73, indicates that evasion increased as people learned how to deal with assessors; also, Dyer, 'Taxation and com-

munities', 171–2; on the scale of the fall from the lay subsidy of 1290, see Maddicott, 'The English peasantry and the demands of the crown', 290; Ormrod, 'Crown and the English economy', 153.

106. *Nonarum Inquisitiones in Curia Scaccarii*, ed. G. Vanderzee (Record Commission, 1807), 208.

107. *Court Rolls of the Manor of Wakefield. Vol. 4*, ed. Lister, 139–40.

108. *Ibid.*, 137.

109. See p. 59; also Maddicott, 'The English peasantry and the demands of the crown', 294–5.

110. R. B. Goheen, 'Peasant politics? Village community and the crown in fifteenth-century England', *American Historical Review*, 96 (1991), 51–2.

111. Hyams, 'Edwardian villagers', 77.

112. *Statutes of the Realm*, vol. 1, 96.

113. Hyams, 'Edwardian villagers', 76, and, for an interesting case, *ibid.*, 77, n.28.

114. Brown, *Governance*, 188–201; see also I. M. W. Harvey, 'Was there popular politics in fifteenth-century England?', in R. H. Britnell and A. J. Pollard, *The McFarlane Legacy. Studies in Late Medieval Politics and Society* (Stroud, 1995), 162–3.

115. See pp. 163–4.

116. Hyams, 'Edwardian villagers'; Schofield, 'Peasants and the manor court'; R. M. Smith, 'Some thoughts on "hereditary" and "proprietary" rights' in land under customary law in thirteenth and early fourteenth century England', *Law and History Review*, 1 (1983).

117. E. Duffy, *The Stripping of the Altars. Traditional Religion in England, 1400–1580* (New Haven, CT, 1992), 71; see also pp. 209, 214, 215 for further discussion of this source.

118. Harvey, 'Was there popular politics?'.

119. Hilton, 'Peasant movements', 83–4; Dyer, 'Memories of freedom', 287.

120. Carpenter, 'English peasants in politics'.

121. I. M. W. Harvey, *Jack Cade's Rebellion of 1450* (Oxford, 1991); also *idem*, 'Was there popular politics?'

122. Dyer, 'Social and economic background', 12, 38.

123. A. Harding, 'The revolt against the Justices', in Aston and Hilton (eds), *English Rising of 1381*.

124. For example, the so-called manifesto of the earls, 1297, for discussion of which, see, for example, *Lincolnshire Assize Roll*, ed. Thomson, x–xi, lxxxi–ii; the author of the *Annals of London*, for 1309, in describing the background to the Statute of Stamford, notes that, 'On account of [the return of Piers Gaveston], as well as the prises and oppressions exacted by the king's servants, the people were on the verge of rising', *Chronicles of the Reigns of Edward I and II*, ed. W. Stubbs (Rolls series, 2 vols, 1882–3), vol. 1, 157; similarly, the preamble to the Ordinances of 1311 includes the warning that the 'kingdom of England [is] on the point of rebelling because of oppressions, prises and molestations', *English Historical Documents, 1189–1327*, ed. H. Rothwell (London, 1975), 527.

125. *Thomas Wright's Political Songs of England from the Reign of John to that of Edward II*, ed. P. Coss (Cambridge, 1996), 85–6.

126. Maddicott, 'The English peasantry and the demands of the crown', 306.
127. For an example of its work, *Lincolnshire Assize Roll*, ed. Thomson.
128. Maddicott, 'The English peasantry and the demands of the crown', 307.
129. Z. Razi and R. M. Smith, 'The origins of the English manorial court rolls as a written record: a puzzle', in Razi and Smith (eds) *Medieval Society and the Manor Court* (Oxford, 1996), 48–9.
130. Carpenter, 'English peasants in politics', 27–9, 42; for some background to this, see also Maddicott, 'Magna Carta and the local community', 45–8.
131. Maddicott, 'The English peasantry and the demands of the crown', 320.
132. Hilton, *Bond Men Made Free*, 231–2.

CHAPTER 9   PEASANTS AND RELIGION

1. M. Rubin, *Charity and Community in Medieval Cambridge* (Cambridge, 1987), 85 and n.188.
2. For instance, J. le Goff, *The Birth of Purgatory* (Aldershot, 1984).
3. R. N. Swanson, *Religion and Devotion in Europe, c.1215–c.1515* (Cambridge, 1995), 16.
4. B. F. Harvey, 'Work and *festa ferianda* in medieval England', *Journal of Ecclesiastical History*, 23 (1972), 295.
5. For the impact of papal taxation in England, see, for example, C. H. Lawrence, 'The thirteenth century', in *idem* (ed.), *The English Church and the Papacy in the Middle Ages* (Stroud, 1999), 133–7; W. M. Ormrod, 'The crown and the English economy, 1290–1348', in B. M. S. Campbell (ed.), *Before the Black Death* (Manchester, 1991), 159–67. For discussions of the rivalry between common law and canon law in this period, see J. A. Brundage, *Medieval Canon Law* (Harlow, 1995), 176–8; P. R. Hyams, 'Deans and their doings: the Norwich inquiry of 1286', *Proceedings of the Berkeley Congress of Medieval Canon Law, 1980* (Monumenta Iuris Canonici, Series C, Subsidia, 7, Vatican City, 1985).
6. For one such example, *The Chronicle of Jocelin of Brakelond*, ed. H. E. Butler (London, 1949), 48.
7. R. W. Southern, *Western Society and the Church in the Middle Ages* (Harmondsworth, 1970), 20–1, 125–6, 154, 156.
8. See, for instance, C. T. Maier, *Preaching the Crusades. Mendicant Friars and the Cross in the Thirteenth Century* (Cambridge, 1994), 106–7.
9. For the text of the 1208 interdict, see *Documents of the Christian Church*, selected and edited H. Bettenson (Oxford, 2nd edn, 1963), 161–2.
10. W. Ullmann, *The Origins of the Great Schism. A Study in Fourteenth-Century Ecclesiastical History* (London, 1948), 97, also 98–9.
11. For a brief discussion, see Swanson, *Religion and Devotion*, 21–6.
12. J. Scammell, 'The rural chapter in England from the eleventh to the fourteenth century', *English Historical Review*, 338 (1971), 15–16.
13. A. H. Thompson, *The English Clergy and their Organization in the Later Middle Ages* (Oxford, 1947), 110–11, 112.
14. R. K. Morris, 'The church in the countryside: two lines of inquiry', in D. Hooke (ed.), *Medieval Villages* (Oxford, 1985), 59.
15. V. R. Bainbridge, *Gilds in the Medieval Countryside. Social and Religious Change in Cambridgeshire c.1350–1558* (Woodbridge, 1996), 71–2.

16. J. R. H. Moorman, *Church Life in England in the Thirteenth Century* (Cambridge, 1946), 26–7.
17. For an example of the implications of this, see *The Chronicle of Lanercost*, ed. and trans. H. Maxwell (Glasgow, 1907), p. 158, cited by Moorman, *Church Life in England*, 27, n. 3; see also pp. 200, 210–11.
18. See, for example, the comments of Bainbridge, *Gilds in the Medieval Countryside*, ch. 6.
19. R. M. Smith, 'Marriage processes in the English past: some continuities', in L. Bonfield, R. Smith and K. Wrightson (eds), *The World we have Gained. Histories of Population and Social Structure* (Oxford, 1986), 57.
20. *Court Rolls of the Manor of Wakefield. Vol. 4*, ed. J. Lister (Yorkshire Archaeological Society, vol. 78, 1930), 33; see also Chapter 6.
21. *Court Rolls of the Manor of Wakefield. Vol. 1*, ed. W. Baildon (Yorkshire Archaeological Society, vol. 29, 1900), 281–2.
22. R. N. Swanson (ed.), *Catholic England. Faith, Religion and Observance before the Reformation* (Manchester, 1993), 53–64; also Duffy, *Stripping of the Altars*, 58–60.
23. R. N. Swanson, *Church and Society in Late Medieval England* (Oxford, 1989), 256.
24. E. Mason, 'The role of the English parishioner, 1100–1500', *Journal of Ecclesiastical History*, 27 (1976), 17.
25. Swanson, *Church and Society*, 210–15.
26. T. Lomas, 'South-east Durham: late fourteenth and fifteenth centuries', in P. D. A. Harvey (ed.), *The Peasant Land Market in Medieval England* (Oxford, 1984), 319; discussed by Swanson, *Church and Society*, 211.
27. Swanson, *Church and Society*, 215; on churching, see also L. R. Poos, *A Rural Society after the Black Death* (Cambridge, 1991), 121–7.
28. See p. 190.
29. Swanson, *Church and Society*, 217; see also p. 118.
30. Scammell, 'Rural chapter in England', 17–18.
31. E. Duffy, *The Stripping of the Altars. Traditional Religion in England, 1400–1580* (New Haven, CT, 1992), 134; also E. Mason, 'The role of the English parishioner, 1100–1500', *Journal of Ecclesiastical History*, 27 (1976), 23–5.
32. W. O. Ault, 'Manor court and parish church in fifteenth-century England: a study of village by-laws', *Speculum*, 42 (1967).
33. Mason, 'Role of the English parishioner', 24–5.
34. Swanson, *Church and Society*, 1–5; D. M. Owen, *Church and Society in Medieval Lincolnshire* (History of Lincolnshire, vol. 5, Lincoln, 1971), 36; Moorman, *Church Life in England*, 135.
35. F. A. Gasquet, *Parish Life in Mediaeval England* (London, 1906), ch. 5; University of Chicago Library, Bacon Ms., 117.
36. C. Dyer, 'The English medieval village community and its decline', *Journal of British Studies*, 33 (1994), 413; Owen, *Church and Society in Medieval Lincolnshire*, 114.
37. Owen, *Church and Society in Medieval Lincolnshire*, 117.
38. J. M. Bennett, 'Conviviality and charity in medieval and early modern England', *Past and Present*, 134 (1992), 26–8.
39. Dyer, 'English medieval village community', 416.

40. B. A. Kumin, *The Shaping of a Community. The Rise and Reformation of the English Parish, c.1400–1560* (Aldershot, 1996), 22–42; also Sir F. Pollock and F. W. Maitland, *The History of English Law before the Time of Edward I* (2 vols, Cambridge, 2nd edn, 1968), vol. 1, 614.

41. For example, N. Tanner (ed.), *Heresy Trials in the Diocese of Norwich, 1428–1431* (Camden Society, 4th ser., vol. 20, 1977) 10ff.; Swanson, *Catholic England*, 268; on heresy and unorthodoxy, see pp. 208–9, 210.

42. A. E. Levett, *Studies in Manorial History* (Oxford, 1938), 224–34; see, for example, the will of William Dogett, 1395/6, *ibid.*, 225.

43. *Court Rolls of the Manor of Walsham le Willows, 1303–1350*, ed. R. Lock (Suffolk Records Society, vol. 41, 1998), 135.

44. Duffy, *Stripping of the Altars*, 145; this looks to contrast rural guilds with their urban equivalents, cf. G. Rosser, 'Communities of parish and guild in the late Middle Ages', in S. J. Wright (ed.), *Parish, Church and People. Local Studies in Lay Religion, 1350–1750* (London, 1988), 33–4.

45. Bainbridge, *Gilds in the Medieval Countryside*, 117–18.

46. Bennett, 'Conviviality and charity', 27–8.

47. Most obviously, M. Rubin, *Corpus Christi. The Eucharist in Late Medieval Culture* (Cambridge, 1991).

48. Rubin, *Corpus Christi*, 57–63; also *idem*, 'The eucharist and the construction of medieval identities', in D. Aers (ed.), *Culture and History, 1350–1600. Essays on English Communities, Identities and Writing* (Detroit, 1992), 50–3.

49. University of Chicago Library, Bacon Ms. 117; *Court Rolls of the Manor of Walsham le Willows*, ed. Lock, 220.

50. *The Medieval Lindsey Marsh. Select Documents*, ed. A. E. B. Owen (Lincoln Record Society, vol. 85, 1996), 15–16; Owen, *Church and Society*, 125–6. On pilgrimage more generally see also R. C. Finucane, *Miracles and Pilgrims. Popular Beliefs in Medieval England* (London, 1977); D. Webb, *Pilgrimage in Medieval England* (London, 2000).

51. See pp. 87–9.

52. Duffy, *Stripping of the Altars*, 141ff.; Owen, *Church and Society*, 128.

53. Le Goff, *The Birth of Purgatory*; see also the useful summary by R. Horrox, 'Purgatory, prayer and plague: 1150–1380', in P. C. Jupp and C. Gittings (eds), *Death in England. An Illustrated History* (Manchester, 1999).

54. *Court Rolls of the Manor of Walsham le Willows*, ed. Lock, 135, and see Chapter 8, this volume.

55. Bainbridge, *Gilds in the Medieval Countryside*, 67; for Elm and its parish church, see also *Victoria County History of Suffolk*, vol. 4, 180–6.

56. Levett, *Studies in Manorial History*, 224, 226, 233, 234.

57. Duffy, *Stripping of the Altars*, 132.

58. See, for instance, M. Aston, 'Lollards and literacy', *History*, 62 (1977), repr. in *idem*, *Lollards and Reformers. Images and Literacy in Late Medieval England* (London, 1984), 207 (from which this and subsequent references are taken); also Swanson, *Catholic England*, 267.

59. Owen, *Church and Society*, 123–5.

60. *Thomas Wright's Political Songs of England from the Reign of John to that of*

Edward II, ed. P. Coss (Cambridge, 1996), 268–72; *Court Rolls of the Manor of Walsham le Willows*, ed. Lock, 135.

61. See pp. 179, 183–5, for exhortations to the faithful at times of national distress and the concomitant association of godlessness with one's enemies, R. Horrox, *The Black Death* (Manchester, 1994), 118–19; C. Harper-Bill, 'The English church and English religion after the Black Death', in M. Ormrod and P. Lindley (eds), *The Black Death in England* (Stamford, 1996), 108.

62. Swanson, *Church and Society*, 37–8.

63. Swanson, *Church and Society*, 36–7; also Moorman, *Church Life in England*, 25.

64. Webb, *Pilgrimage in Medieval England*, 143–4.

65. J. van Engen, 'The Christian Middle Ages as an historiographical problem', *American Historical Review*, 91 (1986), 549–50.

66. M. R. James, 'Twelve medieval ghost-stories', *English Historical Review*, 37 (1922), 418.

67. *The Commonplace Book of Robert Reynes of Acle*, ed. C. Louis (New York, 1980); Duffy, *Stripping of the Altars*, 71–3, 75.

68. Aston, 'Lollards and literacy', 199–200.

69. A. Hudson, 'The mouse in the pyx: popular heresy and the eucharist', in N. Crossley-Holland (ed.), *Eternal Values in Medieval Life* (Trivium, 26, 1991), 46, 48.

70. Hudson, 'Mouse in the pyx', 46–7.

71. Swanson, *Church and Society*, 259.

72. Owen, *Church and Society in Medieval Lincolnshire*, 140–2.

73. *Court Rolls of the Manor of Hales, 1272–1307. Part 1*, ed. J. Amphlett and S. E. Hamilton, (Worcestershire Historical Society, 1910), 31–2.

74. See p. 198.

75. D. Plumb, 'The social and economic spread of rural Lollardy: a reappraisal', *Studies in Church History* 23 (1986); see also p. 210.

CHAPTER 10   CONCLUSION

1. *Court Rolls of Walsham le Willows, 1303–1305*, ed. R. Lock (Suffolk Records Society, vol. 41, 1998), 35, 37, 41, 45, 46, 47, 50, 51, 53, 56, 58, 62, 66, 85, 132–5.

2. E. Duffy, *The Stripping of the Altars. Traditional Religion in England, 1400–1580* (New Haven, CT, 1992), 71–3.

3. M. K. McIntosh, *Controlling Misbehavior in England, 1370–1600* (Cambridge, 1998).

4. J. M. Bennett, *A Medieval Life. Cecilia Penifader of Brigstock, c.1295–1344* (McGraw-Hill, 1999).

FURTHER READING

Community and Peasantry

There is a substantial literature on the theory of community, a major early contribution being F. Tönnies, *Community and Association (Gemeinschaft und Gesellschaft)* (1887). A very useful introduction to this can be found in Susan Reynolds, *Kingdoms and Communities in Western Europe, 900–1300* (2nd edn, Oxford, 1997); see also, M. Rubin, 'Small groups: identity and solidarity in the late Middle Ages', in J. Kermode (ed.), *Enterprise and Individuals in Fifteenth Century England* (Stroud, 1991); R. M. Smith, ' "Modernization" and the corporate village community' in A. H. R. Baker and D. Gregory (eds), *Explorations in Historical Geography* (Cambridge, 1984). For more general statements, see C. Calhoun, 'History, anthropology and the study of communities', *Social History*, 3 (1978); C. Calhoun, 'Community: towards a variable conceptualization for comparative research', *Social History*, 5 (1980).

For the theory of peasantry and the peasant economy, see E. R. Wolf, *Peasants* (London, 1966); D. Thorner, 'Peasant economy as a category in economic history', in T. Shanin (ed.), *Peasants and Peasant Societies* (Harmondsworth, 1971); also D. Thorner, B. Kerblay and R. E. F. Smith (eds), *A. V. Chayanov on the Theory of Peasant Economy* (Madison, WI, 1986). On the issue of 'peasantry' as a viable concept in the context of high and late medieval England, see the views of A. Mac-Farlane, *The Origins of English Individualism* (Oxford, 1978) and his detractors, for example, S. H. Rigby, *English Society in the Later Middle Ages. Class, Status and Gender* (Basingstoke, 1995); also, R. M. Smith, 'Some issues concerning families and their property in rural England, 1250–1800', in *idem* (ed.), *Land, Kinship and Life-Cycle* (Cambridge, 1984).

Sources

There are numerous published examples of the type and range of sources which might cast useful light on the medieval peasantry. Of prime importance are manorial court rolls. For fairly recent examples of these (all translated), see *The Court Rolls of Walsham le Willows*, ed. R. Lock (Suffolk Record Society, vol. 41, 1998); *Court Roll of the Manor of Downham, 1310–1327*, ed. M. Clare Coleman (Cambridge, 1996); *Select Cases in Manorial Courts, 1250–1550. Property and Family Law*, ed. L. R. Poos and L. Bonfield (Selden Society, 1998). For a recent attempt to list some of the surviving rolls, see J. Cripps, R. Hilton and J. Williamson, 'Appendix: a survey of medieval manorial court rolls in England', in Z. Razi and R. M. Smith (eds), *Medieval Society and the Manor Court* (Oxford, 1996). See also P. D. A. Harvey, *Manorial Records* (British Records Association, Archives and User no.5, London, 1984). The development of this source, and of the courts of which it is a record, is an important element of historical discussion of the peasantry, for which see J. S. Beckerman, 'Procedural innovation and institutional change in medieval English manorial courts', *Law and History Review*, 10 (1992); Z. Razi and R. M. Smith, 'Introduction: the historiography of manor court rolls', in Z. Razi and R. M. Smith (eds), *Medieval Society and the Manor Court* (Oxford, 1996); Z. Razi and R. M. Smith, 'The origins of the English manorial court rolls as a written record: a puzzle', in Z. Razi and R. M. Smith (eds), *Medieval Society and the Manor Court* (Oxford, 1996).

Aside of manorial court rolls, a host of other source types provide important material for the study of the peasantry. Manorial and seigneurial records other than court rolls, such as manorial account rolls, writs to local administrators, collections of charters (cartularies), custumals and extents, all contain relevant information. See, for example, **accounts**: *Manorial Records of Cuxham, Oxfordshire, 1200–1359*, ed. P. D. A. Harvey (Oxfordshire Record Society, vol. l, 1976) (which includes examples of manorial accounts and court rolls); *The Pipe Roll of the Bishopric of Winchester, 1301–1302*, ed. M. Page (Hampshire Record Series, vol. 14, 1996); **writs**: *Documents Illustrative of the Rule of Walter de Wenlok, Abbot of Westminster, 1283–1307*, ed. B. F. Harvey (Camden, 4th ser., vol. 2, 1965); **cartularies, custumals, extents**: *Carte Nativorum. A Peterborough Abbey Cartulary of the Fourteenth Century*, ed. C. N. L. Brooke and M. M. Postan (Northamptonshire Record Society, vol. 20, 1960); *Custumals of Battle Abbey in the Reigns of Edward I and Edward II (1283–1312) from MSS in the Public Record Office*, ed. S. R. Scargill-Bird (Camden Society, 1887). Beyond the manor, there is a range of records, judicial and governmental, fiscal and spiritual, which contain material relevant to the study of the peasantry. **Judicial and governmental**: borough courts and county courts include mention of peasant litigants in towns as well as villages other than their own, *Rolls from the Office of the Sheriff of Bedfordshire and Buckinghamshire, 1332–1334*, ed. G. H. Fowler (Bedfordshire Historical Record Society, 4to, 1929); *Court Rolls of the Borough of Colchester*, ed. I. H. Jeayes (4 vols, Colchester, 1921–41). The records of central courts (king's bench and common pleas) might also contain evidence of peasant litigants. In particular, collective action against landlords found its way into central courts, as discussed by R. H. Hilton, 'Peasant movements in medieval England', *Economic History Review*, 2nd ser., 2 (1949). Sources here include *Curia Regis Rolls* (HMSO); *Select Cases in the Court of King's Bench*, ed. G. O. Sayles (Selden Society, 7 vols, 1936–71). Also useful are the Calendars of Patent and Close Rolls (HMSO). We are also likely to find peasants in the records of itinerant justices and criminal jurisdictions in the countryside, as, for instance, *A Lincolnshire Assize Roll for 1298 (P. R. O. Assize Roll no. 505)*, ed. W.S. Thomson (Lincolnshire Record Society, vol. 36, 1944); *Royal Justice and the Medieval English Countryside. The Huntingdonshire Eyre of 1286, the Ramsey Abbey Banlieu Court of 1287, and the Assizes of 1287–88*, ed. A. R. Dewindt and E. B. Dewindt (Toronto, 1981); *Proceedings before the Justices of the Peace in the Fourteenth and Fifteenth Centuries. Edward III to Richard II*, ed. B. H. Putnam and T. F. T. Plucknett (Ames Foundation, London, 1938). The records of governmental inquiries and commissions also are particularly revealing, see especially (for the source which underpins E. A. Kosminsky, *Studies in the Agrarian History of England in the Thirteenth Century* (Oxford, 1956)) *Rotuli Hundredorum Temporibus Henrici III et Edwardi I in Turri Londinensi et in Curia Receptae Scaccarii Westmonasterii Asservati*, ed. W. Illingworth (Record Commission, 2 vols, 1812–18); also, *Nonarum Inquisitiones in Curia Scaccarii*, ed. G. Vanderzee (Record Commission, 1807), a source discussed in, *inter alia*, J. Masschaele, *Peasants, Merchants and Markets. Inland Trade in Medieval England, 1150–1350* (Basingstoke, 1997). Finally, the rulings of central government have much that is relevant, *Rotuli Parliamentorum (1278–1503)* (6 vols, Record Commission, London, 1783); *Statutes of the Realm (1101–1713)*, ed. A. Luders *et al.* (11 vols, Record Commission, London, 1810–28). **Fiscal**: Records issuing from the Exchequer, especially the late thirteenth and early fourteenth-century assessments of lay subsidies, offer important material on peasant wealth and standards of living, amongst numerous examples, see *A Suffolk Hundred in the Year 1283. The Assessment of the Hundred of Blackbourne for a Tax of One Thirtieth, and a Return Showing the Land*

Tenure there, ed. E. Powell (Cambridge, 1910); *Hertfordshire Lay Subsidy Rolls. 1307 and 1334*, ed. J. Brooker and S. Flood, with an introduction by M. Bailey (Hertfordshire Record Society, vol. 14, 1998). Also of utmost importance are the late fourteenth-century poll-taxes, C. Fenwick, *The Poll Taxes of 1377, 1379, and 1381. Pt 1: Bedfordshire–Leicestershire* (Oxford, 1998). **Spiritual**: records of church courts, wills, churchwarden accounts, all mostly dating from the fifteenth century, afford some sense of the religiosity of the peasantry. See, for examples of each, A. Gransden, 'Some late thirteenth-century records of an ecclesiastical court in the archdeaconry of Sudbury', *Bulletin of the Institute of Historical Research*, 32 (1959); A. E. Levett, 'Wills of villeins and copyholders', in *idem, Studies in Manorial History* (Oxford, 1938); *Churchwardens' Accounts of Croscombe, Pilton, Yatton, Trintinhull, Morebath, and St. Michael's, Bath, ranging from AD 1349 to 1560*, ed. E. Hobhouse (Somerset Record Society, vol. 4, 1890). For sources relating to heresy and instruction to priests on appropriate dealing with their flock, see the examples in *Catholic England. Faith, Religion and Observance before the Reformation*, ed. R. N. Swanson (Manchester, 1993); on heresy more particularly, N. Tanner (ed.), *Heresy Trials in the Diocese of Norwich, 1428–1431* (Camden Society, 4th ser., vol. 20, 1977).

Finally, literature and chronicles provide incidental details, *Thomas Wright's Political Songs of England from the Reign of John to that of Edward II*, ed. P. R. Coss (Cambridge, 1996); for the value of chronicles as a source for the Peasants' Revolt, see the collection of relevant material in *The Peasants' Revolt of 1381*, ed. R. B. Dobson (2nd edn, London, 1983); also for commentary on the condition of the peasantry, *The Vision of William concerning Piers the Plowman in Three Parallel Texts*, ed. W. W. Skeat (Oxford, 2 vols, 1886). We have little that is evidently the direct voice of the peasantry; for something that still does not come close but at least is evidence of choice in the compilation, see *The Commonplace Book of Robert Reynes of Acle*, ed. C. Louis (New York, 1980).

General Works on the English Peasantry in the Middle Ages

There are relatively few works that address the topic of the medieval peasantry directly. Most of those that do exist were also written more than a generation or two ago. The most obvious, as well as the best, are R. H. Hilton, *The English Peasantry in the Later Middle Ages*

(Oxford, 1975); G. C. Homans, *English Villagers of the Thirteenth Century* (Harvard, 1941); H. S. Bennett, *Life on the English Manor. A Study of Peasant Conditions, 1100–1400* (Cambridge, 1937). There are also more general texts which have a great deal to say about the peasantry and agrarian conditions; see, for example, S. H. Rigby, *English Society in the Later Middle Ages. Class, Status and Gender* (Basingstoke, 1995); E. Miller and J. Hatcher, *Medieval England. Rural Society and Economic Change, 1086–1348* (Harlow, 1978); R. H. Britnell, *The Commercialisation of English Society, 1100–1500* (Cambridge, 1993); C. Dyer, *Standards of Living in the Later Middle Ages. Social Change in England, c.1200–1520* (Cambridge, 1989). The relevant volumes of the *Agrarian History of England and Wales* are also invaluable, H. E. Hallam (ed.), *The Agrarian History of England and Wales. Volume 2, 1042–1350* (Cambridge, 1988); E. Miller (ed.), *The Agrarian History of England and Wales. Volume 3, 1348–1500* (Cambridge, 1991).

Estate, Regional and Urban Studies

A good deal of historical discussion of the peasantry has been couched in terms of tenantry. **Estate studies**, especially of the larger ecclesiastical and monastic estates, shed much light on the tenurial aspects of peasant life. There are numerous examples: for ecclesiastical estates, A. E. Levett, *The Black Death on the Estates of the See of Winchester* (Oxford, 1916); for monastic estates, F. M. Page, *The Estates of Crowland Abbey* (Cambridge, 1934); R. H. Hilton, *The Economic Development of some Leicestershire Estates in the Fourteenth and Fifteenth Centuries* (Oxford, 1947); E. Miller, *The Abbey and Bishopric of Ely. The Social History of an Ecclesiastical Estate from the Tenth to the Early Fourteenth Century* (Cambridge, 1951); J. A. Raftis, *The Estates of Ramsey Abbey. A Study in Economic Growth and Organization* (Toronto, 1957); F. R. H. DuBoulay, *The Lordship of Canterbury. An Essay on Medieval Society* (London, 1966); E. King, *Peterborough Abbey, 1086–1310. A Study in the Land Market* (Cambridge, 1973); B. F. Harvey, *Westminster Abbey and its Estates in the Middle Ages* (Oxford, 1977); C. Dyer, *Lords and Peasants in a Changing Society. The Estates of the Bishopric of Worcester, 680–1540* (Cambridge, 1980). Secular estates are discussed by G. A. Holmes, *The Estates of the Higher Nobility in Fourteenth-Century England* (Cambridge, 1957); J. M. W. Bean, *The Estates of the Percy Family, 1416–1537* (Oxford, 1958); J. Hatcher, *Rural Economy and Society in the Duchy of Cornwall, 1300–1500*

(Cambridge, 1970). Studies of individual magnates also offer some discussion of their tenants, for example, J. R. Maddicott, *Thomas of Lancaster* (Oxford, 1970); J. R. S. Phillips, *Aymer de Valence, Earl of Pembroke* (Oxford, 1972). **Regional studies**: studies of particular regions and administrative units, such as counties, also provide a great deal of information on the condition of the peasantry. See, for example, D. C. Douglas, *Social Structure of Medieval East Anglia* (Oxford, 1927); H. C. Darby, *The Medieval Fenland* (Cambridge, 1940); R. H. Hilton, *A Medieval Society. The West Midlands at the end of the Thirteenth Century* (Cambridge, 1966); G. Platts, *Land and People in Medieval Lincolnshire* (Lincoln, 1985); A. J. Winchester, *Landscape and Society in Medieval Cumbria* (Edinburgh, 1987); M. Bailey, *A Marginal Economy? East Anglian Breckland in the Later Middle Ages* (Cambridge, 1989); L. R. Poos, *A Rural Society after the Black Death. Essex, 1350–1525* (Cambridge, 1991). **Urban studies** also offer useful additional and incidental comment on such issues as marketing of peasant produce, migration, urban investment in the countryside; see, for example, R. H. Britnell, *Growth and Decline in Colchester, 1300–1525* (Cambridge, 1986); B. M. S. Campbell, J. A. Galloway, D. Keene and M. Murphy, *A Medieval Capital and its Grain Supply. Agrarian Production and Distribution in the London Region, c.1300* (London, 1993); M. Kowaleski, *Local Markets and Regional Trade in Medieval Exeter* (Cambridge, 1995).

Manorial Studies

Inevitably, some of the most important and directive work on the English peasantry has been carried out within micro-studies of particular manors or small groups of manors, typically within single estates. Such work has a long and illustrious pedigree: F. G. Davenport, *The Economic History of a Norfolk Manor (Forncett) 1086–1565* (Cambridge, 1906); P. D. A. Harvey, *A Medieval Oxfordshire Village. Cuxham, 1240–1400* (Oxford, 1965); E. B. Dewindt, *Land and People in Holywell-cum-Needingworth. Structures of Tenure and Patterns of Social Organization in an East Midlands Village, 1252–1457* (Toronto, 1971); E. Britton, *The Community of the Vill* (Toronto, 1977); C. Howell, *Land, Family and Inheritance in Transition. Kibworth Harcourt, 1280–1700* (Cambridge, 1983); M. J. McIntosh, *Autonomy and Community. The Royal Manor of Havering, 1200–1500* (Cambridge, 1986); S. Olson, *A Chronicle of All that Happens. Voices from the Village Court in Medieval*

England (Toronto, 1996). Local studies are not infrequently directed at particular issues, as for instance J. M. Bennett, *Women in the Medieval English Countryside. Gender and Household in Brigstock before the Plague* (Oxford, 1987); J. Whittle, *The Development of Agrarian Capitalism. Land and Labour in Norfolk, 1440–1580* (Oxford, 2000). The most extreme of the micro-studies, the biography, is generally lacking for the medieval peasant but, for a recent attempt to exemplify a range of issues through one peasant's life, see J. M. Bennett, *A Medieval Life. Cecilia Penifader of Brigstock, c.1295–1344* (McGraw-Hill, 1999).

Detailed studies abound for particular aspects of the peasant economy and society. Some indicative and important works provide useful introductions to the following research areas. **Tenure, serfdom and villeinage**: R. H. Hilton, *The Decline of Serfdom in Medieval England* (Cambridge, 1966); J. Hatcher, 'English serfdom and villeinage: towards a reassessment', *Past and Present*, 90 (1981), repr. in T. H. Aston (ed.), *Landlords, Peasants and Politics in Medieval England* (Cambridge, 1987); R. H. Hilton, 'Freedom and villeinage in England', *Past and Present*, 31 (1965), reprinted in R. H. Hilton (ed.), *Peasants, Knights and Heretics. Studies in Medieval English Social History* (Cambridge, 1976); T. H. Aston and C. H. E. Philpin (eds), *The Brenner Debate. Agrarian Class Structure and Economic Development in Pre-Industrial Europe* (Cambridge, 1985); P. R. Hyams, *Kings, Lords and Peasants in Medieval England. The Common Law of Villeinage in the Twelfth and Thirteenth Centuries* (Oxford, 1980). **The peasant land market**: M. M. Postan, 'The charters of the villeins', in *idem*, *Essays on Medieval Agriculture*; D. Thorner, B. Kerblay and R. E. F. Smith (eds), *A. V. Chayanov on the Theory of Peasant Economy* (Madison, WI, 1986); P. R. Hyams, 'The origins of a peasant land market in England', *Economic History Review*, 23 (1970); P. D. A. Harvey (ed.), *The Peasant Land Market in Medieval England* (Oxford, 1984); R. M. Smith (ed.), *Land, Kinship and Life-Cycle* (Cambridge, 1984). **The peasant family and demography**: G. C. Homans, *English Villagers of the Thirteenth Century* (Cambridge, MA, 1941); Z. Razi, *Life, Marriage and Death in a Medieval Parish. Economy, Society and Demography in Halesowen (1270–1400)* (Cambridge, 1980); *idem*, 'The myth of the immutable English family', *Past and Present*, 140 (1993); R. M. Smith, 'Marriage processes in the English past: some continuities', in L. Bonfield, R. Smith and K. Wrightson (eds), *The World we have Gained. Histories of Population and Social Structure* (Oxford, 1986); B. A. Hanawalt, *The Ties that Bound. Peasant Families in Medieval England* (Oxford, 1986); J. M. Bennett, *Women in the Medieval English*

Countryside. Gender and Household in Brigstock before the Plague (Oxford, 1987). **Peasants and the market**: R. H. Britnell, *The Commercialisation of English Society, 1100–1500* (Cambridge, 1993); J. Masschaele, *Peasants, Merchants and Markets. Inland Trade in Medieval England, 1150–1350* (Basingstoke, 1997); J. A. Raftis, *Peasant Economic Development within the English Manorial System* (Stroud, 1997); for pioneering work on marketing and its networks, see C. Dyer, 'The consumer and the market in the later Middle Ages', *Economic History Review*, 2nd ser., 43 (1990), reprinted in *idem, Everyday Life in Medieval England* (London, 1984); *idem*, 'The hidden trade of the Middle Ages: evidence from the West Midlands', *Journal of Historical Geography*, 18 (1992), reprinted in *idem, Everyday Life in Medieval England* (London, 1994). See also his *Standards of Living in the Later Middle Ages. Social Change in England, c.1200–1520* (Cambridge, 1989). For perceptive comment see also K. Biddick, 'Medieval English peasants and market involvement', *Journal of Economic History*, 45 (1985); *idem*, 'Missing links: taxable wealth, markets and stratification among medieval English peasants', *Journal of Interdisciplinary History*, 18 (1987). **Peasants and politics**: for lord–tenant relations see, for example, R. H. Hilton, 'Peasant movements in medieval England', *Economic History Review*, 2nd ser., 2 (1949), repr. in E. M. Carus-Wilson (ed.), *Essays in Economic History, Vol. 2* (London, 1962); E. B. Fryde, *Peasants and Landlords in Later Medieval England* (Stroud, 1996); inter-tenant relations are dealt with in a number of contexts, see, for instance, E. Britton, *The Community of the Vill* (Toronto, 1977); P. R. Schofield, 'Peasants and the manor court: gossip and litigation in a Suffolk village at the close of the thirteenth century', *Past and Present*, 159 (1998); W. O. Ault, 'Manor court and parish church in fifteenth-century England: a study of village by-laws', *Speculum*, 42 (1967); M. K. McIntosh, *Controlling Misbehavior in England, 1370–1600* (Cambridge, 1998); B. Hanawalt, *Crime and Conflict in English Communities, 1300–1348* (Harvard, 1979). For peasants and the wider community, see the important contributions of D. A. Carpenter, 'English peasants in politics, 1258–1267', *Past and Present*, 136 (1992); J. R. Maddicott, 'The English peasantry and the demands of the crown, 1294–1341', *Past and Present, Supplement 1* (1975); R. B. Goheen, 'Peasant politics? Village community and the crown in fifteenth century England', *American Historical Review*, 96 (1991). On peasants and the law, P. R. Hyams, 'What did Edwardian villagers understand by law?', in Z. Razi and R. M. Smith (eds), *Medieval Society and the Manor Court* (Oxford, 1996), is an especially insightful piece. There is a voluminous literature on 1381 and the Peasants' Revolt; see especially, R. H. Hilton, *Bond Men Made Free. Medieval Peasant Movements and the English Rising of 1381* (London, 1973); R. H. Hilton and T. H. Aston (eds), *The English Rising of 1381* (Cambridge, 1984); S. Justice, *Writing and Rebellion. England in 1381* (California, 1996). For other outbreaks of peasant revolt, see, for example, I. M. W. Harvey, *Jack Cade's Rebellion of 1450* (Oxford, 1991). **Peasants and religion**: the issues are best represented in E. Duffy, *The Stripping of the Altars. Traditional Religion in England, 1400–1580* (New Haven, CT, 1992); E. Mason, 'The role of the English parishioner, 1100–1500', *Journal of Ecclesiastical History*, 27 (1976) also offers valuable comment, as does C. Dyer, 'The English medieval village community and its decline', *Journal of British Studies*, 33 (1994). There are a number of specialist pieces on aspects of religiosity which include some discussion of the church, faith and the peasantry, as, for instance, D. M. Owen, *Church and Society in Medieval Lincolnshire* (History of Lincolnshire, vol. 5, Lincoln, 1971); M. Rubin, *Charity and Community in Medieval Cambridge* (Cambridge, 1987); V. R. Bainbridge, *Gilds in the Medieval Countryside. Social and Religious Change in Cambridgeshire, c.1350–1558* (Woodbridge, 1996).

Index